## The Blackwell Philosophy and PopCulture Series
*Series editor William Irwin*

A spoonful of sugar helps the medicine go down, and a healthy helping of popular culture clears the cobwebs from Kant. Philosophy has had a public relations problem for a few centuries now. This series aims to change that, showing that philosophy is relevant to your life – and not just for answering the big questions like "To be or not to be?" but for answering the little questions: "To watch or not to watch *South Park*?" Thinking deeply about TV, movies, and music doesn't make you a "complete idiot." In fact it might make you a philosopher, someone who believes the unexamined life is not worth living and the unexamined cartoon is not worth watching.

**SOUTH PARK AND PHILOSOPHY**: YOU KNOW, I LEARNED SOMETHING TODAY
*Edited by Robert Arp*

**METALLICA AND PHILOSOPHY**: A CRASH COURSE IN BRAIN SURGERY
*Edited by William Irwin*

**FAMILY GUY AND PHILOSOPHY**: A CURE FOR THE PETARDED
*Edited by J. Jeremy Wisnewski*

**THE DAILY SHOW AND PHILOSOPHY**: MOMENTS OF ZEN IN THE ART OF FAKE NEWS
*Edited by Jason Holt*

**LOST AND PHILOSOPHY**: THE ISLAND HAS ITS REASONS
*Edited by Sharon M. Kaye*

Forthcoming

**24 AND PHILOSOPHY**: THE WORLD ACCORDING TO JACK
*Edited by Jennifer Hart Weed, Richard Davis, and Ronald Weed*

**BATTLESTAR GALACTICA AND PHILOSOPHY**
*Edited by Jason T. Eberl*

**the office and philosophy**
*Edited by J. Jeremy Wisnewski*

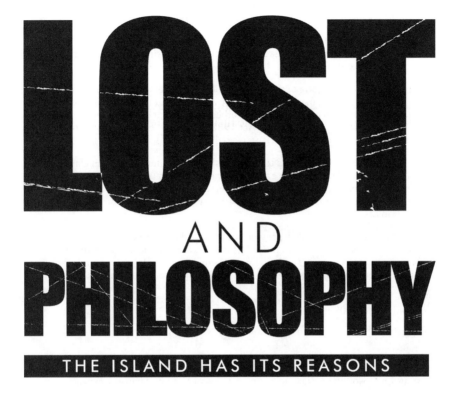

# LOST

## AND

# PHILOSOPHY

## THE ISLAND HAS ITS REASONS

*Edited by Sharon M. Kaye*

**Blackwell**
Publishing

BLACKWELL PUBLISHING
350 Main Street, Malden, MA 02148–5020, USA
9600 Garsington Road, Oxford OX4 2DQ, UK
550 Swanston Street, Carlton, Victoria 3053, Australia

First published 2008 by Blackwell Publishing Ltd

2   2008

Library of Congress Cataloging-in-Publication Data

Lost and philosophy : the island has its reasons / edited by Sharon Kaye.
      p. cm. — (The Blackwell philosophy and popculture series)
   Includes bibliographical references and index.
   ISBN 978–1–4051–6315–6 (pbk. : alk. paper)   1. Lost (Television program)   I. Kaye, Sharon M.

   PN1992.77.L67L67 2008
   791.45'72—dc22

                                                                                          2007031230

A catalogue record for this title is available from the British Library.

Set in 10.5/13pt Sabon
by Graphicraft Limited, Hong Kong
Printed and bound in the United States of America
by Sheridan Books, Inc.

The publisher's policy is to use permanent paper from mills that operate a sustainable forestry policy, and which has been manufactured from pulp processed using acid-free and elementary chlorine-free practices. Furthermore, the publisher ensures that the text paper and cover board used have met acceptable environmental accreditation standards.

For further information on
Blackwell Publishing, visit our website at
www.blackwellpublishing.com

# Contents

# PART I

## L IS FOR LOVE

# PART II

## O IS FOR ORIGIN

# PART III

## S IS FOR SURVIVAL

# PART IV

## T IS FOR TRANSFORMATION

# Introduction
# L.O.S.T. in *Lost*

## *Sharon M. Kaye*

As an avid fan of *Lost* I've been trying to figure out what it is about this show that has such a hold on me. Other fans I've talked to feel the same way. It sinks its teeth into you and won't let go. After wondering about it for some time now, I think I finally figured out what it is. And so I have a question for you.

Have you ever been lost? Or rather, how did you feel when you were lost? Because you have been. We all have. Few of us have been stranded on a tropical island. But we have all had those moments when, far from home, we are suddenly struck by the horror that we will never find our way back.

[Fade to flashback.] It was a meltingly hot, sunny day, June 1974, and we were at the annual summer carnival. The carnival came to Madison, Wisconsin for ten days every summer. It was the highlight of the year. Kids spent long, gruelling hours babysitting, mowing lawns, and begging their parents for cash to buy the longest possible strip of tickets. One ticket would only get you on a baby ride; the best rides – the ones that gave you bat belly and brought you closest to the mystical transcendence – cost four.

[Carnival music. Chillingly alluring. Then children's voices.]
"Are you going on the Zipper this year?"
"No way!"
"Wus!"
"Well, not if they have that same guy strapping people in."
"It's never the same guys."
"That's true. Okay, I get the outside seat . . ."

1

At the carnival there are dangers of every kind and each child is called upon to perform at least one truly outstanding feat of bravery. But I didn't know any of this. I was just three years old, tagging along with the big kids for the first time.

True, I spent most of my time with my parents, observing my sisters and their friends, sampling the cuisine, and taking in the occasional baby ride. But my special challenge came at the end of the day.

There were seven of us, all sweaty and a bit dazed but still chattering away, as we trooped through the converted farmer's field back to our car. It was a 1967 Volvo. A midnight blue two-door with a brick red vinyl interior and no seatbelts. This was the age of innocence when you packed as many people into cars as you could fit, the littlest ones perching on the biggest ones' laps.

Getting everyone in was a bit of a trick that day with all of our carnival paraphernalia and the seats being hot enough to burn striped patterns on your butt right through your terrycloth shortshorts. Everyone vied for the best positions and there was some bickering. But soon enough the little Volvo was on its way. Windows were cranked all the way down and a windy discussion of the plan for the rest of the evening commenced.

Then, half way home, Marcy, the neighbour girl, suddenly said, "Where's Sherri?"

"She's in the front."

"No she isn't. She's in the back."

"Come on, quit kidding around."

"We're not kidding. She isn't here."

"Oh my gosh! We left her."

It never occurred to anyone, not even to my parents, that I may have been snatched up by a pervert. (Such was the age of innocence.) Their only theory was that I must have somehow been hit by a car. As they speeded back to the fairgrounds, my mother scanned for emergency vehicles. Everyone was asking the same question: Why didn't she get in the car?

Why indeed. It remains a mystery.

There were no emergency vehicles in the parking lot and I was nowhere to be seen amid the cars. Upon reentering the carnival gates, however, my dad soon spotted me. I was sitting serenely on a bench between two old ladies. They had apparently found me wandering and bought me a soda. Although I was not crying, my face was red and streaked.

When I heard my name and caught sight of my family, a crushing wave of mixed emotions passed across my face. I welcomed their enthusiastic hugs and kisses, but I didn't answer anyone's questions and I was quiet for the rest of the night.

Once you have been lost you are never quite the same.

The ABC hit drama *Lost* speaks to our deepest fear: the fear of being cut off from everything we know and love, left to fend for ourselves in a strange land. This fear is a philosophical fear because it speaks to the human condition. It forces us to confront profound questions about ourselves and the world.

And this is just what the 22 essays contained in this volume aim to do. I have organized them loosely into four main groups.

## Part I: L is for Love

The first set of essays examines a number of ethical issues raised by the show. Ethics is the branch of philosophy that concerns values along with the nature of right and wrong. Being in such extreme circumstances, the characters on *Lost* face difficult decisions that reveal insights for the rest of us to consider in our own moral lives.

Michael Austin looks into the relationships Jack and Locke have with their fathers. He argues that the failures of all four demonstrate that parents and children have a duty to meet each others' unique needs. Rebecca Vartabedian, however, questions whether Michael took his duty to his son Walter too far when he traded Walter's life for the lives of others. She shows how two different ethical theories provide the framework for evaluating his action. Robert Arp and Patricia Brace apply three different ethical theories to the many instances of moral objectification that occur on *Lost*. Their analysis suggests that, while moral objectification is sometimes alright, it is sometimes wrong. Deborah Barnbaum investigates whether the Dharma Initiative conforms to widely held ethical principles, concluding that it is entirely unjustifiable and therefore wrong. But are actions that depend on values ever really right or wrong? George Wrisley maintains that, though it is tempting to suppose not, this position is ultimately untenable. He argues that the show challenges us to develop justifications for our own moral perspectives.

## Part II: O is for Origin

The second set of essays explores a number of metaphysical issues raised by the show. Metaphysics is the branch of philosophy that concerns phenomena lying beyond the explanation of science. The smoke monster is, of course, the most obvious example. But really the island's smoke monster is just an external representation of the metaphysical mysteries within us all.

Sander Lee discusses issues of faith, reason, and free will in the stories of four of the characters. He concludes that the show's philosophical value may lie more in the questions it raises than the answers it presents. Charles Taliaferro and Dan Kastrul take on the problem of self-knowledge. They propose that, paradoxically, we can find out who we really are only by determining what we would do if we were someone else, such as someone stranded on a remote tropical island. Charles Girard and David Meulemans, however, suggest that the most important lesson all the characters on *Lost* learn is how difficult it is to free themselves from their past. Jessica Engelking argues that *Lost* aims to change the way the viewer sees things. In so doing, she casts fiction as a vehicle of reinvention. Tom Grimwood turns the spotlight on the mystery of fiction. How does it communicate its messages and why do we, the viewers, listen?

## Part III: S is for Survival

The third set of essays looks at a number of social and political issues raised by the show. Social and political philosophy concerns all of the difficulties that arise when humans try to live together and form a unit larger than the individual. The island is a microcosm of the power dynamics we observe in our own communities.

Sandra Bonetto provides a philosophical interpretation of the Others on the island. They constitute a definitive conflict for the survivors of Flight 815, forcing them to face their fear of the human condition. Karen Gaffney argues that the Others symbolize and draw attention to the prejudice in our own society. Though not castaways, we all have our Others, and we would do well to think about why. Scott Parker considers Shannon's position on the island and her relative healthcare rights. To what lengths should her friends go to protect her rights? Do certain situations justify torture? Peter Fosl and Richard Davies trace the history of the philosophical thought experiment known as the "state of nature," which is directly reflected in the *Lost* predicament. Fosl sees something dark in the show's use of this device, but he also sees hope in the passions and feelings of the characters. Davies claims that trust is the only way out.

## Part IV: T is for Transformation

The fourth set of essays investigates a number of religious issues raised by the show. Philosophy and religion are historically two sides of the same coin. By applying a rational analysis to some of the mystical moments portrayed on the show we can more fully appreciate their significance.

Shai Biderman and William Devlin make the surprising proposal that Locke represents the eastern spirituality of Taoism. Brett Patterson, in contrast, sees *Lost* as a staging ground for the theme of redemption found in the Christian tradition. We find another point of debate between the next two authors. David Werther contends that, by constructing a world in which everything happens for a reason, *Lost* makes a powerful case for the existence of God. Briony Addey, however, points out that things appearing to happen for a reason may just be a coincidence. She suggests that our proclivity toward conspiracy theory may be prompting us to read too much into the show. Following Rose's journey, Daniel Gallagher pursues the question of why we believe what we believe. He concludes that while both faith and knowledge are legitimate forms of belief, there is a difference between them that we all need to keep straight. Finally, Jeremy Barris dissects the meaning of life through the lens of *Lost*. In his view, the experience of asking the question unexpectedly turns out to be its own answer.

I hope you enjoy the essays as much as I did. On behalf of the authors, let me add that we all look forward to watching the show with you again soon.

# PART I

## L IS FOR LOVE

# 1

# What Do Jack and
# Locke Owe their Fathers?

## Michael W. Austin

"You don't have what it takes."

Put yourself in Jack's shoes. Imagine you're in junior high school and you to try to save a friend as he's being beaten up by some older kids. Now imagine your father says, "You don't have what it takes" because he thinks that you should have stayed out of it. You grow up thinking that your father doesn't believe in you. In response you're driven to over-achieve; you even finish medical school an entire year sooner than everyone else. This is Jack Shephard's life before the crash of Oceanic Flight 815.

"You think you're the first person that ever got conned? You needed a father figure, and I needed a kidney. And that's what happened. Get over it. And John, don't come back. You're not wanted."

Put yourself in Locke's shoes. You've grown up in various foster homes, never knowing your biological parents. Now, by mere chance, it seems, you've found them both. You develop a close bond with your father, and then discover it was all a ruse to get one of your kidneys. After the transplant that saves his life, your father shuts you out of that life. Even worse, he later attacks you, pushing you through a window and paralyzing you (not permanently, thanks to the island, you believe).

Perhaps Jack and Locke don't owe their fathers anything (especially Locke!). Most of us haven't been conned out of one of our kidneys, paralyzed, and nearly killed by a biological parent. And even though, like Jack's father, our parents have said things that have hurt us, we've probably benefited in numerous ways from the sacrifices that they made on our behalf. In light of these sacrifices, do we owe our parents anything?

## What Do Jack, Locke, and the Rest of Us Owe Our Parents?

According to contemporary philosopher Jane English, we owe our parents *nothing*.[1] This sounds very strange, because it runs strongly against the traditional, commonsense ethical views of western philosophy. On this traditional morality, adult children owe respect to their parents, as well as letters, phone calls, visits, and financial help (if this is needed and possible). Even if our relationship with our parents is not intimate, honest, and trusting, it is traditionally thought that we owe such things to them because of the sacrifices that they have made for us. Many moral philosophers take it upon themselves to criticize our traditional moral views. Sometimes those views withstand philosophical scrutiny, and sometimes they don't. According to English, the traditional idea that adult children owe a debt to their parents doesn't stand up to critical analysis. We'll have to decide for ourselves if she's right about this.

There are good reasons for saying that Locke didn't owe it to his father to give him a kidney. Just consider the level of sacrifice on Locke's part. And certainly after being conned out of a kidney and paralyzed by him, there are reasons for thinking that Locke owes his father very little or perhaps nothing at all. Of course, this doesn't justify Locke having Sawyer kill his father, but many would say that Locke didn't owe Anthony Cooper anything.

Jack's situation is somewhat different. Through a series of flashbacks we have been given a fuller picture of what has happened between Jack and his father, Christian. During one flashback, Jack is in the operating room and loses a patient. As the circumstances surrounding the patient's death are uncovered throughout the show, we learn that Jack's father was initially performing the surgery. A nurse found Jack and asked him to come to the operating room

---

[1] Jane English, "What Do Grown Children Owe Their Parents?" in Onora O'Neill and William Ruddick, eds., *Having Children* (New York: Oxford University Press, 1979), pp. 351–356.

because Christian was drunk while performing surgery. In his impaired state, Christian accidentally cut an artery and the patient died. Later, he calls Jack to his office and asks him to sign off on a report stating that the patient succumbed to the injuries sustained in the car accident. After Jack shows some resistance, Christian says:

> I know I've been hard on you, but that is how you make a soft metal into steel. That is why you are the most gifted young surgeon in this city . . . this is a career that is all about the greater good. I've had to sacrifice certain aspects of my relationship with you, so that hundreds and thousands of patients will live, because of your extraordinary skills.

Then, putting his hand on Jack's shoulder, Christian continues: "What happened yesterday I promise you will never happen again . . . this is not just about my career Jack. It's my life." After this, Jack signs the report, and his father says, "Thank you son. Thank you."

Jack later revises his statement and comes clean about his father's mistake in the OR. One reason for Jack's change of heart is that he believes his father was insincere in their earlier conversation. Jack sees his father put his hand on the shoulder of the dead woman's husband in the same insincere manner that he did with Jack. Then, in a meeting with hospital officials, Jack learns that the woman was pregnant, a fact that his father chose to conceal from him. At this point, Jack reveals what actually happened.

Jane English would say that certainly Jack and Locke owe nothing to their fathers. But apart from these special types of circumstances, it seems to most people that those of us who have had decent parents at least owe them respect and things like letters, phone calls, visits, and financial support. But English argues that we do not owe such things to our parents, even if they haven't failed us in the ways that Anthony Cooper and Christian Shephard failed Locke and Jack. Why would she make such a claim?

Philosophers are often very picky about language, with the result that much, though not all, of the writing in academic philosophy these days is notoriously dry and emotionally uninspiring. There is, however, a reason for this. A desire for clarity and precision helps uncover the real issue in any philosophical discussion. And when we finally get at the real issue, the hope is that a deeper level of understanding is achieved. Setting aside whether or not her view is true, it

11

is this search for understanding and clarity that leads English to the conclusion that we owe our parents nothing.

According to English, the sacrifices that our parents make for us do not create debts. Instead, those sacrifices tend to create a friendship relationship between parents and their adult children. For this reason, English thinks that using the term "owe" in the context of the parent–child relationship is out of place, and in fact has the consequence of obscuring or even undermining the love that should ideally be the basis for the friendship between parents and their adult children.

## What Sawyer and Kate Can Teach Us About the Ethics of Friendship

When we do a favor for someone, we often expect that they will someday do the same for us if we call in that favor. If I help out an acquaintance, I expect that someday he'll return the favor, if need be. He owes it to me, given my previous act of assistance. English notes, however, that friendship doesn't work this way. True friends don't keep track of the sacrifices they've made for one another. Their motive is not to be repaid someday, but rather to give what they can to one another. Friends don't keep track of favors owed; they help each other simply because they are friends.

As relationships develop on the island, the survivors of Oceanic Flight 815 who become friends don't keep track of the ways that they help one another. For example, at one point Locke and Claire develop a friendship, and Locke builds a crib for Claire's newborn baby. In the context of a friendship like this, such actions aren't done in order to get something in return. Rather, they are done out of affection and care. Similarly, over the first three seasons of the show, Sawyer and Kate have developed some sort of friendship. In the first episode of the third season, they end up in cages about 20 feet from each other, put there by the Others. Sawyer is concerned for Kate, and throws her some food that he was able to get. And later in the third season, their relationship becomes romantic. Given that they are friends, Sawyer and Kate don't keep track of the ways in which they've helped each other. The motive for helping out a friend is affection and in some cases even love.

## Jack and Christian as Friends?

After Jack reports his father's misconduct to the hospital, Christian flees to Sydney. Jack and his mother talk, and she urges Jack to go to Sydney and bring back his father. Jack tells her that "He doesn't want me to bring him back, I'm not one of his friends." His mother responds that Christian doesn't have any friends, and because of what Jack did, he has to go bring his father back. Jack ends up finding his father in a morgue, dead from an alcohol-induced heart attack. He then pleads his way onto Flight 815 so that he can bury his father back in Los Angeles.

Given that no friendship exists between Jack and his father, it follows for English that Jack doesn't have any obligations to his father. The same applies to all other relationships between adult children and their parents. But it doesn't follow from this that an adult child can treat her parents however she wants to treat them, nor that the sacrifices parents make are entirely irrelevant to the relationship. Ideally, the sacrifices that parents make on behalf of their children will ultimately help create a friendship between parents and their adult children. Friendships can and do begin in this manner.

The idea that English rejects is that the sacrifices made by parents on behalf of their children *create obligations* that those children must fulfill as adults. The amount of parental sacrifice is irrelevant to the adult child's obligations to her parents, because this type of debt is not appropriate to friendship relationships. And the relationship between adult children and their parents should ideally be a friendship relationship. Not only does this mean that the amount and kind of sacrifices made by parents on behalf of their children are irrelevant to the adult child's obligations, but it also means that the biological relationship between parents and children is irrelevant, according to English. So, if the survivors of Oceanic 815 are one day rescued, and Claire asks her son Aaron for some financial help to pay her medical bills, he would not have the obligation to do so simply because of the time, physical labor, and emotional effort that Claire gave to raise him. But if they have an ongoing friendship, a relationship in which there is mutual care, concern, and affection, then Aaron should and will help her out if he can. For English, whether or not there is an ongoing friendship will determine the obligations that Aaron has to Claire.

*Michael W. Austin*

# The Others

No, not *those* others, but rather the other possible sources of obligation in the parent–child relationship that are worth thinking about. Consider the following from philosopher Henry Sidgwick (1838–1900):

> It would be agreed that children owe to their parents respect and kindness generally and assistance in case of infirmity or any special need; but it seems doubtful how far this is held by Common Sense to be due on account of the relationship alone, or on account of services rendered during infancy, and how far it is due to cruel or neglectful parents. Most perhaps would say, here and in other cases, that mere nearness of blood constituted a certain claim: but they would find it hard to agree upon its exact force.[2]

Sidgwick offers a view that contrasts with that of English. His words reflect the traditional view that children do owe respect, kindness, and special assistance to their parents. He is more tentative regarding the sources of these obligations, however, though he notes several possibilities: (1) the quality of the relationship; (2) the biological connection; and (3) as a debt of gratitude for parental services rendered during childhood.

Sidgwick is in agreement with English that the quality of the parent–child relationship itself plays a role in the existence and extent of the obligations that the adult child has to the parent. From this source, it looks like neither Jack nor Locke are obligated in any way to their fathers. A disagreement arises between Sidgwick and English insofar as Sidgwick grants that the biological relationship and the services rendered by parents in the care of their children both play a role in dictating the existence and extent of these obligations. Do Jack or Locke owe their fathers anything based on these considerations?

Many people think that the biological connection that exists between parents and children is also a moral connection. If you are related "by blood," then you have some obligations to each other because of that kinship relationship. On this view, one need not think that Locke owes his biological father a kidney, nor that Jack owes it

---

[2] Henry Sidgwick, *The Methods of Ethics* (Indianapolis: Hackett, 1981), p. 248.

to his father to keep silent about his medical malpractice. But it seems that on this approach to the parent–child relationship, Jack and Locke both do owe their fathers at least some respect, kindness, and care. Moreover, on the grounds that they are related by blood, on this approach Jack does owe it to his father to bring him back home from Sydney, as his mother told him to do. On the biological approach, those of us who have had decent parents do owe them phone calls, visits, and financial support (if they need it and we're able to provide it). In opposition to the biological approach, it seems initially plausible that even when a biological relationship exists, if one's parents have seriously failed in their parental role then this relieves an adult child of at least some of his obligations, as the case of Jack and his dad makes plain. And if biology is relevant to the obligations that parents and children have to one another, factors such as the quality of the relationship play a large role in the extent of those obligations. The significance of the quality of the relationship over against the biological ties can be clearly seen when no such biological connection exists, as in the case of adopted children.

The other approach alluded to by Sidgwick emphasizes the debt adult children owe their parents due to the sacrifices made by the parents in raising the children. David Mellow has recently developed an argument for the conclusion that adult children do owe their parents a debt based on gratitude.[3] Most parents have benefited their children in many ways that have required major sacrifices on the part of the parents. Moreover, most parents have the right intentions and motives when making sacrifices on behalf of their children, such as the desire that their children have good and happy lives. With these thoughts in mind, it is again clear that Locke would owe nothing to Anthony Cooper based on a debt of gratitude. As Locke puts it, his father "pretended to love me just long enough to steal my kidney and dropped me back in the world like a piece of trash . . . just like he did on the day I was born!" Locke's biological father has made no sacrifices on Locke's behalf, ever. But on this understanding of family obligations, Jack does owe his father something. Still, how much Jack owes Christian is unclear. We know Christian is Claire's biological father, though he has kept this to himself. We also know from a conversation that Christian had in Sydney with Ana Lucia that he loves

---

[3] David Mellow, "Sources of Filial Obligation," unpublished paper.

and respects Jack, but is unable to tell him. So it seems likely that during Jack's childhood Christian did make some sacrifices with Jack's best interests in mind. If so, we can say that Jack does owe it to his father to go to Sydney and bring him back to Los Angeles.

## What Locke Needs, and What We Owe

After the transplant surgery, Locke wakes up in the hospital room he shared with his father, and his dad is gone, having checked out and returned home under private care. After learning what has occurred, that his own father has selfishly manipulated the entire situation and conned him out of one of his kidneys, Locke leaves the hospital and goes to his father's house. Bleeding from the spot where his kidney was removed, Locke is turned away by the security guard. Locke drives away, and in anger and despair he pulls over on the side of the road and weeps. The scene fades into Locke weeping in the same way at the hatch, which he has tried unsuccessfully to open. Locke cries out that "I've done everything you wanted me to do. So why did you do this?" It seems like the island at this point in the show's second season has become a surrogate father for Locke. Given that his own father not only manipulated him but also tried to kill him, it makes sense that Locke would look elsewhere! Just as he did all that he could do to obtain his father's love, he has tried to do all that the island has asked of him to learn why it brought him to itself. This observation might sound like it belongs in a book entitled *Lost and Psychology*, but this scene does have philosophical significance.

Locke's desire for his father's love, while perhaps too extreme, illustrates a need we have as human beings. For some reason, human nature is such that we long to have loving parental figures in our lives. If we don't have them, we deeply miss them, even as adults.[4] Children need their parents, especially early in life. And parents need their children and long for a close relationship with them, sometimes especially later in life. Given these facts, perhaps what parents owe their children and what children owe their parents rests not just on the quality of the relationship they share, the sacrifices that they make

---

[4] For a fuller discussion of this and other issues related to family ethics, see my *Conceptions of Parenthood: Ethics and the Family* (Aldershot: Ashgate, 2007).

for each other, or the biological relationship that exists. Instead, what parents and children owe one another depends on the needs they have that parents and children are uniquely situated to meet for one another. Clearly, Jack and Locke both need more from their fathers than they received. Their fathers have, in fact, failed to fulfill their parental obligations to their sons. It's also clear that the parents of adult children have a very human need that only their adult children can meet, the need for respect and love from one's children. Perhaps the recognition and true appreciation of this need can go a long way in telling us what Jack, Locke, and the rest of us owe our parents.[5]

---

[5]  I would like to thank Cameron Griffith, Brett Patterson, Jonathan Boyd, and Bill Irwin for their comments on earlier versions of this chapter.

# 2

# Should We Condemn Michael for Saving Walt?

## *Rebecca Vartabedian*

In the closing moments of season two's finale, Michael leads Jack, Kate, Sawyer, and Hurley to the Others in exchange for his son, Walt. As Walt and he putter away in a tugboat pointed in the direction of safety, Michael exchanges a long look with Jack, Kate, and Sawyer, who sit – bound and gagged – on the dock, now apparently prisoners of the Others.

Perhaps we should condemn Michael's actions. Then again, perhaps we find ourselves sympathetic to Michael's situation. In fact, we might say that in a similar situation we would be inclined to make the same kind of trade.

With its use of flashbacks, *Lost* is clearly concerned with why characters make the choices they do. As viewers, we have already subjectively evaluated Michael's actions, but how can Michael's actions be understood and objectively evaluated in the context of *Lost*'s island? In this chapter we'll consider two candidates for an adequate evaluative framework on the island: utilitarianism and an ethic of *prima facie* duties. An adequate framework accounts for the variety of features any situation presents, and accounts for the variety of reasons and the special obligations one might have for making any decision. The adequate framework "fits the facts" in this way.

## Consequences, Goods, Decisions: A Look at Utilitarianism

Utilitarianism is a version of hedonism, the philosophical perspective that pleasure ought to be maximized and pain minimized. John Stuart

Mill's (1806–1873) version of utilitarianism maintains that one ought to act in order to bring about the best consequences for the greatest number of people, where the best consequences are understood as an increase in overall happiness. This principle, known as the Greatest Happiness Principle, is the fundamental tenet of utilitarianism, serving as a decision-making principle and as a tool for evaluating actions.

Mill's utilitarianism calls on us to act as impartially as possible. "As between his own happiness and that of others, utilitarianism requires him to be as strictly impartial as a disinterested and benevolent spectator."[1] That is, each individual's interests count equally in our decision-making process. Consider Hurley, who is responsible for the food pantry in the hatch. Tired of the strict control over food, Hurley decides to distribute it. He shares the food because he believes sharing – rather than rationing – would be better for everyone.

What about Michael's situation? First, in order for Michael to be justified in a course of action he must consider Walt's and his interests as equal to those of Jack, Kate, Sawyer, and Hurley. Then he should determine which course of action would bring the greatest amount of happiness to the most people. Imagine that each survivor is allotted one unit of happiness. On the requirement of satisfying happiness, making decisions becomes simply a matter of calculating units of happiness. In the situation at the dock, we have the balance of four units of happiness to two. On this calculation, the interests of the captives on the dock outweigh the interests of father and son. So utilitarianism would forbid Michael to do what he did.

This requirement for impartiality seems awfully demanding. Michael's status as Walt's father seems like a factor that should count in his decision. We tend to think that the special relationship parents have with their children should be given more weight in our moral calculations and decisions. A utilitarian might attempt to account for the special nature of Michael's relationship to Walt in a decision-making process by identifying the "contingent significance of special relationships."[2] This "contingent significance" is the idea that our special relationships provide a handy way of being able to bring

[1] John Stuart Mill, *Utilitarianism*. In *Utilitarianism and On Liberty*, 2nd edn., Mary Warnock, ed. (Oxford: Blackwell, 2003), p. 194.

[2] Diane Jeske and Richard Fumerton, "Relatives and Relativism" in *Philosophical Studies* 87 (1997), pp. 147–148.

about the good. Putting what we know about Michael's and Walt's past aside, the simple fact that Michael is Walt's father puts him in a position to make choices that would satisfy the good and serve Walt's interests by bringing his perspective as a parent to the utilitarian decision process.

When Jin, Sawyer, and Michael prepare to sail off the island on the raft, it's reasonable to assume Walt will come along too. Presumably, Michael brings Walt along because he perceives it would be in Walt's best interests to get off the island. At least until their plan is foiled by the Others and Walt is captured, this decision serves the overall good too, since the idea was not just to get Walt off the island but to rescue the group once they arrived safely at their destination. Here a concern for Walt's well-being contributes to the overall purpose of leaving the island. The same might be said about Jin's motives for leaving Sun behind. These special relationships are only of contingent significance – that is, these special relationships are not important to the situation because they reflect our intuitive notions of the obligations parents have to children and husbands to wives. Instead, the parent-child (or husband-wife) relationship is acknowledged as instrumental in promoting the best consequences for all.

The scenario at the dock illustrates the difficulty with this perspective. If Michael is responsible for bringing about the greatest happiness for the greatest number, his parental perspective is still only secondary to the overall best outcome. On this view, the courses of action available to Michael on the dock either benefit the fewest number (Walt and him) or they require Michael to leave aside his obligation to Walt. This results in a kind of stalemate.

The impartiality requirement prevents Michael from acting to promote Walt's interests. Even if he was planning an alternate (and more benign) course of action than the one he undertook, Michael could not act unless the interests of everyone were equally accounted for. Further, the happiness requirement indicates that Michael would be risking more by putting others in jeopardy simply to rescue Walt, who counts equally in the equation. From this end of the analysis, Michael's prospects for saving Walt look fairly bleak.

Additionally, Michael runs into another problem on the utilitarian account. If it's the case that the right course of action is that which benefits the most people, then any action or set of actions might be justified as long as the actions yield good outcomes for everyone concerned. For utilitarianism, the end can justify the means. Sayid's torture of "Henry Gale" (Ben) could be justified on this analysis if such actions resulted in a way off the island, or some large-scale benefit for Oceanic 815's survivors. As long as the actions themselves lead to the best outcome, theft, murder, and even torture can be justified.

Michael clearly fails here since his actions – leading all the way back to the (deliberate) murder of Ana Lucia and the (accidental) killing of Libby – have brought about bad consequences for the group, culminating in the effective loss of Jack, Kate, and Sawyer to the Others. It would appear, then, that the outcomes-focused analysis of utilitarianism only leads us to blame Michael for what seems to be an intuitive duty of a parent – saving Walt.

## Ross's Intuitionism and *prima facie* Duties

The utilitarian system relies on one principle to do all the moral work. But the survivors (like all of us) face a messy situation that demands more complicated analysis than one principle can provide. So let's consider W. D. Ross's (1877–1971) theory of *prima facie* duties, which is *agent-specific*. Broadly speaking, the theory employs several principles (rather than just one) that are flexible, not in their nature, but in their relative applicability to a situation. Ross proposes that an adequate moral framework must "fit the facts" of our experience.[3] In the same vein, he rejects frameworks that seek to maximize good outcomes, since all acts that are identified as good or right under utilitarian analysis ignore whatever reasons may accompany or precede the action itself.

Ross proposes a system that accommodates a variety of moral principles available to us on reflection. The flashbacks on *Lost* give unique access to each character's "moral memory," pieces of information that are relevant – if not absolutely necessary – for understanding an action. Ultimately, these flashbacks have the substance of reasons. In telling us what they do about each character, the flashbacks are an important resource for understanding morally

---

[3]  W. D. Ross, *The Right and the Good*, Philip Stratton-Lake, ed. (Oxford: Oxford University Press, 2002), p. 19.

significant choices. We know how Michael will act when it comes to Walt, because we have access to moral reflection and relevant moral experience recorded in the flashbacks.

By acknowledging a variety of relevant moral principles, Ross thinks his theory "fits the facts" better than utilitarianism does. Ross recognizes six *prima facie* duties, which are really dispositions (or attitudes) toward certain kinds of acts:[4]

1   Our recognition that both keeping promises and telling the truth are good yields the *prima facie* duty of fidelity.
2   Related to the idea that keeping promises should be valued is the idea that previous wrongful acts should be put right. This view about previous wrongs introduces the *prima facie* duty of reparation.[5]
3   A recognition that goods of various sorts ought to be properly distributed forms the basis for a *prima facie* duty of justice.
4   That there are certain actions we can undertake to improve the situation of others in pleasure, intelligence, or virtue is the foundation for a *prima facie* duty of beneficence.
5   That there are certain actions we can undertake to improve our own situation introduces a *prima facie* duty of self-improvement.
6   A recognition that one ought not bring harm to others leads to the *prima facie* duty of non-injury (non-malfeasance), which is stricter in scope than that of beneficence.

The reasons for upholding these *prima facie* duties emerge from our moral experience, since we only come to know these principles in particular situations.

## The Button: How *prima facie* Duties Work

The *prima facie* duties don't tell Michael precisely what to do about Walt. Rather, these duties provide a way of deciding how to act by

---

[4]   The substantial discussion from which this summary is taken can be found in Ross, pp. 20–21.
[5]   Ross handles these duties together and so the first "duty" is really two. I've separated them here for consistency and clarity.

sorting through the features of a situation (including the relationships in play) and assessing reasons for or against competing courses of action. In any given situation one acts according to the weight of reasons, and in doing so Michael "sorts" among his *prima facie* duties. As Ross points out,

> When I am in a situation, as perhaps I always am, in which more than one of these *prima facie* duties is incumbent on me, what I have to do is to study the situation as fully as I can until I form the considered opinion (it is never more) that in the circumstances one of them is more incumbent on me than any other; then I am bound to think that to do this *prima facie* duty is my duty *sans phrase* in the situation.[6]

Our actual duty (what Ross means by the term "duty *sans phrase*" above) in any situation is a matter of judgment that is determined by our assessment of *prima facie* duties. Consider an analogy. If each individual has a transmission (as in a car) with six gears, these gears run in neutral until we need to move the moral car forward. This shift and the subsequent movement constitute our actual duty.

Think of John Locke's refusal to continue pushing the button. After seeing the video at the Pearl station, he comes to see the Dharma Initiative as an insult to his own intelligence and virtue. In this situation, John's act was *prima facie* right because he acted according to the duty of self-improvement. But note that the *prima facie* rightness of his action does not guarantee any sort of outcome, nor can we immediately evaluate the act. According to Ross, the evaluation cannot be immediately known (or counted for or against our reasons for acting).[7] In this case, John's refusal ultimately destroyed the hatch. In order to evaluate his act we must wait until we know the impact of this event on the castaways.[8]

Michael's moral transmission has shifted to beneficence in order to save Walt. Speaking broadly, their relationship is governed by this *prima facie* duty of beneficence and so Michael is obligated to improve Walt's overall situation in pleasure, intelligence, or virtue.

---

[6] Ross, p. 19.
[7] See Ross, pp. 31–32.
[8] In chapter four, "Research Ethics and the Dharma Project," Deborah Barnbaum gives an analysis of another of John Locke's actions according to the *prima facie* principles identified in the contemporary theory of Beauchamp and Childress.

Just as Michael has this duty, Walt has a right to Michael's doing this kind of work on his behalf.[9] The relationship between duties and rights is mutually reinforcing, and so *prima facie* duties can be clarified as a responsibility, which is ultimately a more accurate way of describing what *prima facie* duties are. His responsibility to his son has required Michael to override his other duties in favor of saving Walt. Michael's actual duty – Ross's designation for what we do, in fact, choose to do – involves potential injury to Jack, Kate, and Sawyer.

## Saving Walt: *Prima facie* Duties, Actual Duty, and Equilibrium

When Michael overrides his other duties in favor of beneficence to Walt, he does not eliminate his other duties. Instead, his other duties are drawn into perspective accordingly. Ross explains the relationship between *prima facie* duties and actual duties this way:

> When we think ourselves justified in breaking a promise to relieve someone's distress, we continue to recognize a *prima facie* duty to keep our promise, and this leads us to feel not shame or repentance, but compunction, for behaving as we do; we recognize, further, that it is our duty to make it up somehow to the promisee for the breaking of the promise.[10]

Note carefully what Ross is saying here. We don't have a blank check to act however we want. Our relationships to others bind us to them, so *prima facie* duties construct a system within which one is able to act, as well as be held accountable for actions. Consider Michael's long look as an acknowledgment of what he has done *and to whom he has done it*. Hurley returned to the group and relayed what Michael has done. The group will be justified in restoring the equilibrium, acting according to the duty of justice if and when they encounter Michael again.

Actual duties, when they require us to discern between two *prima facie* duties, demand what Ross terms a "moral risk," especially since *prima facie* duties aren't themselves a guarantee or guide for what

---

[9]  See Ross, p. 48.
[10]  Ross, p. 28.

comes next. Michael's actions certainly fit this bill. Michael's actual duty in this situation is based on his acknowledgment of his role as Walt's father. This actual duty has arisen from his reflection on past events. His duty of beneficence to Walt has overridden his other duties but not eliminated them. There's no telling what the group will do when confronted with Michael's apparently treasonous behavior, but *prima facie* duties give a way for them to sort out what is important in order for them to act on behalf of Jack, Kate, and Sawyer.

So, should we condemn Michael for saving Walt? It's a close call, but no. Michael's reasons for acting as he did were closely aligned with a duty to beneficence and care for his son. Unfortunately, Michael's actions opened the possibility for Jack, Kate, and Sawyer to be harmed. Michael is bound to these three by duties of reparation and justice. The group also has *prima facie* grounds for holding Michael accountable for his actions, based on these same duties. It will be interesting to see how they react when Michael returns.[11]

[11] My thanks to Karen Adkins, Michael Austin, Deborah Barnbaum, Chip Case, Nancy Hollenback, Sharon Kaye, Andrew Vartabedian, Matthew Vartabedian, and George Wrisley for providing comments and helpful suggestions on several drafts of this chapter.

# 3

# Moral Stand-offs:
# Objectification on *Lost*

## *Robert Arp and*
## *Patricia Brace*

## The Right and Wrong of Objectification

Objectification is the act of treating a person like an object. People can use objects like hammers, cars, and computers to get what they want, fulfill goals, or gain pleasures. On *Lost* the characters consistently use each other to gain information, power, trust, or sexual pleasure. For example, Sawyer seduces the unhappy wives of rich men in order to subject them to phony oil well scams ("Two for the Road"). Such behavior strikes us as wrong because we think of people as rational beings – worthy of dignity and respect – who never should be treated like mere objects. In fact, in the history of western philosophy there are at least three distinct grounds for thinking that objectification is morally wrong, namely Kantian ethics, utilitarian ethics, and virtue ethics. Things are not that simple, however. As we'll see, each of these three ethical approaches can also be used to argue that objectification is sometimes morally right. So in the end what can we say about the morality of objectification?

## You Respect Me for My Mind, Right?
## Kant and Moral Sanctity

Followers of Immanuel Kant (1724–1804) ground moral decision-making in the fact that persons are conscious, rational beings, capable of making their own free and informed decisions. He tells us that we should "act in such a way that you always treat humanity, whether in your own person or in the person of another, never simply as a means, but always at the same time as an end." Kant is not ruling out the moral possibility of treating people as means. After all, we have to use people for goods, services, information, and such things in order to live our daily lives. What Kant is ruling out is treating a person as *nothing but a means* for such ends. In other words, a person must always be treated as an end in him or herself even while also being used as a means to some other end. Because we are conscious, rational beings, persons have an *intrinsic* value (as ends) and not just an *instrumental* value (as a means to an end) like some object, tool, thing, or instrument. From this perspective, morally right decisions are those decisions that treat a person as an end, and morally wrong decisions are those that treat a person as a mere instrument or means to an end.[1]

Characters in *Lost* constantly are portrayed as having instrumental value, to be used like mere things. For example, Charlie Pace, the has-been British rock star, is a heroin addict, and we see through flashbacks that he was a user of people as well as drugs. In the episode "Homecoming," after his one-hit wonder band DriveSHAFT goes bust, he is forced to become a sort of hustler based on his former fame. At a bar one night, a fellow addict instructs him to find a rich woman and take her for as much as he can get. When he's recognized by a group of Sloane Ranger types – well-to-do young British women – he joins them for a round of drinks and his hit song, "You All Everybody," on the jukebox. His object becomes Lucy, and we learn that her father owns a very successful company. When Charlie is invited to dinner at their well appointed home, he cases the place for any readily portable, pawnable small items. A silver and gold case that belonged to Winston Churchill fits the bill, but Charlie can't quite bring himself to steal it – yet. After bonding with her father over dinner, Charlie admits to him and Lucy that his band is over and he's

---

[1] See Immanuel Kant, *Foundations of the Metaphysics of Morals*, trans. Lewis White Beck (Upper Saddle River, NJ: Prentice-Hall, 1989). A classic exposition of Kant's moral philosophy can be found in Onora O'Neill, *Constructions of Reason: Explorations of Kant's Practical Philosophy* (Cambridge: Cambridge University Press, 1990).

out of work. He returns to his furious drug buddy with only a job offer from Lucy's father, selling copiers. Without any items to fence, the buddy reminds him, they are now out of heroin: "A weekend without a fix. Monday should be bloody wonderful. Let's see how the future treats you then, hey, Charlie?"

Not well. Monday arrives, and at her house in the new suit Lucy has purchased for him, Charlie is sweating out withdrawal. Because of the kindness that Lucy and her family have shown him, once again, he's presented with the choice to be a moral person, but this time he fails. He waits for an opportune moment and slips the gold Churchill case in his jacket. He may be telling himself that it's "just in case" the job doesn't work out, but it's a lie. Lucy, her father, and their property are the means to his end – more drugs – plain and simple. He can't escape yet, however, as Lucy cheerfully volunteers to drive him to work because it's his first day. Forced to go through with his sales spiel, he tries to sell a copier series 815 (same number as the doomed flight) and, unfortunately, ends up vomiting all over the copier and passing out. Even more unfortunately for Charlie, the ambulance crew taking him to the hospital finds Churchill's case in his coat and it's returned to Lucy.

## A Kantian Stand-off: Sanctity versus Autonomy

Charlie Pace is an obvious example of a self-centered user of people and drugs, and you don't need to be Immanuel Kant to see that his actions are immoral! But things get a little more hairy when we consider other aspects of Kant's moral theory. Given that persons are conscious, rational beings, capable of making their own free and informed decisions, Kant also notes that they must be considered as *autonomous* beings. The word *autonomy* comes from two Greek words meaning self (*auto*) and law (*nomos*), highlighting the facts that a rational person is "self-ruling" and his or her own informed decisions should be respected. Since a person's innate dignity and worth are tied to rational autonomy, some post-Kantian philosophers argue that what is most significant in making a moral decision has to do with whether a person's *freedom in rationally informed decision-making* has been respected.[2] The idea here is that if a fully rational person chooses to engage in some action – as long as the action doesn't harm anyone else – then that person is fully justified in making that decision, even if the decision puts that person in the position of being used by another person or group of persons.

Consider when Claire allows herself to be used as "bait" to help capture her kidnapper, the devious representative of the Others, Ethan Rom ("Other Man"). Think of fully rational adults joining the army of a nation knowing that they may be sacrificed for the sake of that nation's winning a war. Or think of persons getting hired at a huge corporation knowing full well that the ultimate goal of the company is to make money, and that they may lose their jobs in a downsizing that would keep the corporation afloat. For that matter, there would be nothing immoral about one spy using another spy as a sexual conduit for information, since both spies freely and autonomously have agreed to engage in these behaviors knowing full well that they are using and being used.

This seems to set up a conflict in Kant's moral decision-making process between, on one hand, the idea that one should never use another person as an instrument, and on the other hand, the idea that fully rational persons have the freedom to make their own well-informed decisions, even if those decisions include using or being used by another person. So, there is one camp of "moral sanctity" Kantians who would argue that it's immoral to objectify a person, no matter what.[3] And there is another camp of "moral autonomy" Kantians who would argue that, as long as all parties are fully aware of the parameters, risks, and consequences of the situation, nothing immoral occurs in the whole using/being used process. In fact, these same thinkers often argue that to deny a person the freedom to choose to be of use to someone else would itself be immoral because such a denial violates a person's autonomy as a rational, wholly free

2   See Thomas Hill, *Autonomy and Self Respect* (New York: Cambridge University Press, 1991); Christine Korsgaard, *The Sources of Normativity* (New York: Cambridge University Press, 1996); Timothy Madigan, "The Discarded Lemon: Kant, Prostitution and Respect for Persons," *Philosophy Now* 21 (1998), pp. 14–16.
3   Andrea Dworkin, *Pornography: Men Possessing Women* (New York: Perigee Press, 1981); Catherine MacKinnon, *Feminism Unmodified: Discourses on Life and Law* (Cambridge, MA: Harvard University Press, 1988).

29

decision-maker. In other words, to deny a person the freedom to choose is to reduce that person to an object, since, after all, mere objects lack choices.[4] Here, we have a bit of a stand-off concerning Kant's moral decision-making process. From the moral sanctity perspective, objectification is morally wrong; from the moral autonomy perspective, objectification can be morally right.

## A Utilitarian Stand-off: Bad Use versus Good Use

Followers of John Stuart Mill (1806–1873) argue that an action is morally good insofar as its consequences promote the most benefit, pay-off, or pleasure for the most persons affected by the decision. This view has been termed *utilitarian* because of the apparent usefulness (utility) to be found in generating the most satisfaction for the group of persons. In opposition to the Kantian view that persons never should be used as a mere means to some end, the utilitarian position justifies treating persons as means to the greater good of achieving benefit for the majority.[5] For example, if the greater consequence of saving the group from some evil-doer requires killing one, two, or even a hundred people in the process, then, on utilitarian grounds, this may be deemed morally correct. On *Lost*, John Locke often keeps vital information from the majority of the survivors in order to accomplish his goals: "what they don't know won't hurt them" (see, for example, "Do No Harm"). Locke is of course wrong about the harmlessness of secrets, as disastrous consequences follow. Thus, he violates the utilitarian view.

One prime example of the utilitarian position can be found in the actions of the *Lost* character Danielle Rousseau. Shipwrecked on the island 16 years ago when her research vessel ran aground, the Frenchwoman has lived there most of the time alone, in part because the others kidnapped her newborn daughter, Alex, but mostly because

---

4   Ann Garry, "Pornography and Respect for Women," in John Arthur, ed., *Morality and Moral Controversies* (Upper Saddle River, NJ: Prentice-Hall, 1993), pp. 395–421; Madigan, "The Discarded Lemon"; Sibyl Schwarzenbach, "On Owning the Body," in James Elias, Vern Bullough, Veronica Elias, and Gwen Brewer, eds., *Prostitution: On Whores, Hustlers, and Johns* (New York: Prometheus Books, 1998), pp. 345–351.

5   John Stuart Mill, *Utilitarianism* (Indianapolis: Hackett, 2002); Peter Singer, *Practical Ethics* (Cambridge: Cambridge University Press, 1993).

she killed the rest of her crew. We first meet her in person in the episode "Solitary," where she captures and interrogates Sayid. Part of the reason Sayid was out in the jungle was that he'd intercepted the distress call she had set to broadcast continually for the last 16 years. When he goes searching for the source of the transmission she traps him and proceeds to torture him, trying to find out if he knows where her child is. Ironically, we know from the previous episode, "Confidence Man," the other reason Sayid left camp was because of *his* part in torturing Sawyer in the mistaken belief that the con man was hoarding medicine. Torture is perhaps the ultimate objectification. And those who attempt to justify it do so by focusing on the end rather than the means – it achieves a "greater good." Sayid's greater good was supposed to be finding asthma medicine for Shannon; Rousseau's is finding her daughter and ultimately preserving her own life.

Previously, we noted that Kant's theory presents us with a moral stand-off because the same grounds of conscious rationality – and hence, autonomy – can be used to justify the morality and immorality of objectification. A stand-off also arises from the utilitarian perspective, as one can sometimes argue on utilitarian grounds *both* that objectification is good and bad. If consequences are the key to determining whether objectification is morally wrong, then we can see that treating persons as objects has negative ramifications and, hence, is morally unacceptable. Think of all of the instances of slavery throughout human history and all of the negative consequences that follow. Or think of instances of totalitarian regimes – like Stalin's Soviet Union or Hitler's Third Reich – where persons were tormented, tortured, unjustly treated, displaced from their homes, and murdered, all for the greater "good" of some state or ideology. Further, consider the consequences to our communities of treating women or men like sex objects, as is common in advertising, television shows, and movies. Such objectification has been linked to violence against women, date-rape, eating disorders, and a general disrespect for the sanctity of intimate relationships.[6]

---

[6]  See the resources, videos, and articles at www.vawnet.org; also, Lisa Tessman, "Critical Virtue Ethics: Understanding Oppression as Morally Damaging," in Peggy DesAutels and Joanne Waugh, eds., *Feminists Doing Ethics* (Lanham, MD: Rowman and Littlefield, 2001) pp. 79–99; Kathleen Barry, *The Prostitution of Sexuality* (New York: New York University Press, 1995); Susan Dwyer, *The Problems of Pornography* (Belmont, CA: Wadsworth, 1995).

However, as crazy as it may first seem, it's possible to argue that objectification sometimes has had – and does have – good consequences. Hence, on utilitarian grounds, one can argue that forms of objectification are moral and should be promoted. One could argue that the objectification of persons, as on *Lost*, sometimes has good consequences for the community.[7] One could say that *Lost* stories act as foils to real life, teaching folks a lesson on how *not* to treat people. This is nothing new in storytelling, and has been used as a valuable teaching tool throughout recorded human history, from the ancient Hindu Vedic scriptures, through the Hebrew/Christian scriptures, to Grimm's fairy tales, and into this century with the rise of film. Characters are presented in situations where they act in ways that bring about their own suffering or demise, and we learn from their inappropriate behavior how to act appropriately. *Lost* stories, then, have the good consequence of teaching a moral lesson.

A darkly humorous example of this is the know-it-all high school science teacher, Mr. Leslie Arzt. He spends most of his short on-screen time telling the other characters what they are doing wrong. In the episode "Exodus, Part 1," when a group decides to follow Rousseau into the jungle to salvage enough dynamite to blow open the hatch, Arzt pushes his way into the party by explaining how dangerous dynamite is to handle. He berates Jack, Locke, and Kate, and then delivers a schoolhouse style lecture on the history of dynamite. We find it ironic, initially shocking, and then oddly satisfying when, during a demonstration of correct practice in dynamite transport, he blows himself up. On the *Lost* island, the arrogance of thinking one has all the answers often leads to dangerous twists of fate. Arzt's death does serve a purpose: it's an excellent warning for the rest of the party who now must *carefully* transport the dangerous explosives back across the island to successfully blow the hatch. And it teaches the viewer the valuable lesson that one has to be careful not to let "know-it-all" emotional arrogance get in the way of true, careful assessment.

---

[7] For utilitarian arguments defending objectification, see Sarah Bromberg, "Feminist Issues in Prostitution," in *Prostitution: On Whores, Hustlers, and Johns*, pp. 294–321; Marti Hohmann, "Prostitution and Sex-Positive Feminism," in *Prostitution: On Whores, Hustlers and Johns*, pp. 322–331.

One could also argue that the actions and values associated with objectification in *Lost* stories could be good for persons trying to simply survive or survive successfully in this world. The fact of the matter is that it's beneficial to use and manipulate people, at times, so as to get what you need or want. This is the way it works in most societies, and you can either play the game and make it in life, or not play the game and get crushed by the others who are playing.

For example, the episode "The Long Con" is all about gamesmanship. The star of the tale is Sawyer and, even though he is still in conflict with Jack about the medical supplies, at the start of the episode, Sawyer has been semi-redeemed in the mind of many of the survivors for his part in the failed raft expedition. On the raft Sawyer took a bullet while trying to protect Walt from the Others (unusual self-sacrifice, considering his previous track record) and saved Michael from drowning. These actions earned him a place in Kate's good graces as she nurses him back to health. Sawyer is a player, and he finds a way to use all this good will to his advantage. Sawyer knows that Jack and Locke are at odds over control of the large weapons cache discovered in the hatch armory. Ana Lucia wants the guns to start an army to go after the Others, but not everyone perceives the threat to be as dire as she does. When Sun is attacked in an apparent kidnapping attempt, Sawyer leads Kate to believe it was a set-up perpetrated by Ana to force Locke and Jack's hand about the armory. It works – just the way Sawyer intended. Kate sends him to warn Locke that Ana and Jack are coming for the guns. Locke is manipulated into moving the guns while Sawyer remains behind in the hatch (pushing the all-important and mysterious button). After finding the armory empty, Jack confronts Locke on the beach, demanding two guns. As they argue, shots ring out from the tree line and out strolls Sawyer, gun in hand. He delivers a self-serving speech in which he rails against them for raiding his stash while he was on the raft and says he won't take orders from Jack and Locke, ending with, "New sheriff in town, boys! You-all best get used to it."

In this episode, Sawyer has played well, and he has won. We might even admire his willingness to do directly and boldly what the rest of us try to do in a more tentative and ineffective way.

# Lost Souls?

We have seen that the attempt to determine the moral status of objectification on Kantian and utilitarian grounds has led to moral stand-
offs, as one can sometimes argue that objectification is either right or
wrong depending upon what aspect of Kantianism or utilitarianism
one emphasizes. Kantianism and utilitarianism are known as *action-
based* moral theories whereby the issues surrounding the moral
action (Kantianism) and its consequences (utilitarianism) are central.
In contrast to these action-based moral theories is a moral theory
dating back to Aristotle (384–322 BCE) which places emphasis on the
soul/psyche/mind/disposition/character (for our purposes these all
mean the same thing, but we'll continue to use the word *character*)
from which the moral action stems.

Because the concern is to promote a good or *virtuous* character,
this moral position is known as *virtue ethics*. The central idea is that
if one has a virtuous character, then not only will one likely perform
morally right actions, but also these actions likely will have good
consequences.[8] If someone is sick or hurt, the survivors can count on
Jack (who is caring and reliable) to treat that person and usually with
good results. Like Jack, we want not only to perform right actions
that have good consequences; we also want to be *virtuous persons*.
You can get a demon (or Sawyer) to do the right thing yielding good
consequences – however, he's still a demon (or a con man). Wouldn't
it be better instead if we could turn demons into angels?! Thus, virtue
ethics can act as a kind of complement to the Kantian and utilitarian
positions, rounding out our moral lives.

Followers of Aristotle conceive of virtues as good habits whereby
one fosters a kind of balance in one's character. The idea is to promote the "not too much" or "not too little," but the "just right" in
our characters so that our actions and reactions to situations reflect
this hitting of the mean between two extremes. The virtuous person
has cultivated the kind of character whereby she knows how to act
and react in the right way, at the right time, in the right manner, and

---

[8] Aristotle, *Nicomachean Ethics*, trans. Martin Oswald (Upper Saddle River, NJ:
Prentice-Hall, 1962); Alasdair MacIntyre, *After Virtue* (Notre Dame, IN: University of
Notre Dame Press, 1981).

for the right reasons in each and every moral dilemma encountered. And the way in which one cultivates a virtuous character is through choosing actions that are conducive to building that virtuous character. So, for example, if one wants to cultivate the virtue of self-control so that one can actually be a self-controlled person, then one needs to act with self-control time and time again so that the virtue can "sink in" to the person's character. The more Charlie actually abstains from taking drugs, the more he cultivates the virtue of self-control. The more Sawyer lies when asked whether he has done something wrong, the more he cultivates the vice of dishonesty.

Important virtues include honesty, courage, prudence, generosity, integrity, affability, and respect, to name just a few. Respect is the key virtue for our purposes here. The person who has cultivated respect for persons in his or her character naturally will not objectify another person. When one treats a person as an object, one empties another of their intrinsic dignity, value, and worth, affecting both the one doing the objectifying and the one being objectified. In effect, the problem lies in the psychological ill-effects of treating another as less than a person.[9]

Some contemporary thinkers in the virtue ethics camp have argued for the cultivation of a different set of virtues. For example, Whelehan and Hohmann link objectification to psychological, social, and economic dynamics whereby *power* is envisioned as a virtue.[10] The idea that power – and with it, cleverness, manipulation, scheming, and well-placed aggression – act as virtues can be traced back to philosophers like Thomas Hobbes (1588–1679), Niccolò Machiavelli (1469–1527), and especially, Friedrich Nietzsche (1844–1900).[11]

---

[9]   See Elizabeth Brake, "Sexual Objectification and Kantian Ethics," in *Proceedings and Addresses of the American Philosophical Association* 76 (2003), pp. 120–131; Tessman, "Critical Virtue Ethics"; Barbara Andrew, "Angels, Rubbish Collectors, and Pursuers of Erotic Joy: The Image of Ethical Women," in *Feminists Doing Ethics*, pp. 119–134; Marilyn Friedman, *What Are Friends For? Feminist Perspectives on Personal Relationships and Moral Theory* (Ithaca, NY: Cornell University Press, 1993).

[10]   Imelda Whelehan, *Modern Feminist Thought: From Second Wave to 'Post-Feminism'* (New York: New York University Press, 1995); Hohmann, "Prostitution and Sex-Positive Feminism."

[11]   Thomas Hobbes, *Leviathan*, ed. C. B. MacPherson (New York: Penguin Books, 1982); Niccolò Machiavelli, *The Prince*, trans. Daniel Donno (New York: Bantam Classics, 1984); Friedrich Nietzsche, *Beyond Good and Evil*, trans. Walter Kaufmann (New York: Random House, 1966) and *The Will To Power*, trans. Walter Kaufmann (New York: Random House, 1967).

Nietzsche argued that power should be cultivated and, if exercised in the right way, can be conducive to a well-balanced character.

For Nietzsche, power can be understood in the context of a dominating master-slave relationship. Different people have different characters; an idea that can be traced back to Plato's (427–347 BCE) *Republic*.[12] Some people have the kind of character necessary to be in power, control others, or rule; while others have the kind of character that leads them to be powerless, controlled by others, or ruled. Another way of saying this is that there are types and degrees of personality. A well-balanced character is cultivated by a person being what she is naturally disposed to be. To be something that you are not would be the result of and would result in a disordered character. Following Nietzsche we might say that on *Lost* Locke, Sawyer, Sayid, Shannon, and Eko exhibit the virtue of power and sometimes rightly subjugate, control, and objectify powerless people like Boone, Charlie, and Hurley. In fact, all of this objectification is right and good since the dominant character is fulfilling his or her natural station in life as master and the one doing the objectifying, and the folks being used are fulfilling their natural stations in life as slaves and the ones being objectified.

## Lost in a Sea of Souls, What Kind of Character Do You Want to Foster?

We must now ask whether, from the virtue ethics perspective, one can successfully argue for the morality or immorality of objectification without falling into the same stalemate trap as that of the Kantian and utilitarian positions. The answer depends upon what one takes to be a virtue. From the Aristotelian-based virtue ethical perspective, *mere* objectification will be detrimental to character-building. From the Nietzschean-based virtue ethical perspective, however, objectification will be conducive to character-building.

So which virtue ethics perspective is the better one to uphold and foster in one's life? In other words, which kind of person should we strive to be, an Aristotle or a Nietzsche? It may seem sensible, from a

---

[12]  Plato, *The Republic of Plato*, trans. David Bloom (New York: Basic Books, 1991), Book 4.

practical perspective, for one to just be what one is naturally destined to be, as the Nietzschean-based perspective instructs. So, if you do not have the skills to become a pro basketball player, then don't bother beating yourself up – you'll never make it as a pro player and instead, only will find misery. In the same way, if you are naturally a master or a slave, then just go with it; be *who* you are as a master or a slave.

However, this may be where the Nietzschean-based perspective relies too much upon *what is* the case, and neglects *what ought to be* the case. It seems that, even if you are destined to be slave-like, people around you should not treat you as such for Aristotelian, as well as Kantian and utilitarian, reasons. We honestly must ask ourselves these four questions:

1   As a fully rational and autonomous person, should I treat myself or another fully rational and autonomous person as a means, rather than as end in him or herself? (The Kantian perspective)
2   What kinds of consequences will result for other persons affected by my action and me if I do decide to treat myself or another fully rational and autonomous person as a mere means, rather than as an end in him or herself? (The utilitarian perspective)
3   Do I want to foster a virtue in myself, my kids, my family, my community, and/or in my world whereby others are seen as persons worthy of respect, fundamentally equal to myself, making it such that one person is not permitted to objectify another person? (The Aristotelian virtue ethics perspective)
4   Do I want to foster a virtue in myself, my kids, my family, my community, and/or in my world whereby certain others are seen as emptied of the intrinsic dignity, value, and worth afforded to me as one of the lucky persons who happens to be endowed with a naturally powerful disposition, such that I am permitted to objectify another person? (The Nietzschean virtue ethics perspective)

Of course, these questions are "loaded" to a great extent; but this is done to make a point. It seems that, if (1) and (2) do not halt us in our tracks and stop us from objectifying ourselves or one another, then (3) and (4) give us pause to consider what kind of person we would become if we continually objectify other people. After all, a Nietzschean-minded position, in combination with versions of social

Darwinism, has been the distorted rationalization for many a totalitarian regime throughout human history including, most obviously, the Nazi Final Solution which led to the Holocaust.[13] Countless people have been killed because they weren't considered persons, under the justification of "survival of the fittest." (Although it may not be clear yet, the Others may be guilty in a similar way.) So, think of the various *Lost* personalities who exhibit Nietzsche-like or Aristotle-like characters. Ask yourself: "Do I want to be more like the Nietzschean Ana Lucia and Charlie Pace, or more like the Aristotelian Jack Shepherd and Boone?"

[13] See Robert Bannister, *Social Darwinism: Science and Myth in Anglo-American Social Thought* (Philadelphia: Temple University Press, 1989).

# 4

# Research Ethics
# and the Dharma Initiative

## Deborah R. Barnbaum

There are several incidences of experimenting on humans on *Lost*: the Dharma Initiative's observations of people punching in numbers at one hatch while being watched from another, Ben's experimentation on pregnant women, and Juliet's experiments on her own sister to induce fertility after cancer treatment. Some aspects of these experiments – such as kidnapping Claire to test her during her pregnancy – are morally repugnant. Yet much of what we know about medicine and psychology comes from experiments on humans, and we are grateful for that knowledge. Because advances in medicine and psychology require researchers to experiment on humans, ethical safeguards have been put in place to protect the interests of those human research subjects.

The modern era of human research subject protections commenced in 1948 with the adoption of the Nuremberg Code, a response to Nazi atrocities in which humans were brutally experimented on without their permission. The Nuremberg Code begins with the following statement: "The voluntary consent of the human subject is absolutely essential."[1] One cornerstone of the ethical use of human research subjects is informed consent from all research participants. However, there are several cases in which informed consent is either inappropriate or impossible to procure, such as research on very young children,

---

[1] Reprinted in Deborah R. Barnbaum and Michael Byron, *Research Ethics: Text and Readings*, (Upper Saddle River, NJ: Prentice-Hall, 2001), pp. 28–29. The Declaration of Helsinki can be found in this volume on pages 30–32, and the Belmont Report on pages 33–43.

the mentally ill, emergency room patients, and "deception research," where explaining the experiments to the subjects would undermine the experiment. Some aspects of the Nuremberg Code have been superseded by more recent codes, such as the World Medical Association's Declaration of Helsinki (first adopted in 1964; most recently revised in 2004), and the United States' governmental paper on human research ethics, the Belmont Report (1979), both of which allow for cases in which informed consent might ethically be waived.

This chapter examines one of the most shadowy experiments on the island – the Dharma Initiative's observation of people punching numbers into a computer – and asks if it is a morally acceptable project.

## Informed Consent I: What It Is, and Why It's Important

Informed consent requires that three conditions be met: (1) the subject has knowledge of certain facts about the proposed experiment; (2) the subject offers affirmative agreement to participate based upon an understanding of those facts; and (3) the subject's participation is completely voluntary.

Without knowledge of certain facts, the research subject isn't consenting in an informed manner. The extent of the participation, the risks and benefits of participating, the alternatives to participating, and the protections of the subject's confidentiality all should be known to the participant before the experiment starts. Absent this knowledge, there is no sense in which consent to participate is *informed*. It's pretty clear that no human subjects in the Dharma Initiative were informed about the extent of their participation, or the risks and benefits.

The second component of informed consent is that the subject must agree to participate *based upon an understanding* of the facts mentioned above. Being told a set of facts and nodding in agreement isn't sufficient for informed consent. Mere agreement is *assent*, but agreement based upon understanding is *consent*. It is assumed, for example, that young children are in a position to assent to some research studies, but that they cannot yet fully understand the risks and benefits, and thus cannot consent to participation. Walt, for example, wouldn't be able to consent to participation in the Dharma

Initiative – only assent to participate – though Michael could consent on his behalf. Given the severity of Libby's mental disorder, she would not have been able to consent. Desmond, by contrast, is not a child, nor does he have a mental disability that would prevent him from fully grasping any aspects of the Dharma Initiative. He could have consented, but he was never given the chance.

Finally, the participation of the research subject must be completely voluntary. The research subject cannot be limited by external constraints, such as threats or attractive inducements (like lots of money), nor can the subject be limited by internal constraints, such as a mental disability, which might affect his ability to make a clear decision. It would be interesting to consider whether Juliet's sister consented voluntarily to experimental fertility treatments. Was the prospect of becoming pregnant so alluring so as to be coercive? Was Juliet's sister really in a position to say no to *her own sister* about an experimental procedure? In addition to these considerations, voluntariness must be ongoing. It is unethical to voluntarily enroll a subject in an experiment, with no way to exit once the experiment is in progress. If the subject wants to leave, it is immoral to keep him in the study against his will.

With each of these three elements in place – sufficient information, affirmative agreement based upon an understanding of that information, and voluntary participation – the subject is said to offer informed consent to participate.

## Four Principles of Biomedical Ethics

Informed consent has its moral basis in the principles of biomedical ethics. Tom Beauchamp and James F. Childress propose that there are four principles of biomedical ethics, each of which needs to be weighed against the others in determining what the right action should be in any given circumstance.[2]

*The principle of autonomy* dictates that we should respect persons, their decisions, and their privacy; that we should remove

[2]   Tom Beauchamp and James F. Childress, *Principles of Biomedical Ethics* (New York: Oxford University Press, 2001).

impediments to knowledge, understanding, and voluntariness; and that we should protect those who are not autonomous, such as children or the mentally disabled.

*The principle of nonmaleficence* dictates that we should not harm others. Some versions of the Hippocratic Oath, the ancient oath taken by Jack and other physicians, famously begin with a caution to "First do no harm."

*The principle of beneficence* dictates that we should promote good for others. This principle works against unrelenting selfishness and indifference.

*The principle of justice* dictates that we should treat people fairly, or equally, or in keeping with what they deserve. This is perhaps the most difficult principle to articulate, because there are competing notions of justice.

Beauchamp and Childress's theory is that each applicable principle should be weighed against the others in each case in order to determine the morally right action in a given situation. Consider this question: Should John Locke donate one of his kidneys to Anthony Cooper, his long-lost father? Beauchamp and Childress would ask that we consider the following questions: Is Locke's decision fully informed? How harmful will the donation be for Locke? How beneficial will it be for Cooper? Is the situation fair? According to Beauchamp and Childress, the answers to these questions should be weighed against each other to determine an answer. (See chapter one in this volume for another way to answer this thorny problem.)

It would be a mistake to say that just because three principles weigh in favor of keeping the kidney (autonomy, nonmaleficence, and justice) whereas only one principle weighs in favor of the alternative (beneficence), the right action is to keep the kidney. Beauchamp and Childress's theory doesn't simply say whatever action is guided by the greater number of principles wins. Rather, after examining the situation, we are supposed to apply our moral intuition to arrive at the answer. Locke made the wrong decision not because three principles of bioethics counted against the decision. He made the wrong decision because moral intuition demonstrates that the action that upholds the principles of autonomy, nonmaleficence, and justice are more stringent in this case than the action that upholds the principle of beneficence.

## Informed Consent II: If It's So Important, How Can We Ignore It?

Although the principles of biomedical ethics typically require informed consent, they may not in some circumstances. There are three types of research that seem morally permissible even without informed consent:

Some research is performed on *people who are by definition not autonomous*. For example, research is done on very young children with childhood leukemia, or on persons with mental disorders that may affect their decision-making capacity, such as advanced Alzheimer's, so that we might one day conquer these horrible diseases.

Some research is performed on *people who were autonomous, but who are in circumstances that temporarily render them non-autonomous, the very circumstances under study*. For example, a person could end up in an emergency room after a massive head trauma in a car accident. Imagine that this person was taken to a hospital that is researching a new therapy to reduce brain damage after head trauma.

Some research is performed on *people who, if they knew that they were research subjects, or if they knew what aspect of their behavior was being studied, might perform differently*. This is referred to as "deception research" – research that can only be accomplished if the experimental subject is deceived in some way. Studies that examine how people respond to unexpected, stressful situations wouldn't have reliable results if subjects were told "As part of this experiment we will be exposing you to a stressful situation" before the research began.

Deception may be justified if the benefit of the knowledge gained outweighs the risks of harm to the subjects, and that benefit also outweighs the subject's loss of autonomy in not giving informed consent. Deception in research can be justified for many of the reasons that deception is justified in non-research circumstances. So, for example, Rose may have rightly deceived Bernard into believing the faith healer cured her so that they could live out her remaining time in happiness, but Sawyer's long con of Cassidy that deceived her out of

$600,000 was not justified. Both cases involved a failure to respect the principle of autonomy, but Rose did so for the sake of beneficence, whereas Sawyer failed in his moral duty of nonmaleficence. Justice shouldn't be violated in deception research, by using vulnerable subjects who could not have said "no" even if they wanted to. Notice the weighing of principles here: beneficence outweighs both nonmaleficence and autonomy in ethically acceptable deception research, and justice is protected. But in cases in which the gain in knowledge is *outweighed* by the harm to subjects, coupled with their lack of autonomy, the deception research is not morally acceptable.

The Hanso Foundation's Dharma Initiative is a deception research project, designed to test participants' adherence to a strict regimen that doesn't necessarily follow rational rules. The Dharma Initiative asks the inhabitants of the "Swan" hatch to enter a meaningless sequence of numbers on a computer at regular intervals. Meanwhile, the inhabitants of the "Pearl" hatch must observe the activities in the Swan and submit reports. That the activities in the Pearl were just as meaningless as the activities in the Swan became evident when the reports were discovered, abandoned carelessly in the jungle. However, both parties *were* observed, and *those* observations were part of the Dharma Initiative (someone *was* watching the watchers). Would the participants, either the ones in the Swan or the Pearl, fulfill their roles if they weren't deceived? If either of those parties knew the truth behind their participation, they might have acted differently. Hence, deception was an integral part of Dharma.

Informed consent isn't possible in a deception project, but other research protections can and should apply when informed consent is waived. The Code of Federal Regulations (CFR) for the use of human research subjects, known as the Common Rule, states that it is permissible to waive informed consent only if:

1 the research is expected to yield only "minimal risks" (risks not beyond those of everyday life, including routine medical or psychological tests);
2 the rights and welfare of the subject are protected;
3 the research could not be done any other way than without informed consent; and, when appropriate,
4 additional pertinent information is made available to the subjects after participating. This is called "debriefing."

Given these rules, how does the Dharma Initiative stack up against three other famous experiments that tested behavioral and psychological responses?

## Questionable Research, or Just More Questions?

Stanley Milgram wanted to understand how it was possible for Germans during World War II to plausibly claim that they were "just following orders" when acting in ways that were obviously morally wrong.[3] Milgram designed an experiment in which research subjects were asked to follow an authority figure's orders, orders that the subjects knew that they should not follow. In the experimental set-up a subject, designated the "Teacher," entered a room and sat in front of a machine that supposedly administered electric shocks to a person – the "Learner" – who was seated in the next room. The "Teacher" couldn't see the "Learner," but could hear him. The "Learner" was supposedly being tested on his memory of word pairs – with each incorrect response the "Teacher" was told to shock the person, creating negative reinforcement so as to provoke correct answers. An experimenter stood over the "Teacher's" shoulder, urging him to give progressively more powerful shocks to the "Learner" with each wrong answer. A dial on the machine was marked clearly – the shocks steadily became more painful, then debilitating, then lethal – and yet the "Teacher" was urged by the authority figure to continue shocking the "Learner." The subject could hear the "Learner" screaming, and then eventually heard nothing but silence (suggesting that the "Teacher" killed the "Learner"). In fact, 65 percent of the "Teachers" administered what appeared to be lethal shocks to the "Learners," on the advice of an authority figure standing next to them.

Of course, this was all a deception – Milgram didn't really hurt or kill people in an attempt to show that other people will follow the advice of authority figures. Milgram demonstrated that otherwise normal people could be urged to do horrible things when an authority figure told them to do so, but Milgram wouldn't have

[3] Lauren Slater, *Opening Skinner's Box: Great Psychological Experiments of the Twentieth Century* (New York: W. W. Norton, 2004).

*Deborah R. Barnbaum*

been able to make this point unless the subjects were deceived. Many people would call the study an unethical deception: experiencing pressure to hurt or kill someone is deeply traumatizing, both during and afterward. Imagine how a debriefing session of the Milgram experiment might have concluded – "Oh, by the way, there wasn't really a person getting shocked, and you didn't really kill anybody. Have a nice day."

There are two parallels between the Milgram experiment and the Dharma Initiative. Both require deception, and thus preclude informed consent; both are designed to test the subjects' willingness to adhere to a regimen simply because they were told to do so.

The Tearoom Trade Study involved two parts, both of which incorporated deception. Laud Humphreys, a doctoral candidate at Washington University, investigated why men had anonymous sex in public bathrooms, a practice once known as "tearoom trade."[4] Humphreys offered to act as a guard to watch for police or intruders while other men had sex in a public bathroom. After they did so, Humphreys attempted to learn more about them, disclosing his role as a researcher. But in cases in which Humphreys was unable to learn more about the men, Humphreys surreptitiously followed the men into a parking lot to copy license plate numbers off their cars. Humphreys was then able to trace their identities. A year later, disguised as a public health worker conducting interviews, Humphreys presented himself at the men's homes. Through the interviews Humphreys learned that a significant number of men who have sex with other men in public restrooms were married, considered themselves heterosexual, and were Catholic or were married to women who were Catholic.

It's unlikely that Humphreys would have discovered this information if he had not practiced deception, both in the public restrooms and while disguised as a public health worker. However, it isn't clear that the benefits of knowledge gained from the study outweighed the possible risk of harm to the research subjects. Furthermore, no debriefing occurred in which the researcher let the subjects know that they were actually part of a research study. This project, like the Dharma Initiative, is a deception study. Additionally, both Tearoom Trade and the Dharma Initiative do not merely violate autonomy by

---

[4]   Joan E. Seiber, *Planning Ethically Responsible Research: A Guide for Students and Internal Review Boards* (Newbury Park, CA: Sage, 1992), p. 8.

failing to obtain informed consent, but also by significantly violating the privacy of the subjects.

In the Stanford Prison Experiment 24 male college students were recruited and randomly assigned to be either prison guards or prisoners for a two-week period in a makeshift prison created on the campus of Stanford University.[5] "Prisoners" were given numbers and uniforms. Every aspect of their lives was controlled by "guards," including meals, sleeping, and even what the prisoners were allowed to wear. After only six days the researcher shut the experiment down, in the wake of a prisoner rebellion, the mental break-down of one prisoner, what was called "pathological" behavior on the part of those playing prisoners, and what was called "sadistic" containment techniques on the part of those playing guards. The "prisoners" had so internalized their roles in the study that they were convinced that they could not leave the experimental situation. The experiment was designed to study prison culture, but the benefit from that knowledge was determined to be outweighed by the harm to the subjects in the study.

Unlike the Milgram experiment or Tearoom Trade experiments, the Stanford Prison Experiment was not a deception study. However, there is one significant similarity between the Stanford Prison Experiment and the Dharma Initiative: both studies limited the voluntary participation of the subjects. Autonomy was not compromised in the way that it is for deception research, but the loss of voluntariness is nonetheless a significant erosion of autonomy. In the Milgram study the subjects knew that they were part of an experiment, ostensibly one about negative reinforcement and electric shocks. They were deceived, but they could walk out any time they wanted. No one forced the Tearoom Trade participants to have anonymous sex in bathrooms, or to let a "public health worker" into their homes for an interview; even though they were deceived, and thus not informed participants, they acted voluntarily. In the Stanford Prison experiment the "prisoners" were treated in such a way that all autonomy was wrung out of them. They were miserable and believed that they could not leave. In a similar fashion, no one is able to opt out of the Dharma Initiative. Voluntary participation is not even a question.

---

[5]  A comprehensive discussion of the project can be found at www.prisonexp.org/.

*Deborah R. Barnbaum*

# Dharma is Unethical Research

Not all research without informed consent is unethical, despite the Nuremberg Code's strong admonition. Some research simply cannot be done with informed consent, such as research on young children, on persons with certain permanent or temporary mental disabilities, or on subjects who must be deceived in order for the experiment to work. Granting that such cases violate the principle of autonomy, this violation must be weighed against the principles of nonmaleficence, beneficence, and justice. If the experiment doesn't hurt anyone, helps someone, and is fair to everyone then it may still be considered ethical. How does the Dharma Initiative score?

Not very well. First and foremost, people are getting hurt. Worse yet, some have been killed. So nonmaleficence isn't being observed. Second, beneficence isn't being upheld: there is little good that can come out of the psychological research in the Dharma Initiative. Even if the Initiative is about observing people who are being asked to follow orders, it hardly seems that the value of the knowledge gained outweighs the harm or loss of autonomy. Finally, it is not clear that the principle of justice was adequately observed when the subjects were placed in the study. Much like the Tearoom Trade study, the passengers on Oceanic Air Flight 815 were very much in the wrong place at the wrong time.

Informed consent is a value that can and should be protected. When it is not protected, overriding applications of the principles of nonmaleficence, beneficence, and/or justice are needed. The creators of the Dharma Initiative haven't demonstrated that these *prima facie* principles can be invoked to offer a compelling rationale for subjecting people to the Dharma Initiative without their consent. Without a reasonable justification, the Dharma Initiative is unethical.

# 5

# The Island of Ethical Subjectivism: Not the Paradise of *Lost*

## *George Wrisley*

*Lost* is permeated with ethical situations, ones in which it is difficult to remain neutral. For example, Michael's relationship with his son Walt has been a troubled one. But while Michael isn't perfect, he certainly seems to be a "good guy." His efforts to make up for lost time, to protect and to connect with his son are praiseworthy. But then Michael does something shockingly violent: he shoots and kills Ana Lucia and Libby out of his love for his son. What are we to make of such actions? Another example: What are we to make of Locke's manipulating Sawyer into killing Locke's father? Perhaps it was understandable, but was the action praiseworthy or good? In contrast to a number of movies and other TV shows where good and evil are clearly and unrealistically demarcated, *Lost* shows the ethical complexities of individuals and the situations in which they find themselves. Life and life's questions can be difficult because, as *Lost* demonstrates, things are rarely black and white. It can be extremely difficult to know what to do or whether something is right or wrong. Given the complexities and the inevitable disagreements, and given our natural desire for possessing answers, it's easy to unreflectively assume that the answers to ethical questions are merely a matter of opinion. Thus, someone will say that, for example, when it comes to abortion there really is no right or wrong; it's just a matter of opinion. Or someone will say that it is right in Michael's eyes to shoot Ana Lucia and it's wrong in Jack's eyes. When someone says these kinds of things they most likely mean that there really is no "objective" right or wrong – no right or wrong that we could discover that is independent of how a person or people feel.[1] In other words, it's all relative. When it is claimed that right and wrong are relative to an individual, we'll call that view *ethical subjectivism* or just *subjectivism*. When it is claimed that right and wrong are relative to a society or culture, we'll call that view *ethical relativism* or just *relativism*.[2] In this chapter, we'll focus on whether either subjectivism or relativism is a viable position by looking at some of the ethically charged situations in *Lost* – situations that provide excellent opportunities for moral reflection.[3]

## How Important Might it be What Jack or the Others Think?

According to the most basic form of subjectivism, when I say "It was wrong of Michael to shoot and kill Ana Lucia and Libby in order to save Walt" I am simply describing my attitude or how I feel. I really mean something like "I disapprove of Michael's shooting Ana Lucia and Libby in order to save Walt." What makes the judgment true is simply the fact that I have the attitude that I say I do in the moral judgment. Thus, under subjectivism, it is not any aspect of the shooting itself that I am describing by calling it wrong. The idea is that while "Michael's killing Ana Lucia is wrong" has the same grammatical form as "Michael's hair is dark," the similarity is misleading. The description of Michael's hair predicates a certain property of Michael's hair, but what appears to be a description of Michael's action does not actually predicate any properties of that action. Rather, the ethical judgment is a claim concerning the subject's own attitudes.

---

[1] By "how a person or people feel" I am thinking of feelings like those of approval and disapproval, not feelings like pleasure and happiness or their opposites. This is important since on some "objective" ethical views (for example, some versions of consequentialism), which we won't talk about, what is right or wrong is a product of how people feel in terms of pleasure or happiness.

[2] Much of my description and evaluation of subjectivism and relativism are inspired by James Rachels' *The Elements of Moral Philosophy* (Philadelphia: Temple University Press, 1986) and Michael P. Lynch's *True to Life* (Cambridge, MA: MIT Press, 2004). I imagine similar approaches can be found elsewhere as well.

[3] While a distinction could perhaps be made between "moral" and "ethical," I am using them interchangeably.

According to the most basic form of relativism, when I say "Sayid's *forcefully* interrogating 'Henry Gale' was right," I am simply describing my culture's or society's attitude toward *forceful* interrogation (or *forceful* interrogation in situations similar to the one involving "Henry Gale").[4] I really mean something like "My culture approves of Sayid's *forceful* interrogation of 'Henry Gale.'" What makes the judgment true is the fact that my culture does approve of forceful interrogation. Thus, as with subjectivism, it is not any aspect of the interrogation itself that I am describing by calling it right. I am merely describing my culture's approval of such interrogations.

As you will surely notice, subjectivism and relativism are very similar. The main difference seems to lie merely in what each view takes ethical judgments to be describing. That difference, however, will become important when we look at possible objections to each view.

## Tolerance and the Importance of Disagreement

Before looking at possible problems with subjectivism and relativism, let's consider what might motivate one to hold either position. A possible motivation for endorsing subjectivism or relativism is the desire to avoid intolerance and closed-mindedness concerning others' views while promoting diversity. It seems clear that people within and across cultures sometimes disagree, for example, about the best way to live, what religion is the true religion, and what actions are right and wrong. Think about the differences between the survivors. Sayid, Locke, Sun and Jin, and Mr. Eko, for example, have diverse backgrounds. While none of them come from *radically* different cultures, there are still important differences. For example, Sayid is Muslim, Locke comes from a decidedly individualistic culture, and Sun and Jin come from a culture that values highly certain kinds of honor and duty. We can easily imagine the negative consequences that would

---

[4] Henceforth, when I write of something being relative to a culture, I am including the idea of societal relativism. While important for a detailed account, I am not concerned here with differences between societies and cultures, or what exactly delineates one culture from another. Also, we know that "Henry Gale" is named Ben, or at least that is what he is called by the other Others. I will refer to him as "Henry Gale" in the examples where that is the name by which he is known.

result if Sayid, Locke, or Jin acted intolerantly by uncompromisingly imposing their views on the other survivors. Perhaps if any of them were convinced that there was no other way to do things, that he had the *one* Truth, then each would try to impose that "Truth" on everyone else. Thus one might worry that if some kind of ethical *objectivism* were true, if the *actual* rightness or wrongness of an action were independent of anyone's or any culture's attitudes or feelings, then someone or some culture might feel justified in trying to impose what she or they see as the one true ethic on others. By holding and encouraging either subjectivism or relativism, it might seem that we can diffuse this worry, for then individuals or cultures seem to be accorded the right to their views.

In response to this motivation, we should note, first, that while intolerance and closed-mindedness should be discouraged and avoided, neither necessarily go hand in hand with objectivism. It is surely true that historically those who have been intolerant and closed-minded, not to mention imperialistic, also thought that they were in sole possession of the truth. However, notice that it is certainly possible to think that ethical truth is *not* subjective or relative *and* to hold that we should be tolerant and open-minded about the views of others – just as Jack can disagree with but still respect the decision of those survivors who want to remain on the beach right after the crash. We can believe we are right while at the same time acknowledging both that we may be wrong and that there might be something to learn from the views of others – just as Locke *could* acknowledge that he might be wrong about the meaninglessness of pushing the button and that Mr. Eko might have a point about how meaningful it actually is despite what they have seen in the Dharma Initiative film in the Pearl. Such a willingness to recognize that we may be wrong or not have the whole truth is in many ways the wisdom the ancient Greek philosopher Socrates most extolled: the wisdom that comes from admitting what we don't know and realizing that we could be quite wrong about what we think we know.

Nevertheless, there is an argument that one might offer in favor of subjectivism or relativism. Let's call it "the argument from disagreement." Again, it seems obvious that people within and across cultures disagree about what is ethically right and wrong. For example, it would be easy to find fans of *Lost*, both within our culture and outside it, who would disagree about whether Sayid should have tortured

Sawyer. Moreover, there are not only disagreements in and across cultures, but there are also ethical disagreements across time. For example, in general, slavery was seen as morally unobjectionable to the ancient Greeks (or at least those in power). Today, slavery is considered reprehensible. What are we to make of such rampant ethical disagreement? One thing we might do is argue that since there is ethical disagreement between people and across history and cultures, there is no objective truth about whether any action is right or wrong. Right and wrong are relative to subjects or cultures. In order to evaluate this argument, let's lay it out explicitly:

*Premise:*   There are ethical disagreements within and across cultures and history.
*Conclusion:*   Therefore, there are no objective ethical truths. Ethical truth is relative to either a subject or a culture.

The first step in evaluating an argument is to ask how strongly the premises support the conclusion. The most direct way to do that is to ask whether the truth of the premises implies or guarantees the truth of the conclusion. Assuming the argument from disagreement's premise is true, it is fairly easy to see that its truth does not guarantee the truth of the conclusion.

The main problem is that the argument from disagreement's premise has to do with what people feel or think, while the conclusion has to do with what actually exists. What does this mean? A non-ethical analogy might help to clarify it. Think of the second season's finale. Mr. Eko and Locke disagree about whether the button should be pushed. Locke has come to believe that it is all a twisted psychological experiment and *nothing will happen* if they don't push the button. Mr. Eko, however, clearly wants to keep pushing the button. Let's assume he believes the world will end if they don't push the button. Thus, Locke and Mr. Eko disagree about what will happen if they don't push the button. Clearly, what they believe has no bearing on what exists, namely, what will or will not happen if they don't push the button. In a similar fashion it is a mistake to draw a conclusion about the non-existence of objective ethical truth from a premise concerning what people think and feel. There could be objective ethical truth despite ethical disagreement: persons or groups could simply get it wrong.

53

Not only can we question whether the premise guarantees the conclusion, we can also question whether the conclusion is what we might call the "best explanation" for the phenomena of ethical disagreement across cultures and time. An alternative explanation for ethical disagreement is that while there is objective ethical truth, it is simply hard to come by. The idea is that while objective truth may allow for agreement, it does not always go hand in hand with agreement. For example, even some non-ethical objective truths are very difficult to figure out. If Michael had not acted in a way that tipped off Sayid that he had been "compromised" and if Michael had not been so quick to confess that he killed Ana Lucia and Libby, it probably would have been very difficult, if the idea occurred to one of them, for the other survivors to come to a consensus about whether Michael shot Ana Lucia and Libby. Given the situation on the island and the expertise of the survivors, it simply would be a difficult task to prove whether he shot them. Similarly with ethical truth: it may just be that ethical truth is something that is very hard to figure out in a way that even a majority of people could agree about what is right or wrong.

One final concern regarding the motivations for subjectivism and relativism: insofar as either view is motivated by the valuing of diversity, tolerance, and open-mindedness, consider whether these values themselves are only subjectively or relatively valuable. That is, doesn't an appeal to the importance of diversity, tolerance, and open-mindedness as a motivating force for subjectivism or relativism require that diversity, tolerance, and open-mindedness be objectively valuable? If it does, then in what sense can subjectivism or relativism be true?

You may be unconvinced by these responses to the motivation and argument for subjectivism and relativism. There are, however, serious problems for the views themselves to which we now turn.

## Why Locke's or the Others' Attitudes Don't Make It So

Let's consider the problems to which subjectivism leads and why the *Lost* island is a veritable paradise in comparison to the crippling isolation of subjectivism. Subjectivism implies that whether you approve or disapprove of an action, you speak the truth if you truly describe your attitude. That is, if you approve of Michael's actions and you say "Michael was right to shoot Ana Lucia and Libby," then it is true that Michael's actions were right. The main problem with this view is that it implies that you cannot be wrong about your ethical judgments as long as you accurately describe your approval or disapproval. Further, not only can you not be wrong, but no one else can be wrong either. This is an unacceptable consequence for at least two reasons. First, as we see in *Lost*, the ethical situations that we may confront in life are terribly complex and difficult – even if we aren't lost on an island. Can we honestly expect infallibility from ourselves or others in such situations? Further, if we are honest with ourselves, we will admit that there are a number of ethical dilemmas that we are not sure about. If you are sure about abortion, then what about euthanasia or capital punishment? Or imagine that Locke could save Jack, Claire, Charlie, and Sayid from the island's "monster" but only by sacrificing Hurley by pushing him in front of them? Are you sure about the right thing for Locke to do? The point is that there are certainly times when we are unsure of the right action in a given situation. If we are unsure and subjectivism is true, then it is neither true nor false that an action is wrong until we "make up our mind." Second, there are instances when we would presumably not want to say that it's possible that others are making true ethical judgments. For example, certainly some of the ethical judgments of Stalin, Hitler, or Pol Pot were not true.[5]

This brings us to another problem for subjectivism. If all Boone is doing when he makes an ethical judgment is describing his attitude and all Sayid is doing is describing his attitude, it is unclear how they could disagree. That is, it seems that an important aspect of our ethical talk is to express disagreement with one another. Imagine Sayid, regretting what he did, says it was wrong of him to torture Sawyer. In response, let's imagine Boone defends the action and says, "No, it wasn't wrong." They seem to disagree. But are they disagreeing if subjectivism is true? Think of a non-ethical analogy to descriptions of one's attitudes. If Locke describes his head as bald and Jack describes

---

[5]  A subjectivist could bite the bullet, and a rather large bullet it would be, and say that even Hitler spoke the truth (at least relative to his attitudes). But as we will see, there are still further problems with subjectivism.

his own head as not bald, are they disagreeing? No, they aren't, since there is no conflict in Locke's describing his own head as bald and Jack's describing his own head as not bald. Moreover, they can actually agree with each other's descriptions. There would only be a problem if Locke described *his own* head as bald and Jack described *Locke's* head as *not* bald. Similarly, under subjectivism there is no conflict when Sayid says it was wrong of him to torture Sawyer and Boone says that it wasn't wrong. Since all they are doing is describing their individual attitudes they can actually agree with each other. That is, Sayid can agree that Boone approves of the torture and Boone can agree that Sayid regrets and disapproves of it. Again, this is a problem if we think that there can be genuine ethical disagreement.

To be fair, the subjectivist can say that what people disagree about when making ethical judgments are the relevant non-ethical facts. By "non-ethical facts" I mean facts that do not involve evaluative features such as *good*, *right*, *should*, and *approve* or their opposites. Disagreement about non-ethical facts is important since our attitudes and other beliefs are often based on what we believe those facts to be. Presumably, if you approve of Michael's shooting Ana Lucia that approval is based on a number of non-ethical beliefs. For example, your approval might be based in part on your belief that he had no other choice but to kill Ana Lucia in order to free "Henry Gale"; and if he didn't free "Henry Gale," he would never see Walt again. Now, say I disapprove of Michael's actions. Initially, under subjectivism it might seem we cannot disagree with each other. However, it turns out that I believe that Michael had other options for freeing "Henry Gale." He could have volunteered to guard him and then let him go. Thus, we disagree with each other insofar as we disagree about the non-ethical facts that inform our ethical attitudes. Such disagreement might surface in discussion of the action in question.

A possible problem with this response is that it is unclear whether we cannot still have different ethical attitudes even though we agree on all the relevant non-ethical facts. Let's consider Jack's operating on Ben's cancerous spine and his using Ben's vulnerable position on the operating table as leverage to free Kate and Sawyer as an example. What if we agreed on all the relevant non-ethical facts? This is not an exhaustive list, but let's say we agree that Kate and Sawyer will be killed if Jack doesn't try the ploy with Ben's life. Further, we agree that Ben will probably die even if the operation is successful. It's at least possible that we could agree on all such relevant facts while we disagree about whether it is wrong of Jack to manipulate the Others using Ben's life. The point is that while our beliefs about the non-ethical facts may have an influence on our ethical attitudes, there may still be a disconnect between our attitudes and our "factual" beliefs. And if that is the case, then the disagreement that seems to be involved in all cases of one person saying "Action X was wrong" and another person saying "Action X wasn't wrong" cannot be accounted for by appealing to disagreement over non-ethical facts.

Relativism faces problems similar to those of subjectivism. Under relativism, an ethical judgment is true if it accurately describes a culture's approval or disapproval of an action. This avoids the first problem that subjectivism faced. That is, since it is the culture that either approves or disapproves of an action, an individual person can make mistaken ethical judgments insofar as she *inaccurately* describes the culture's stance.[6] Thus, if we take the survivors on the island to form a culture, then an action is right or wrong depending on whether they as a group approve or disapprove of the action. So, let's say that the group approves of blowing up the Others who are coming to take Sun and anyone else who is pregnant. If Rose were to say, "It's not right for us to blow up the Others," she is wrong because she is inaccurately describing the group's position. Thus, it is possible under relativism for individuals to be mistaken in their ethical judgments.

The problem is that while the individual can be wrong, it's not possible for the culture to be wrong – cultures as wholes become infallible. This kind of infallibility is troubling for two main reasons. First, if the Others as a group approve of torturing Walt, then within that society it is right to torture Walt. If relativism is true, then the Others cannot be wrong for doing so. If that is not objectionable, then think of Nazi Germany's Final Solution or ancient Greece's approval of slavery.[7]

The second problem with cultural infallibility, and one that ties into the first one, is that it makes it unclear on what basis an individual

---

[6]  I am glossing over important questions concerning how to draw the boundaries between cultures. There are also issues concerning the number of a culture's members that need to be in consensus for the culture as a whole to have a particular attitude (if that idea even makes sense).

[7]  Again, one could just bite the bullet here. But the next problem is not so easily swallowed.

can go against her culture in order to try to make changes. For example, let's imagine Rousseau's daughter, Alex, tries to petition for the rest of the Others not to torture Walt. She is in a poor position to do so, since she is, under relativism, automatically wrong in her view that it is wrong to torture him. Thus relativism makes it difficult to make sense of the notion of reform. If we look at Martin Luther King Jr., the most straightforward way to make sense of what he was doing is to say that he worked toward trying to get our culture as a whole to see the truth concerning the wrongness of racism and discrimination. If relativism is true, however, then Martin Luther King Jr. could not have been working to get others to see the truth concerning the wrongness of racism. At the time, the society at large still approved of it in various forms and thus, under relativism, Martin Luther King Jr. was simply wrong.

Since the forms of subjectivism and relativism that we have looked at lead to unacceptable consequences, they should be rejected. The question then becomes: Where do we go from here?

## If Not on the Island of Ethical Subjectivism, Then Where?

*Lost* does not, in and of itself, show the untenability of subjectivism or relativism. Nevertheless, with its excellent writing, its morally charged and sometimes morally ambiguous situations, *Lost* presents one opportunity after the other for moral consideration. It is difficult not to react with moral judgment to Michael's killing Ana Lucia and Libby, Sayid's torturing Sawyer, the Others' treatment of a captured Kate and Sawyer, or Locke's pushing Mikhail into the sonic defense barrier, seemingly killing him. Upon reflection we can see that the simple forms of subjectivism and relativism lead to unacceptable consequences: infallibility of persons or cultures, inability to disagree with each other, and no possibility of ethical progress.

But if simple forms of subjectivism and relativism are untenable, where does this leave us? When we see Michael kill Ana Lucia and Libby out of desperation to save Walt, and we judge those actions to be wrong, what could it be that makes those actions right or wrong? Philosophers have long struggled with this question, and I cannot begin to answer it here. Instead, I leave you with some questions to consider – questions that bring us closer to figuring out what it is that makes our actions right or wrong. When watching and talking about *Lost* with others, think about the following: If the simple forms of subjectivism and relativism that we have examined don't work, is it possible that more sophisticated forms might work? What ways could subjectivism, for example, be modified to meet the objections? Perhaps when Jack accuses his father of moral wrongdoing in the operating room he is not saying anything true or false, but rather just *expressing* his feelings (he's not describing anything). If that is so, how might that help subjectivism? What role should the consequences of Locke's blowing up the submarine, for example, play in the rightness or wrongness of his action? What kinds of consequences are important? Is it the happiness of everyone or perhaps just Locke's own happiness? Is he perhaps not culpable, or at least less culpable, if he had good intentions? What difference does Mikhail's survival make to the rightness or wrongness of Locke's pushing him into the sonic defense barrier presumably with the intention of killing him? Lastly, when you watch *Lost* and it provokes an ethical judgment, ask yourself, "Why do I think that?" and "Are those good reasons?" See how long you can keep challenging your answers with "Why?" and see where it leads you.

# PART II

O IS FOR ORIGIN

# 6

# Meaning and
# Freedom on the Island

## *Sander Lee*

*Lost* is an exciting show that combines adventure and romance with an array of mysteries and puzzles. It has spawned an unprecedented reaction from its devoted fans, a reaction which includes message boards, podcasts, online "experiences," and even novels supposedly written by fictional characters (*Bad Twin* by Gary Troup). Is it a political thriller, science fiction, or a mystical tale of supernatural forces? It may be all or none of these, but one thing is for certain. *Lost* raises philosophical questions that place it above most television shows and connect it with themes found in the works of a number of philosophers such as John Locke, David Hume, Søren Kierkegaard, and Jean-Paul Sartre. Let's look at four of the characters (Jack, Locke, Mr. Eko, and Desmond) to see how philosophy may help us to better understand them.

## Jack Shepard

All *Lost* fans know that Jack and Locke fundamentally disagree on the proper roles of reason and faith. While Locke is the "man of faith," Jack is the "man of science." As a doctor, Jack only trusts the experiences of his senses. In this way, Jack has as much in common with the British philosopher David Hume (1711–1776) as does the character who bears his name, Desmond David Hume. Like Jack, Hume was very skeptical of any claims that are not based on empirical data. For example, Hume argues that our common belief that every event has a cause has more to do with our human desire to explain everything rationally than with the evidence of our senses. The same may be said for our belief in God or miracles.

Thus, when Jack first encounters Locke's claim that the island has brought them there for a purpose, he rejects it vehemently, even telling Kate in the first season finale that they have a "Locke problem." The conflict between Jack and Locke manifests itself in their differing attitudes toward the button in season two. While Locke is quick to believe Desmond's assertion that the button must be pushed every 108 minutes, Jack would probably never push the button if it were left only to him.

Jack's conflict with Locke is rooted in Jack's belief in free will. Existentialist philosophers such as Jean-Paul Sartre (1905–1980) claim that each of us is fundamentally free to choose our values and our actions and thereby create ourselves and construct the meaning of the world. We are completely responsible for our own actions. For Jack, as for Sartre, an acceptance of individual freedom and responsibility is the cornerstone of moral integrity. Anyone who denies his or her freedom is engaging in a form of hypocrisy that Sartre calls "bad faith." A person in bad faith lies to himself and thereby refuses to accept his freedom and the responsibility that goes with it.

In Jack's view, his father Christian's greatest flaw is his abdication of personal responsibility. The very first time we see Christian he is lecturing a young Jack on the liabilities of caring. He tells Jack that he watched a boy die on the operating table that day and asks rhetorically how, after this, he can stand to come home in the evening and enjoy himself with his family. His answer is to detach himself emotionally from the events he witnessed and any concern for his own potential responsibility in the death. For Christian, only by not caring can Jack grow up to be a "real man," one who "has what it takes." Although Christian suggests that his attitude makes him "strong," as opposed to Jack (whose caring for others makes him "weak"), we can see that Christian's "strength" comes out of a bottle.

In his "bad faith," Jack's father refuses to acknowledge his capacity for free choice and his own moral responsibility for his mistakes. Jack identifies this moral failure with a belief in determinism, the claim that our actions are the result of destiny. Such a belief in fate can be used as an excuse to escape one's moral complicity in the results of one's acts. Symbolic of these views is Christian's use of the motto, "that's why the Red Sox will never win the World Series." In saying this, Christian is claiming that events in life are beyond our control. It doesn't matter what the Red Sox do or which players they put on the field, it's their fate to be eternal losers. They might come one strike away from winning the World Series (as they did in 1986), but fate will inevitably intervene to destroy their hopes. Those who superficially appear to be the causes of these failures are not really responsible. So Red Sox fans must forgive Bill Buckner and there's no reason to hate Aaron Boone or even Bucky F. Dent. Ironically, given the fact that Oceanic 815 crashed on September 22, 2004, these references to the Red Sox's fate take place only a few weeks before the team reversed the curse and won their first World Series in 86 years.

This point is hammered home in "The Glass Ballerina" when Ben tries to convince Jack that he is in contact with the outside world. Jack only believes Ben after he watches a video of the Red Sox celebrating their victory, a victory which seems to nullify all of Christian's excuses for his personal failures.

Because of his extreme commitment to existential notions of freedom and responsibility, Jack is contemptuous of Locke, whose belief in destiny can only remind him of his father. For philosophers like Sartre, and especially the German philosopher Martin Heidegger (1889–1976) whose methods greatly influenced Sartre, the person who fully accepts his or her freedom and corresponding responsibility is on the road to "authenticity." The opposite of "bad faith" is not "good faith," as all forms of faith entail self-deception, but complete honesty, even when such honesty reveals unpleasant truths.

This explains why Jack is so intolerant of those who lie to him. Jack blames Locke for Boone's death because Locke not only lied about the circumstances of the accident, he also ran away. In disappearing immediately after delivering Boone, Locke not only deprived Jack of the medical information needed to treat Boone's injuries correctly, he also, like Jack's father, abdicated personal responsibility.

As a person committed to moral integrity in a world seemingly without divine purpose, Jack takes it upon himself to become a savior. As his father tells him, Jack's tragic flaw is that he cares too much. Like the doctor in Albert Camus' novel *The Plague*, Jack can't let go even when the circumstances seem to demand it. When he succeeds, Jack's persistence makes him appear to be a miracle worker. Against all odds he cures his wife of her injuries and later, during season two, he revives Charlie despite Kate's belief that it is too late. However, when he fails, as he does with Boone, Jack must attribute blame. His father must be held accountable for killing a patient just as Locke must pay for the death of Boone.

Throughout his ordeal in season three, first as a prisoner of the Others, then as Ben's doctor, and, finally, as the leader in the war against the Others, Jack continues to judge himself, and everyone else, by these rigid standards. In the season three finale, we see a flash forward into a future where Jack has become a suicidal, pill-popping drunk who bitterly regrets his decision to leave the island. This suggests that despite everything, Ben wasn't lying when he told Jack that leaving the island was a mistake. Clearly, Jack now believes that he failed as a leader, and he is punishing himself by becoming what he hates the most, a man just like his father.

# John Locke

In presenting Locke's story, the creators of *Lost* explore the moral dimensions of situations in which an apparently good man is confronted with the realization that life can be randomly haphazard and morally indifferent. Locke desperately seeks meaning and purpose for his life yet, again and again, he ends up disappointed and filled with anguish.

Through flashbacks we discover how Locke's desire for a genuine relationship with his father (who he never knew as a child) led him to give up one of his kidneys. Only after the operation does he discover that his father has conned him. Once he's received the kidney transplant, he has no interest whatsoever in maintaining a relationship with his son. Unable to move on with his life, Locke obsesses over his father, sitting every night in his car outside his father's estate and lying to his girlfriend, Helen, when she demands that he concentrate on her and forget the past.

Locke's initial optimism (some might call it gullibility) resembles some of the beliefs of the philosopher after whom he is apparently named. John Locke (1632–1704) is perhaps best known for his political views and their influence on the founders of the United States, such as Thomas Jefferson and James Madison. Locke views human nature as basically good. For him, the social contract protects the rights of all against the small minority of those who miscalculate their self-interest, mistakenly believing that it is to their advantage to criminally deprive others of their rights. Thus, Locke has faith in a democratic form of government in which the majority can be trusted to decide issues in ways that are best for all.

While the philosopher Locke argued that a belief in God and divine purpose is rational, he did not privilege religious claims or scripture. The study of religion should be approached in the same way as science, no claims should be accepted that are not backed up by empirical evidence and the use of reason.

Throughout his initial days on the island, *Lost*'s Locke shares his namesake's optimism and faith in the basic goodness of others. The miraculous recovery of the use of his legs provides empirical evidence for his belief that he and the other survivors have been brought to the island for a reason. Locke believes he has a destiny to fulfill and he need only wait for the island to reveal this purpose to him. The discovery of the hatch door and his vision of the location of the crashed drug plane in season one seems only to confirm this sense of destiny. When his faith is challenged by Boone's tragic death, Locke returns to the hatch door to pray for a sign. Kneeling with his forehead pressed against the cover in a Muslim-like posture of prayer, he is rewarded by the sudden appearance of light streaming through the hatch door's window. This leads him to believe that the obstacles he encounters (including Boone's death) occur because the island is testing his faith. If he can meet these challenges with his faith intact then the island will tell him what to do in order to fulfill his destiny.

Once Locke makes it into the hatch, meets Desmond, and views the *Orientation* film, everything he has endured finally seems to have been worthwhile. Clearly, it is his fate to make sure that the button is pushed every 108 minutes. In his devotion to the button, Locke moves beyond the rational faith of the philosopher John Locke and into the realm of the Danish thinker Søren Kierkegaard (1813–1855).

Indeed, Locke's role in the death of Boone recalls the biblical tale of Abraham and Isaac, the story of a man who decides, against both his desires and his reason, to blindly follow God's command to sacrifice the life of his son. Kierkegaard used this story to illustrate his belief that the only life worth living, and capable of delivering us from despair, is one that results from a "leap of faith." One must rely on an intuitive belief in God. A leap of faith requires us to do what we know in our heart is right, despite the fact that society will ridicule us, and despite the fact that no empirical evidence exists to prove such a choice is justified. Locke takes just such a leap into the belief that he has been chosen to play a special role on the island and invites the ridicule and scorn of his fellow survivors because of his devotion to the button.

Kierkegaard contrasts the leap of faith with two unsuccessful ways of living, the aesthetic and the ethical. Those leading the aesthetic lifestyle, like Sawyer and Charlie in season one, seek fulfillment solely through the gratification of their senses. The aesthetic way of life ultimately leads to despair, as the empty pursuit of pleasure alone always leaves one hungry for more. Kierkegaard sees the ethical life as equally unsatisfactory. Building on a foundation of hypocrisy, the ethicist (Jack) pontificates about life's eternal truths while simultaneously realizing that such unfounded claims are dependent upon one's subjective perceptions.

Kierkegaard further contended that traditional religious institutions are actually more of a hindrance than a help in coming face to face with God. Locke indicates his agreement by his lack of interest in relating his beliefs to those of traditional Christianity as represented by Mr. Eko. When Mr. Eko tells Locke he has something to show him and then brings out a copy of the Bible, Locke's disdain is evident. Of course, once Mr. Eko pulls a film from inside the book, Locke's interest is rekindled. While he has no faith in Christianity, a message from the Dharma Institute may contain the received words of the prophets.

Thus, Locke feels an obligation to reveal the true nature of the island's collective ethical dilemmas in spite of his passionate desire to believe that answers exist for the most profound metaphysical questions. This is why Locke is so angry and self-critical in the final episodes of season two. By this point, the fake Henry Gale (Ben Linus) has claimed that he didn't input the numbers during the crisis in "Lockdown" and that the button is "just a joke." In the episode "?," Locke visits a new hatch with Mr. Eko and absorbs all its evidence, evidence which suggests that the button-pushing was never any more than a psychological experiment. From all this, Locke concludes that he allowed his burning desire for a spiritual purpose (and the apparent "miracle" of his legs) to overcome an honest realization of his bleak situation, and it explains his unwillingness to listen to the arguments of Mr. Eko and, ultimately, Desmond.

Always one to swing to extremes, Locke becomes as dogmatic in his nihilism – a belief in nothing – as he once was in his devotion. Determined to brook no opposition in his quest to prove that the button is a hoax, he uses Desmond to lock out Eko. As the countdown progresses, Locke refuses to hear Desmond's rational explanation of the button's true purpose and his compelling evidence that it was his own failure to push the button on September 22, 2004 that caused the crash of Oceanic Flight 815. In Locke's anger and despair he destroys the computer monitor, leaving Desmond only one option once it becomes clear that their failure to push the button has triggered a catastrophe.

Locke's error lies not in his rejection of the button but rather in his unwillingness to trust that a path exists by which he can find meaning and fulfill his sense of moral duty. Too late, he realizes that he has failed the most important test of his faith. When he finally encounters Mr. Eko at the end of the second season finale, all he can say is, "I was wrong."

In season three, Locke's faith in the mystic power of the island has returned and this leads him to try to destroy all possible means of escape from the island. Locke's renewed spiritualism and over-confidence allow Ben to manipulate him onto the road that leads to his shooting. Like so many others on the island, Ben's relationship with his father was ghastly. Blamed throughout his childhood for his mother's death in childbirth, Ben patiently waits, planning the murder of his father and the deaths of everyone in the Dharma community in the great "Purge" by the "Hostiles."

Viewing Locke as a rival threatening his leadership, Ben "tests" Locke by demanding that he kill his kidnapped father just as Ben himself did. Although Locke's father has recently used the name "Anthony Cooper" (the real John Locke's seventeenth-century patron), Richard Alpert reveals that he is also the original "Sawyer," the man responsible for the deaths of James Ford's parents. Using this information, *Lost*'s Locke is able to manipulate *Lost*'s Sawyer into killing Cooper, thus allowing Locke to fulfill Ben's demand.

When he deposits his father's body at Ben's feet, Ben at last agrees to take Locke to meet Jacob, who Locke sarcastically calls "The Man Behind the Curtain." In *The Wizard of Oz*, "The Man Behind the Curtain" turns out to be a powerless charlatan, and when Ben seems to be talking to an empty chair, Locke concludes that Ben is equally powerless and probably insane. Unfortunately, as usual, Locke has gotten it completely wrong. Jacob is very real and when Ben realizes that Locke has the power to hear Jacob's pleas for help, he shoots Locke at the mass grave of his earlier Dharma victims. Locke should have paid more attention when Alex gave him a gun and warned him that he would need it if Ben was taking him to meet Jacob. As at the end of season two, Locke again arrogantly refuses to believe until it is too late.

Ben's initial inability to understand Locke's words ("Help me!") mirror Locke's confusion over the meaning of the last words said to him by Mr. Eko, the character we will examine next. Just before his death, Eko whispered to Locke that "You're next." Locke tells his companions that Eko said "We're next," not realizing that the message was meant for him alone.

In the season three finale, Locke is stopped from committing suicide by the sudden appearance of Walt, who convinces him that he is not really injured and that he must stop Jack from leading everyone off the island. The end of the finale suggests that, for once, Locke is right. Presumably, in seasons four through six, Locke will remain on the island to unravel its mysteries and, perhaps, find his spiritual salvation.

# Mr. Eko

As one of the "tailies," Mr. Eko first appeared in the second season, but he quickly became one of the series' most intriguing characters. Like Locke, Mr. Eko is torn by his experience of the world as a place void of meaning and moral purpose despite his desperate desire for meaning and purpose. Although Locke's experiences with his father were certainly tragic, Mr. Eko's story, as first presented in "the 23rd Psalm," is infinitely more horrific.

When a gang of warlords appears in Eko's village in Nigeria, he sacrifices himself to save his younger brother, Yemi. His sacrifice is not so much to save Yemi from death, although that is certainly a possibility, but from a more horrible fate, that of losing his soul. Seeing his brother forced to choose between murder and suicide, Eko takes the gun from Yemi's hands and makes the choice for him by instantly killing the old man. Before doing so, however, Eko removes his own crucifix and gives it to Yemi. Eko had been a devout Catholic, but by taking his brother's place he was choosing to forsake his own salvation. In joining the warlords and eventually becoming one of their leaders Eko turns his back on God to live in a world empty of meaning. But, unlike Locke, Eko never really stops believing. Where Locke is capable of thinking and acting like a nihilist, Eko cannot. He may do terrible things but he always accepts that those acts carry with them a heavy spiritual price. In other words, where Locke chooses to deny the very existence of meaning, Mr. Eko, even when he was a warlord, continued to accept that meaning and redemption exist, just not for him.

Having escaped from Nigeria disguised as a priest, Eko tentatively starts to believe that, despite his many sins, redemption may still be possible. This rebirth of hope is illustrated by his encounter with the Australian girl, who claimed to have been resurrected from the dead. Initially very skeptical, Mr. Eko is clearly shaken by this encounter. Once on the island, he starts to actively seek redemption through a variety of acts of penance (his period of silence, his carved staff, the knots in his beard, his plan to build a church, and his plea for forgiveness from the fake Henry Gale).

The Jewish theologian and philosopher Martin Buber (1878–1965) suggested that God only enters the lives of those who wish it. If one chooses to live one's life without God, then no evidence of God's existence will appear. But once one chooses to open oneself up to the possibility of God by initiating a genuine dialogue with Him, Buber contends that a true relationship is possible. Only allowing oneself to be completely vulnerable before God can one construct a meaningful life.

For Mr. Eko, like Buber, the price of a secular moral relativism is not eternal damnation but emptiness and despair. Strange as it may seem, certain damnation is preferable in Mr. Eko's mind to the nihilism of nonbelief. To follow the instructions given to him by Yemi in a dream, Eko is willing to do anything, as he explains to Locke in the episode "?":

> This cross was worn by my brother, Yemi. Yemi was a *great* man. A priest. A man of God. And because I betrayed him he was shot and died. He was placed on a plane . . . which took off from an airstrip in Nigeria, *half* a world from here. Then the plane *I* was on crashed on this island. And somehow . . . *here* . . . I found my brother again.

71

> I found him in the same plane that took off from Nigeria. In the same plane that lies above us now. That has concealed this place. And I took this cross from around Yemi's neck and put it back on mine. Just as it was on the day I first took another man's life. So let me ask you . . . How can you say this is meaningless? *I* believe the work being done in the hatch is *more* important than anything. If you will not continue to push the button, John . . . *I will.*

Further, in his moment of truth at the end of "The Cost of Living," when he thinks he is facing Yemi for final judgment, he defends himself by saying:

> I ask for no forgiveness, Father. For I have not sinned. I have only done what I needed to do to survive. A small boy once asked me if I was a bad man. If I could answer him now I would tell him that when *I* was a young boy I killed a man to *save* my brother's life. I am not sorry for this. I am *proud* of this. I did not ask for the life that I was given, but it was given nonetheless. And with it I did my best.

Eko speaks honestly even though he believes, as a Catholic, that he may be condemning himself to everlasting damnation. His hopes for understanding are dashed, however, when the figure standing before him responds, "You speak to me as if I were your brother." Eko now realizes that the origin of his dreams and visions has not been divine intervention, but instead forces unrelated to his spiritual quest. "Who are you?" he screams repeatedly in the seconds before the "smoke monster" kills him.

The philosophical and religious issues raised by Eko's story are real, but the events he encounters on the island don't address them. The purpose and meaning of these events are still unknown.

## Desmond

Many observers have pointed out the similarity of Desmond's story to that of Odysseus (Ulysses) from Homer's classic epic the *Odyssey*. While it would be foolish to claim there are exact parallels for each of Odysseus' adventures, there are some clear similarities. Like the *Odyssey*, Desmond's story starts in the middle of the plot and only slowly is his whole story revealed to us through flashbacks. Like

Odysseus, Desmond's love is named Penelope and she is condemned to wait for him for years while being pursued by other suitors attracted by her beauty and wealth. Desmond also must overcome a series of obstacles, including imprisonment (though not by a beautiful nymph named Calypso) and, like Odysseus, he is shipwrecked on an island. In this variation on the myth, Odysseus' nemesis, the god Poseidon, is transformed into Penelope's father, Charles Widmore, the head of the British arm of the enormous Widmore Corporation. Also, like Odysseus, Desmond tells Penelope that, although he would prefer to stay with her, he must finish his journey successfully for the sake of honor. The appearance of the ruined statue with four toes resembles that of ancient Greek statues such as the Colossus of Rhodes or even perhaps Odysseus' own Cyclops Polyphemus. Finally, the similarities between the *Odyssey* and the *Epic of Gilgamesh* remind us of the clue Locke encountered in his crossword puzzle ("friend of Enkidu").

When we see Desmond released from military prison at the end of season two, we learn that his full name is Desmond David Hume. So, like Locke and Rousseau, Desmond shares his name with a famous philosopher. As we discussed earlier, David Hume, a Scott like Desmond, is primarily regarded as a skeptic. Given this, we might expect Desmond to be somewhat skeptical of the claims of others and certainly less gullible than Locke. This expectation is borne out in key moments of his story. While he initially believes Kelvin's claims about the sickness on the island, Desmond eventually uncovers Kelvin's lies when he notices that his hazmat suit is torn and follows him out of the hatch. He is also skeptical of Locke's claims to be an innocent survivor of a plane crash when he first encounters him in the hatch at the beginning of the second season. And, when he reappears at the end of the second season, it is Desmond's skeptical nature that leads him to challenge Locke's assertions that the button has no real function. Despite Locke's violent certainty, Desmond uses the readout from the other hatch to prove empirically that his failure to push the button on September 22, 2004 was responsible for the crash of Oceanic Flight 815.

Yet, on the other hand, unlike the philosopher David Hume, Desmond is open to the possibility of omens and miracles. We learn that Desmond at one point contemplated suicide, but was deterred by the sounds of Locke banging on the hatch cover and his discovery

73

of Penelope's letter. Ironically, their conversation about this incident has opposite effects on Locke and Desmond.

Locke initially interpreted the light streaming through the hatch window to be a miraculous omen. But, by the time Locke talks about this with Desmond at the end of season two, he is so bitter and disillusioned that he dismisses the significance of the light by suggesting that Desmond was probably just going to the bathroom. Hearing Locke's story has exactly the opposite impact on Desmond. When he learns that Locke caused the banging that prevented him from committing suicide, and led him to turn on the light, he sees it as an amazing confluence of events in which two people received exactly what they needed at exactly the right time through a process of events that overtly appears to have been coincidental. While the philosopher David Hume would no doubt see this to be purely accidental, Desmond appears to be more willing to see this as fate and it is this openness that leads him to eventually conclude that it was his failure to push the button that caused Oceanic 815 to crash.

Thus, by the end of the second season, Locke and Desmond were moving in opposite directions, Locke towards nihilism and Desmond towards faith. Desmond's renewed faith, and sense of moral duty, eventually led him to use the key, at the risk of his own life, in an attempt to save lives and stop the effects of Locke's destruction of the computer. While one might assume that David Hume's skepticism would entail the rejection of morality, in fact Hume argued that all of us have a natural sympathy for others and that moral actions should in fact be made for the sake of the overall public good, what he calls "utility." Thus, Hume would see Desmond's act of self-sacrifice as moral and commendable.

In season three, Desmond's sacrifice has resulted in his seeming "rebirth." Unlike the other survivors of the hatch explosion, Desmond has a mystical experience in which he travels through time and reemerges on the island naked as the day he was born. Desmond is now the one who must struggle most specifically with the dichotomy between free will and determinism.

In "Flashes Before Your Eyes," he encounters Ms. Hawking who tries to convince him that he must act in accordance with a predetermined path. Like her apparent namesake, the physicist Steven Hawking, she is a master of the intricacies of the space-time continuum. She claims that any attempts to change the timeline will ultimately fail, as the universe has a way of "course correcting." Interestingly, she also tells Desmond that if he doesn't go along with his destiny, then "every single one of us is dead." This seems to be an apparent contradiction. If everything is predetermined and the universe will "correct" any attempts to alter fate, then how could it be possible for Desmond to derail destiny sufficiently to kill us all? Perhaps because of his awareness of this paradox, once Desmond returns to the beach he ignores Ms. Hawking's warnings and devotes himself to repeatedly saving Charlie from the death he has foreseen, even when, in the episode appropriately named "Catch 22," he believes that doing so changes the identity of the parachutist from his beloved Penny to Naomi Dorrit.

The biblical tale of Abraham and Isaac, mentioned earlier, is explicitly discussed by Desmond and Brother Campbell in this episode. Desmond tells Brother Campbell that he thinks it's "interesting" that the monastery chose the name "Moriah," the same name as the place where God asked Abraham to sacrifice his son ("Not exactly the most festive locale, is it?"). When Brother Campbell reminds Desmond that God ultimately spared Isaac, Desmond argues that God "need not have asked Abraham to sacrifice his son in the first place," leading Brother Campbell to respond that "then it wouldn't have been much of a test would it Brother? Perhaps you underestimate the value of sacrifice."

Brother Campbell seems to be urging Desmond to accept the need to abandon the ethical and make the Kierkegaardian "leap of faith." But Desmond is not ready to do this. His conscience won't let him abandon Charlie despite his overwhelming desire to see Penny. Like the philosopher David Hume, in this episode, Desmond skeptically rejects the possibility of miracles. He is unwilling to believe that if only he chooses to allow events to unfold without intervention, then his faith might be rewarded. Interestingly, Brother Campbell has a photo on his desk of himself with Ms. Hawking, suggesting that they may be colleagues. This makes sense as they both preach the same message of stoical acceptance of one's fate.

In the final episodes of season three, Desmond convinces Charlie that he must sacrifice himself so Claire and Aaron may be rescued. Yet, when the time comes to make the swim down to the Looking Glass station, Desmond once again changes his mind, demanding that Charlie stay safely in the boat. In the season three finale, despite Desmond's best efforts, Charlie dies exactly as Desmond predicted.

## Does It Matter If *Lost*'s Secrets Are Revealed?

As we have seen, the stories of these four characters are permeated by issues of free will and determinism as well as concerns about the demands of moral duty and honor. They often shift back and forth between periods of faith and despair in ways that raise a variety of interesting philosophical questions. We are all eager to find out how the show's creators ultimately resolve these mysteries; however, I would contend that, like earlier shows such as *The Prisoner* or *Twin Peaks*, *Lost*'s greatest philosophical contributions are to be found in the issues it raises rather than in the answers it may eventually show us.

# 7

# What Would You Do? Altered States in *Lost*

## Charles Taliaferro and Dan Kastrul

## 4, 8, 15, 16, 23, 42, Hike!

Imagine you were on that plane and made it to the island. Life has suddenly become outrageously altered; your health has changed. Perhaps you are now completely healed of some past injury or you now have some new bodily weakness. Rather than interacting with people you are familiar with, you're surrounded by a whole new group of people with different, sometimes shifting, bizarre stories about their past. Are the people you encounter really who they claim to be? Will *you* be the person you claim to be in that altered state? An even more troubling question: Will you be the person you *believe* yourself to be? Reflection on how you would act if you were in the world of *Lost* can shed light on your character. Would you let the numbers run down to zero? If someone kidnapped your son, would you break down, as Michael did? How you *would* handle such different, altered situations is important information about *who you are now*.

## "What would you do if I sang out of tune . . . ?"

Influenced by Aristotle (384–322 BCE), some contemporary philosophers argue that judging a person's character and action at any given time involves judging how the person would act under different conditions. Imagine a neighbor, Fritz, who appears good natured, but who would be a vicious scoundrel if placed in slightly different social circumstances. If we have reason to believe that he would behave horribly under different conditions, don't we have reason to question the current appearance of his respectable nature and character under current conditions? Mr. Eko is a perfect case in point. Whether he was heroically saving lives or brutally and heartlessly snuffing them out seems to have been very much driven by circumstance. For instance, he didn't hesitate to kill an innocent elder villager when he believed such drastic action was necessary to prevent ruthless guerillas from killing his brother. He clearly was a loyal ally in certain situations as well as a formidable adversary in others. Aristotle's view is that many of the ways in which we describe ourselves ethically have distinctive implications for what would happen, or what we would do, under very different conditions. So, for example, the courageous person is not someone who is *always* performing brave acts under all conditions. Even brave people need to sleep once in a while. But being a courageous person means that the person would act bravely if it were the case that she or he was faced with a dangerous situation in which a person could undertake a heroic rescue, for example. In this sense, the term "courage" is like other dispositional terms such as "vain" or "irritable" which imply future, probable behavior. Not necessarily all the time – but at least sometimes – the vain person boasts too much, and the irritable person frequently displays various levels of anger without much provocation.

The most dramatic use of thought experiments involving hypothetical conditions is the famous Myth of Gyges that is presented in dialogue with Socrates in Plato's *Republic*, written in about 380 BCE. In this story, we are to imagine what a person would do if they found a ring that would render them invisible. The thought experiment is intended to bolster the claim that we are not innately good or oriented toward justice. Rather, if we could get away with injustice to our own advantage, we certainly would do so. Because of its historical importance and because we will have reason to return to discuss the case again, we cite the thought experiment at length:

> According to the tradition, Gyges was a shepherd in the service of the king of Lydia; there was a great storm, and an earthquake made an opening in the earth even more incredible than the hatch at the place where he was feeding his flock. Amazed at the sight, he descended into the opening, where, among other marvels, he beheld a hollow brazen horse, having doors, at which stooping and looking in he saw a dead

body of stature, as appeared to him, more than human, and having nothing on but a gold ring; this he took from the finger of the dead and reascended. Now the shepherds met together, according to custom, that they might send their monthly report about the flocks to the king; into their assembly he came having the ring on his finger, and as he was sitting among them he chanced to turn the collet of the ring inside his hand, when instantly he became invisible to the rest of the company and they began to speak of him as if he were no longer present. He was astonished at this, and again touching the ring he turned the collet outwards and reappeared; he made several trials of the ring, and always with the same result – when he turned the collet inwards he became invisible, when outwards he reappeared. Whereupon he contrived to be chosen one of the messengers who were sent to the court; where as soon as he arrived he seduced the queen, and with her help conspired against the king and slew him, and took the kingdom. Suppose now that there were two such magic rings, and the just put on one of them and the unjust the other; no man can be imagined to be of such an iron nature that he would stand fast in justice. No man would keep his hands off what was not his own when he could safely take what he liked out of the market, or go into houses and lie with any one at his pleasure, or kill or release from prison whom he would, and in all respects be like a God among men. Then the actions of the just would be as the actions of the unjust; they would both come at last to the same point. And this we may truly affirm to be a great proof that a man is just, not willingly or because he thinks that justice is any good to him individually, but of necessity, for wherever any one thinks that he can safely be unjust, there he is unjust.[1]

At least initially, the case for human injustice seems quite forceful. If you had such a ring, wouldn't you do at least some things that are considered immoral? If the only reason we do "the right thing" is because we fear being caught, our ethical character is quite weak.

The Myth of Gyges thought experiment would probably expose the true character of more than one person on the island. Sun comes to mind as someone whose character cries out for maturity and moral development. Sun tends to do what she pleases, unless or until she gets caught. Even as a little girl, after she accidentally broke her father's glass ballerina, she did not own up to the truth, and accused the maid of breaking it, resulting in the maid getting fired, a consequence Sun knew was inevitable if she didn't come

---

[1]  Plato, *Republic*, trans. Jowitt, numerous editions (including online), Book II.

forward with the truth. After learning she is pregnant, Sun does not tell her husband Jin about her affair, which she halted initially upon being caught by her father, and which was terminated via the untimely death of her lover. Jin is sterile, but was led to believe that Sun was unable to conceive. Sun is now pregnant. Is her deceased lover the father? Did Jin become fertile due to the magic of the island? Could this be a virgin birth? Might there be some other explanation? If Sun's pregnancy is a result of her extramarital tryst, as evidence to date suggests, imagine what Sun would do if she had the ring of Gyges!

While the Gyges thought experiment would expose Sun's inner character, we disagree with the claim that it describes *what all human beings would do*, let alone even most.

## "What do you see when you turn out the light?"

In a sense, our question of what would you do if you were on the island could be asked of many different settings from television, film, theater, and literature. For example, would you have committed suicide if you were in the position of Anna Karenina? But island narratives are especially effective in bringing to the fore a person's character because they invite us to entertain what we would do when separated from our cultural home. Consider two island narratives from the past that bear some relation to *Lost*: the Homeric epic poetry about Odysseus on Calypso's island, and Daniel Defoe's famous eighteenth-century story of a surviving shipwrecked sailor, *Robinson Crusoe*.

In Homer's poem, the *Odyssey*, Odysseus is on a ten-year journey from the ruins of Troy, back to his homeland, Ithaca, where his wife and son are waiting for him. Early on in his voyage home, Odysseus is washed up on the island of Ogygia where Calypso, a beautiful divine nymph, takes him captive. He is placed under her spell as her lover and bondsman for a full seven years. He is tempted by her beauty and her promise of immortality (eternal youth) to forget his family, but eventually he pleads successfully with Calypso to release him and help him make his journey homeward. This story has been used to illustrate a choice that some of us face: pursuit of the dream of endless youthful pleasure (with Eros) or the choice of domesticity, of coming to have a home and family, and of coming to terms with age. When Odysseus does come home there is (after he rids the palace of rivals and enemies) a scene of enviable, domestic joy. Odysseus and his wife Penelope spend their first night together doing three things: telling each other stories of their time apart, making love, and sleeping. Homer's epic effectively uses the narrative of life on an island so that its main character can come to terms with whom he really loves (Penelope, not Calypso) and compel a decision about whether he will shun immediate gratification and the wonder of appearances in order to be with the person whom he truly loves.

In *The Life and Strange Surprising Adventures of Robinson Crusoe of York, Mariner* (to give the full title of the book), a man of considerable wealth and ambition is completely cut off from his past life when he becomes shipwrecked on an island off the coast of South America. Rather than discover his commitment to true romantic and marital love like Odysseus, he comes to discover the need to understand his life in relationship with God. He moves from someone who earlier had designs to engage in the slave trade, to someone who is oriented to compassion and piety. Defoe suggests that without this radical break from "civilization," this transformation would not have taken place. After two years on the island, Crusoe records in his journal:

> It is now that I began sensibly to feel so much more happy this life I now led was, with all its miserable circumstances, than the wicked, cursed, abominable life I led all the past part of my days; and now I changed both my sorrows and my joys; my very desires altered, my affections changed their gusts, and my delights were perfectly new from what they were at my first coming.[2]

Being on the island provides a unique context for self-awareness and self-transformation.

*Lost* has some resonance with both of these classic works. As with the *Odyssey* there is enchantment and good and bad magic, the opportunity to come to terms with what one truly loves or hates. And as with *Robinson Crusoe* there are transformations (good and bad) and also religious elements at work, brooding hints of mystery and

---

[2] *Robinson Crusoe*, various editions (including online), chapter 9.

providence. There is also something of the existential feel to *Lost* that Defoe achieved in his book. Also, like Crusoe, there is a sense in which the characters are split, carrying some things from their home, but also encountering that which is strange and unpredictable. Consider the following exchange:

> *Sawyer:* You're just wasting your time, trying to save a guy who, last time I checked, had a piece of metal the size of my head sticking out of his bread basket. Let me ask you something. How many of those pills are you going to use to fix him up?
> *Jack:* As many as it takes.
> *Sawyer:* Yeah? How many you got? You're just not looking at the big picture, Doc. You're still back in civilization.
> *Jack:* Yeah? And where are you?
> *Sawyer:* Me? I'm in the wild.
> ("Tabula Rasa")

This fascinating boundary between the wild and the "civilized" places *Lost* squarely in the great tradition of island narratives which explore the questions of character and identity.

*Lost* especially invites the exploration of our key question – What would you do if you were on the island? – for all the characters have a complex relationship between who they were or the kind of life they used to live, and who they are now, interacting with each other and the island itself. We learn, for example, that Michael's past was vexing. The mother of his son, Walt, has run off to Amsterdam to pursue her law career. Many years later, shortly after her death in Sydney, Walt's adopted father asks Michael to assume custody of Walt. Michael is just getting to know Walt when, in the course of the father and son's effort to escape the island, Walt is kidnapped by the Others. Michael serendipitously manages to find Walt, but in so doing, also becomes a captive of the Others. In order for Michael and Walt to be together with one another and be free from the Others, a deal is cut between Michael and the Others. Michael gets Walt back unencumbered providing he rescues the Other (Benjamin aka Henry who was being held prisoner by his fellow survivors) and assures that Sawyer, Hurley, Kate, and Jack end up in the custody of the Others. Michael is now a man on a mission, and in passionately executing this quest to be reunited with his son, he executes two innocent women in cold blood (Ana Lucia and Libby). Prior to that moment, who would think it would come down to such killing? But the fact that it did means that Michael's past constitution was vulnerable and insecure.

Perhaps the opposite of Michael is Charlie. Prior to the island, he is a heroin addict. But on the island he overcomes his addiction (with a little help from his friend, Locke) remaining restrained, despite the fact that there is heroin on the island. Another character whose consistently heroic behavior suggests he has more substance than the con man he was prior to the crash is James Ford, aka Sawyer. A couple more seasons on the island, and who knows? Sawyer could prove to be the true hero of the entire cast of castaways. So, the island invites the question of what-would-you-do, but it also invites what we will describe as the reversal of the myth of Gyges and, ultimately, aligns *Lost* with the *Odyssey*.

Obviously, there are layers upon layers of mystery in *Lost*. How did a polar bear end up on a tropical island? Is this a lone polar bear or are there others? Who is Jacob and who is included on Jacob's list? As of this writing, we know very little about the Others, the "French woman," the Dharma (Department of Heuristics and Research on Material Applications) Initiative, whether many of the stories about the past are credible or how they might be interwoven (Hurley's lottery winning and experience in a psych ward are mystifying), but we believe the whole show is driven by the desire to do the opposite of Gyges: not to make people invisible, but gradually to bring people into focus, to make the past and what is going on in the present visible. This takes a dramatic turn when the numbers are allowed to reach zero, as this threatens to bring about an apocalyptic end to the island itself. But this is quite telling and true to the story of Odysseus: the word *apocalypse* comes from the words "to remove" and "covering." "Calypso," the name of the nymph goddess who kept Odysseus on his island so long, means "covering." So the term *apocalypse* can be interpreted as meaning the removal of Calypso (removing the mere appearances of what you want, to get to what really matters). The fact that discovering the truth about the machine in the hatch might involve real destruction fits in with the longstanding warning in Greek tragedy, that discovering your own identity can bring about disaster (think of Oedipus, who is fearless in his quest to find out his origin until, at last, he discovers the horrifying truth that he killed his father and married his mother, certainly Oedipus' own apocalypse).

Despite the driving force of the role of mystery in the *Lost* narratives and the threat that revelation and the uncovering of appearances may be destructive, there is a hunger in the main characters to uncover appearances and to get at what truly happened or is happening, come what may. Consider this briefly with Kate, Locke, and Jack.

We have a colorful glimpse of Kate's past, blowing up her abusive father, running away from the law resulting in a car crash killing her boyfriend, robbing a bank, and traveling on Flight 815 as a prisoner under federal marshal escort. Yet, somehow, in light of this tumultuous history, we cannot help but be taken with Kate. She hadn't realized the abusive man she killed was her biological father until after the deed was done. She didn't mean for her boyfriend to die and was truly in love with him. She didn't implement the bank heist for money. She was after her deceased boyfriend's toy airplane locked away in safety deposit box #815. How can we not be impressed by this overt display of sentimentality? This is a woman who tries to help out her mother by killing her abuser, is genuinely in love and has that taken away from her, and will go to any extreme to "right" a wrong. Kate manages to fall in love again with a policeman, but realizes she must tell him the truth, that she is a fugitive from the law. Kate is highly intelligent, compassionate, and committed to her beliefs, even when none of this is rewarded by society. In that sense, and based on her behavior while on the island, an argument can be made that she is brave and honorable, even in the face of conflicting evidence. A key motivation in her character is to know both herself and the others. It is as though she would love to have a visibility ring – a ring that would make clear what others are really thinking or wanting – rather than obscurity and secrets.

Locke undergoes a major change on the island and (as of this writing) he seems to be growing in wisdom, but he, too, is seeking revelation. He is more prepared to explore mystical avenues to get to the truth than, say, Jack, but he definitely wants to know why he is there on the island (is he summoned?). Jack was immediately thrust into the leadership role, trying desperately to save lives, heal the injured, and encourage everyone to work together for the common good. Jack is slow to trust, but quick to try to do the right thing. He is a logical thinker thrust into an illogical environment. How does he make sense of his predicament? Can he reconcile the new, bizarre direction his life has taken? In order for Jack to truly understand his fate, he will likely need to first undergo a major paradigm shift regarding the circumstances he now finds himself in. Perhaps the first step in his journey toward reconciliation of his present status is believing the evidence that was presented to him, namely, that the Red Sox had finally won the World Series.

So we propose that the main characters are not mere Lotus Eaters, those creatures in Homer's *Odyssey* who placidly give themselves over to idle, drugged pleasures. They are energized by the quest for self-awareness and values, avoiding what Robinson Crusoe laments as the "Stupidity of his soul, without desire for Good, or Conscience of Evil." They want to come to terms with happiness, joy, and sorrow. And viewers are invited to participate in this quest as we identify with the characters or resonate with their decisions and failures. While we endorse this overriding positive interpretation of the show, we think that *Lost* (so far) is a tad closer to Homer's world rather than Defoe's. Amid all his adventures (and Crusoe, like some of the *Lost* characters, has to rescue a captive), the Crusoe character comes to believe in an all-good, all-powerful, provident God. The realm of *Lost* seems closer to Homer's strange cosmos of competing deities or powers, only some of which are good.

## "Lend me your ears and I'll sing you a song, and I'll try not to sing out of key"

*Lost* is bizarre on many fronts. We have profoundly improbable narratives in terms of persons and nature, but the one thing we do not have is a complete reversal of values. Kidnapping children is still evil, even if the kidnappers think they have a really, really good reason for doing so. If, however, *Lost* involved a complete reversal of values, our thought experiments would collapse. Imagine that the show advanced the following premises: on the island, cruel kidnapping is actually good, as is betraying friends, theft for personal gain, cowardice, and so on. Courage, compassion, fidelity, what we think of as justice and fairness, care for the vulnerable and innocent, and so on, are all evil. Let's further imagine that the show asks us to accept these premises as not just about what is labeled "good" and "evil" but about the morality of the island itself. On this scenario viewers are asked to imagine that cruel kidnapping is actually

85

deserving of praise on the island; it is worthy of love and attention, while compassion truly is worthy of blame. Under this condition of complete reversal, let's go to our question: What would you do on that island?

With such a radical reversal of values, the question would lack sense, for it involves what might be called a moral impossibility. While customs change across cultures (especially in matters of politeness and shame), if morality has *any* normative force, it cannot be regarded as *completely* relative to context. To take an extreme, particularly grotesque claim: if it is truly the case that skinning and salting a child is wrong, this cannot be wrong only in New Jersey. To bring this point home, consider the most-good person you know. If you asked her or him the following question, "If you were on an island where skinning and salting babies is good, would you do it?" what do you think their response would be? Their response would range from horror to an embarrassed, forced laugh thinking that you were (unsuccessfully) making a joke. No person who is good in the sense that she or he is just, compassionate, courageous, and so on, would say that, oh yes, if it turned out that justice and so on were evil, and that skinning and salting babies good, they would get to work right away on such a cruel mission.

You can imagine worlds with radically different technology or laws of nature, but once you try to reverse all values, "the world" you are imagining will slip into what we can only find incoherent. So, in Homer's *Odyssey*, readers for at least the last 2,500 years have enjoyed the story about the enchantress Circe who turned Odysseus' poor, unsuspecting men into swine, and they have cheered Odysseus on when he gets them changed back into human beings. We don't have to believe that there are such enchantresses in order to enjoy the story, but we do have to suppose that transforming humans involuntarily into swine is, well, at least not good, especially if the change is permanent and there is a lively market for pork. Our thesis was stated quite well in a short story, "The Blue Cross," written in 1911 by G. K. Chesterton. In the story, the main character makes the following assertion of the permanency of overriding values:

> Reason and justice grip the remotest and the loneliest star. Look at those stars. Don't they look as if they were single diamonds and

sapphires? Well, you can imagine any mad botany or geology you please. Think of forests of adamant with leaves of brilliance. Think the moon is a blue moon, a single elephantine sapphire. But don't fancy that all that frantic astronomy would make the smallest difference to the reason and justice of conduct. On plains of opal, under cliffs cut out of pearl, you would still find a notice board, "Thou shalt not steal."

We are not claiming that morality is as clear-cut as reading a notice board or that (except in our grotesque case involving salt) it is always obvious what acts are right and wrong. But we are claiming that if we ask our "What would you do if you were in that world?" question about a world in which values are completely overturned, the thought experiment cannot shed light on who you are now.

In the episode "Dave," Hurley struggles with reality. Is Dave real or just some kind of manifestation produced by the overactive imagination of a guilt-ridden individual? He must be real because when he hits Hurley on the head, Hurley experiences pain. Yet how can Dave be real, since no one else can perceive him? Even more radically, is Hurley truly shipwrecked on a remote island, or is the island simply a metaphor representing the confines of a psych ward that serves as a holding place for Hurley's comatose body? Is Libby real? Hurley finds it difficult to believe that a woman so beautiful inside and out could possibly be attracted to him. Apparently, two kisses from Libby are enough to convince Hurley that perhaps he really is on an island and Libby's affection for him is genuine. If he's correct, then he has much to look forward to. If not, why end it all by jumping off a cliff as Dave had suggested, only to find himself waking up in a psych ward, or worse, assuring himself one doozy of a "cluckity-cluck-cluck day" by becoming a rotting mass of out-of-luck-beach-muck? At this juncture, Hurley opts to get by with a little help from his friend Libby, to head back to camp, and to move forward with what appears to be his life. While much is not evident to Hurley, what is clear is that in *Lost* there remains a core realization of basic goods and evils. If Libby lures Hurley to a premature violent death, this is bad. If she turns out to be a true friend and helps him recover, this is good. These value judgments remain stable even when we are not clear about the conditions of our own reality.

So how about it readers? How would *you* fare if faced with situations similar to those experienced by the survivors on *Lost*? Can you look yourself straight in the face, and know in your heart of hearts, that you'd get by with a little help from your co-castaways, with your character and integrity fully intact?[3]

[3] We thank Sharon Kaye for her encouragement of this project and the opportunity to contribute to *Lost and Philosophy*. Thanks, also, to Tricia Little for comments on earlier drafts.

# 8

# The Island as a Test of Free Will: Freedom of Reinvention and Internal Determinism in *Lost*

## Charles Girard and David Meulemans

### From the Eye to the Island

*Lost*'s pilot episode begins with a close-up of Jack Shepard's eye – first closed, and then suddenly open, in a brutal awakening. This is the first shot of the show, before any view of the plane, the beach, or the island itself, and a similar image opens most of the following episodes. Usually still and wide open (since from now on the survivors are awakened), the opening eye seems to invite us to enter its owner's mind, to explore his or her inner thoughts. This introduction is also a warning: what we are about to see for the next 42 minutes will be seen from the point of view of a specific character, be it Kate, Sawyer, Hurley, Ana Lucia, Sun, or another survivor from Oceanic Flight 815. We will not necessarily see through his or her eyes, but we will follow the events occurring on the island from a perspective that is primarily concerned with his or her destiny. The editing of each episode, showing in parallel sequences the traumatic or decisive events of one character's past and the challenging dilemmas the same character is confronted with after the plane crash, builds the interplay between past actions and present choices into one of the show's main themes. These flashbacks, bringing helpful clues and context for our

89

understanding of the character, echo the dilemma he or she is currently confronted with on the island. Beyond the long-term questions (why did the plane crash? who are the others? will the survivors be saved?), a personal conflict dominates each episode. It's usually a challenge or an ordeal that requires the protagonist to free himself from his past. Will Jack overcome his guilt of not being able to fix everything and accept his role as a leader? Will Kate come to terms with her criminal past and stop fleeing? Will Sawyer renounce treachery and betrayal to help his companions in adversity? Will Charlie stop chasing the dragon and help Claire with her baby? Sure enough, this recurring narrative structure could not be more typical of classic TV writing. Will the protagonist overcome all obstacles, internal as well as external, and manage to achieve his goal – as well as to choose the right one?

This type of storyline builds on a classic philosophical question: the problem of liberty and determinism. Is it possible for an individual to act according to his free will without yielding to the influence of determinist factors, either external (his environment) or internal (his personality)? *Lost* does not only exploit a philosophical cliché, it also offers an innovative illustration of this classical problem, as the island on which the plane crashes allows the writers not only to create a suspenseful plot but also to transform a theoretical hypothesis into a narrative device. Isolated on an island where everything is different (the crippled can walk, the sick are cured, the estranged are reunited), separated from their relatives, deprived of the context supporting their daily habits, *Lost*'s characters are not only wrenched from ordinary life, they are freed from the environment that has contributed to making them what they are. As a consequence, the type of determinism each of them is struggling with does not come from the outside but from the inside. On the island, it is not family, community, or society that limits their freedom, but their past actions, and more importantly, their perception of these past actions. Thus, the island in *Lost* appears as an artificial device allowing the writers and the viewers to wonder: How free are we to reinvent ourselves when the only thing that remains from our past is the remembrance of our actions and choices? Lost on the island, but also freed by the island, can we escape the tyranny of our memories?

## "Everyone deserves a fresh start": State of Nature and Second Chance

In the episode appropriately named "Tabula Rasa," Kate offers to give Jack some explanations after he finds her mug shot in the jacket of Marshal Edward Mars:

> *Kate:* I want to tell you what I did, why he was after me.
> *Jack:* I don't want to know. It doesn't matter Kate, who we were, what we did before this, before the crash. It doesn't really . . . Three days ago, we all died. We should all be able to start over.

By isolating them on an island where nothing remains from their past but themselves, and where new conditions of living – or rather, surviving – replace old ones, the plane crash violently separates the characters from the familiar context that has so much contributed to making them who they are. The fact that the new environment it provides them with is a lost island where nature, rather than humans, seems to rule (at least at first sight) transforms this contextual change into a liberation. Like many fictions that set their plot on an island where human civilization hasn't yet prevailed, the show depicts a new state of nature. On *Lost*'s island, social constraints aren't as institutionalized and oppressing as in normal society; personal liberty is wider and opportunities of reinvention are more frequent. Admittedly, the island doesn't make all forms of external determinism disappear – that is simply not possible, and the characters' expectations, prejudices, and demands still exert a deep influence on each other's acts. The state of nature that is the island is not a state where no human community exists, but rather a state where social organization is loose and fragile, and where, as a consequence, there is some space for individual autonomy. Since the island's nature is inhabited by the survivors of the crash (and then some more), it is not a state totally free from social determinism.

For instance, Sawyer, so quick to mock Jack for "not looking at the big picture" and being "still back in civilization" while he, the bad boy, is already "in the wild," cannot in fact emancipate himself from the other survivors' judgments. He doesn't cease to lie, steal, and cheat, acting as if he were afraid of failing his newly acquired reputation as an immoral rebel. However, because *Lost*'s state of nature liberates them from past social determinations and allows them to partially reinvent their social identity, it offers the survivors a second chance. The quest for such a chance is precisely at the core of all the characters' past and present trajectories. This is especially true of Kate, who is non-coincidentally the first to reveal her past to us through flashbacks that go back in time *before* the take-off of the plane ("Tabula Rasa"). The farmer who hosts her while she is on the run confronts her after she tries leaving his farm by night: "I get it, you know, everyone deserves a fresh start." Since traces of their social identity have disappeared, *Lost*'s characters would be unidentifiable if it weren't for the flashbacks. Who could guess, seeing him on the island, that John Locke had been a cardboard firm employee? Certainly not Boone:

> *Boone:* What do you do in the real world, Mr. Locke? . . .
> *Locke:* Why don't you guess?
> *Boone:* Well, you're either a taxidermist or a hit man.

Who could guess, watching him build a church, that Mr. Eko had been a drug trafficker? Who could believe, except for the fact that they are telling us so, that Charlie had been a famous rock star and Hurley a millionaire? Even Charlie can't believe Hurley when he confesses his fortune. Locke's metamorphosis is probably the most impressive: the frustrated handicapped employee becomes, after the crash, a formidable walking hunter. The man who suffered so much from social vexations (by his colleagues) and familial rejections (from his father) is reborn with new skills and possibilities. Of course, the crash (or is it the island?) has reawakened his legs – but at least as important is the fact that no one among the survivors knows that he had been in a wheelchair. It is not only because Locke isn't disabled anymore, but also because he is no longer confronted with social representations of his handicap that the frontiers of the doable and the undoable have significantly moved for him. Embodying the rejection of external determinism, Locke keeps repeating a signature line of the show: "Don't tell me what I can't do" ("Walkabout"). One's freedom of choice and actions should not be determined by anyone other than oneself. Locke thus encourages his co-survivors to use their newly acquired liberty of reinvention, such as when inviting Shannon to let go of her ambiguous relationship to Boone ("In Translation"): "Everyone gets a new life on this island, Shannon. Maybe it's time you start yours." Thus, *Lost*'s island appears to be an artificial device that allows people to partially cut themselves off from social determinism. To that extent, it can be seen as a philosophical as well as a narrative fictional device. Nonetheless, separation from your context and social identity is not enough to emancipate you from your past, as the agonizing Marshal reminds Kate, when mentioning that he was able to arrest her only because she stopped to rescue the farmer that had denounced her:

*Edward:*   You would have gotten away if you hadn't helped him.
*Kate:*   In case you haven't noticed I did get away.
*Edward:*   You don't look free to me.

What does he mean? Of course, Kate and the others are trapped on the island. But that's not all: on the island, where traces from her past have been erased, she keeps hiding and fleeing from something. Being freed from your environment is not enough to set you free: you also have to be freed from yourself.

## "That's not gonna happen": Bad Habits and Second Nature

When Locke discovers that Charlie is a drug addict and has been hiding a stack of heroin, he decides to help him by calling on his free will ("The Moth"). After trading him his drugs for his guitar, Locke tells Charlie that if he asks three times, Locke will give it back to him. This promise puts Charlie's will to the test. To obtain what he desires, he will have to ask for it repeatedly and by doing so he will test his determination. The time involved in the process as well as the prospect of being left alone with his own responsibility after the third demand create conditions for reflection and give Charlie's will a chance to triumph over his urges. As a result, Charlie asks for the heroin three times, only to burn the stack. But kicking his addiction is not a mere question of will, since body and mind have developed a dependency over time. Discovering that a plane containing heroin-filled Virgin Mary statues has crashed on the island, Charlie can't

93

help but get one ("Exodus: Part 2") and then some more. It will take Claire's contempt, Locke's antagonism, and a lot of social frustration to finally throw the heroin into the ocean ("The Long Con") and kick the habit for real.

External factors such as society or family are not the only determining factors inherited from your past. Internal traces remain with you even after a change of context, and Charlie's addiction is only one example. As one episode's title, "Born to Run," indicates, Kate keeps running: she flees alternately from Jack and Sawyer, as she fled, one way or another, from the Marshal ("Tabula Rasa"), the farmer Ray Mullen ("I Do"), her mother ("Born to Run") and Kevin ("I Do"). Having been a con man in his pre-island existence, Sawyer lies and cheats again and again: as he deceived Jessica ("The Confidence Man") or Cassidy ("The Long Con"), he can't help but deceive the other survivors on many occasions, stealing supplies repeatedly and most notably all the guns of the group ("The Long Con"). Marked by his experience as a torturer during the Gulf War ("One of Them"), Sayid finds himself unable, once on the island, to honor his commitment never to torture again: he uses his particular "skills" on Sawyer, in an attempt to recover Shannon's asthma medicine ("Confidence Man") and on Ben, suspected of being one of the Others ("One of Them"). Why are these men and women unable to take advantage of the second chance offered by the island and to impose their free will against their past? In fact, two distinct kinds of mechanisms are at work on *Lost*'s island, echoing two classical explanations of internal determinism in philosophy: second nature and subconscious.

Aristotle defines habit, in *Nichomachean Ethics* (Book II), as a "second nature." Moral virtues, according to him, are acquired by habit: it is not by a single choice, but by repeated practice, that we form our moral nature. As you become a builder by building or a cithara player by playing cithara, it is by accomplishing just actions that you become just. Mere will can't counterbalance tendencies and dispositions that have been built by the force of repetition into a second nature. For instance, it is not natural to be brave, although nature has given us the virtue of courage as a potentiality. To actualize this potentiality, a man has to act bravely again and again in order to transform repetition into a disposition – a tendency to be brave that is as spontaneous and imperious as if it was natural.

Unfortunately, the man who acquires a vicious disposition because of bad habits will be as influenced by his immoral tendencies as the virtuous man will be by his moral ones. *Lost*'s flashbacks show us the past moments during which the characters condemned themselves to be what they are by repeatedly acting in the same, often reprehensible, way. They explain why our protagonists, freed from the context that made them act as they did (Kate's abusive father, Sawyer's traumatic witnessing of his parents' death, Sayid's involvement in the Gulf War) and emancipated from the society that saw them as criminals or monsters, seem condemned to repeat again and again the same acts that disgust them. As a consequence, they share a common guilt and contempt for themselves, as well as an acute belief that they won't be able to stop acting as they do. And they occasionally encounter antagonistic figures who explicitly prophesy the inevitable perpetuation of their bad habits. When Sayid regrets having done what "no human being should ever have to do to another" ("One of Them"), Joe Inman, who forced him to torture for the US army, responds, "One of these days there will be something you need to know. And now you know how to get it." Asked by Kate to stop chasing her ("I Do"), Edward Mars sniggers, "I'll tell you what. If you can really stay put, really settle down, then I'll stop chasing you. But you and I both know that's not gonna happen."

## "Do you think there are horses here?" Subconscious and Psychological Determinism

The characters' inability to do what they acknowledge to be the right thing in *Lost* can't be explained purely in terms of second nature, however, as the dilemmas exposed by each episode also take a psychoanalytic turn. Indeed, the connection that is drawn between the flashbacks and the characters' actions is reminiscent of Freud's psychoanalytical theories. The flashbacks appear sometimes as direct memories which are actually remembered by the character in the present, sometimes as artificial parentheses intended to inform the viewer but of which the character is unaware, and sometimes (most of the time) as some kind of mental representation of the past, somehow summoned by actual events, but not really conscious. As the flashbacks always seem to reveal the hidden biographical logic

95

motivating our heroes' current actions, they appear as mental content unconsciously experienced in the present by the character's mind. Another explanation of the characters' inability to escape from their past is then the influence of their subconscious. In his *Introduction to Psychoanalysis*, Sigmund Freud exposes what he calls "psychological determinism": there is a logical link behind what we think to be free associations of ideas. Mental images or ideas that occur in the mind of a subject are determined by internal mechanisms, which are not unrelated to the ones at the origin of phenomena such as Freudian slips or symptomatic acts. They are part of the subconscious logic that guides many of one's actions without one's knowing it. To that extent, the characters' actions seem influenced by past experiences and traumas, very often rooted in childhood, such as Sawyer's parents' death ("Confidence Men"), Locke's desertion by his parents ("Deus Ex Machina"), Mr. Eko's sacrifice to save his brother ("The 23rd Psalm"), the same Mr. Eko's forced confessions ("The Cost of Living"), or Jack's belittling by his father ("White Rabbit"). Sharon, Kate, Hurley, and almost all the other characters – even Ben – have serious mommy or daddy issues. The apparent "hallucinations" experienced by the characters on the island can be seen thus as additional manifestations of their subconscious lives. Jack's obsession with the evanescent figure of his reproachful father at the very moment when he finds it difficult to accept his new role as a leader ("White Rabbit"), or Hurley's perception of his imaginary friend Dave while he is desperately trying to put an end to his own addiction to food ("Dave"), as well as the many voices that echo past memories through the show, in the woods or through an intercom, are good examples of such "apparitions," interpretable as creations from the characters' minds if not as avatars of the island itself.

The most striking image is the black horse which Kate faces when she exits the hatch with Sawyer, after overcoming the unconscious association that made her mistake him for the abusive father she had murdered ("What Kate Did"). It looks similar to the horse which suddenly appeared on a country highway after she had been arrested for that same murder, forcing the Marshal's car to crash and allowing her to escape. These surreal apparitions, linking the character's present challenge and past trauma, hint at a psychoanalytical explanation of the repeated failures of free will. Of course, the fact that

Sawyer also saw the horse would lead us to believe it is real – and maybe it is. Who could explain where imagination stops and reality begins, on an island where polar bears inhabit a tropical jungle and dark clouds of smoke murder people? In the enigmatic sequence that closes *Lost*'s third season, Jack and Kate are briefly reunited *after* having been rescued from the island ("The Looking Glass"). However, such a rescue is nowhere near certain at that point in the story. What we see is less likely to be a flashforward than a creation from Jack's subconscious, when he is confronted with a difficult choice (whether to use Naomi's phone or not) and dreads making the wrong decision and losing Kate.

## "I'm not a good person": Freedom of Reinvention and Self-Representation

To reduce internal determinism to second nature or subconscious is not enough. When asked by Charlie to explain why he has gone to such great lengths in order to con Jack, Locke, and all the survivors by stealing the guns ("The Long Con"), Sawyer has no better reply than this: "I'm not a good person, Charlie. Never did a good thing in my life." Sawyer's motivation can't be reduced to unconscious tendencies or behavioral patterns – it has also to do with how he understands his own identity. This idea echoes some pages of *Existentialism is a Humanism*, in which Jean-Paul Sartre asserts that man is always alone when confronted with choice. From an atheistic perspective, there is no predefined definition of human nature: no God or Destiny created mankind in order to achieve a preconceived end. No definition of what man is precedes his appearance on earth. On the contrary, it is existence that precedes essence, and thus no determinism can completely cancel one's freedom of choice. To invoke the influence of nature, society, or God to refute freedom of choice is only to deny the inescapable obligation to choose. To refuse to choose, or to blame external or internal forms of determinism in order to excuse one's refusal of the responsibility that comes with free will, is also a choice. It is what Sartre calls "bad faith." This is precisely, in Jack's view, what his father, Christian Shepard, does, as he explains to Sawyer in "Outlaws":

> *Jack:* That's why the Red Sox will never win the series.
> *Sawyer:* What the hell's that supposed to mean?
> *Jack:* It's just something my father used to say so he could go through life knowing that people hated him. Instead of taking responsibility for it, he just put it on fate. Said he was made that way.

A few days earlier, before the crash, the disbarred surgeon and deserting husband met Sawyer in an Australian bar in which he was drinking himself to death and used the exact same words:

> *Sawyer:* So we're in hell, huh?
> *Christian:* Don't let the air conditioning fool you, son. You are here, too. And you are suffering. But don't beat yourself up about it. It's fate. Some people are just supposed to suffer. That's why the Red Sox will never win the damn series.

The conflict between fate and freedom, recurring in *Lost*, takes a specific meaning when considered in relation with internal determinism. While fate is used as an excuse by Christian Shepard ("he said he was made that way"), it is on the contrary invoked by John Locke as a force for personal change. In both cases, a form of freedom is denied. As Locke says when confronting Jack in "Exodus 2," they did not choose the island, the island chose them:

> *Locke:* Do you really think all this . . . is an accident? That we, a group of strangers, survived, many of us with just superficial injuries? Do you think we crashed on this place by coincidence, especially this place? We were brought here for a purpose, for a reason, all of us. Each one of us was brought here for a reason.
> *Jack:* Brought here? And who brought us here, John?
> *Locke:* The island. The island brought us here. This is no ordinary place, you've seen that, I know you have. But the island chose you, too, Jack. It's destiny.

Nonetheless, Locke considers fate a force which allows some elect individuals to change who they are and what they do. Thanks to fate, which picked him and changed him, Locke can deny to others the right to tell him what he can't do. The repeated debates in *Lost* between believers in fate do not exactly oppose partisans of pure determinism and partisans of free will. On the side of fate is Locke, for example, who refuses to "mistake coincidence for fate" ("The

Cost of Living"). On the side of chance is, among others, Mr. Eko in the second season, who refuses, for the opposite reason, to "mistake coincidence for fate" ("What Kate Did"). Fate is used in *Lost* as much to excuse bad faith and justify determinism as to explain the possibility of free will. This is all the more crucial since some of the survivors, like Locke, believe they are "being tested" by the island ("Exodus 2"). The violent death of Mr. Eko, murdered by the island's "monster" ("The Cost of Living"), appears indeed as a punishment, as Eko just refused to repent his past sins: "I ask for no forgiveness, Father. For I have not sinned. I have only done what I needed to do to survive . . . I did not ask for the life that I was given. But it was given, nonetheless. And with it . . . I did my best." Isn't Eko killed for throwing away an opportunity to change as well as to hide behind determinism to flee his responsibility? Sartre asserts that to overcome the influence of external or internal determinism, one needs to reinterpret one's past trajectory. After all, a life doesn't take its full signification until it ends, since, at every moment, what you are can be changed by what you do. Bad faith precisely consists in pretending that what you are determines what you do once and for all. Sawyer is a good example, but almost all characters have displayed that attitude at some point. In Sartre's eyes, free will is possible because what one does defines who one is and not the other way around. Because one is free to create a new interpretation of one's past, one can always act differently and reinvent oneself. Locke can change so radically because he decides that he has been chosen by the island to survive the crash, find the hatch, or press the button. That's the origin of the moral crisis he goes through in "Die Alone": as soon as he starts doubting that he is chosen by the island, he begins to suspect that he cannot really change and that he's still the same, a useless frustrated cripple. Ben makes it perfectly clear when he challenges John to kill his father ("The Brig"): "You're still crippled by the memory of the man you used to be before coming to this island. You'll never be free until you release the hold your father has over you . . . That's why you're gonna have to kill your father." The fact that John's past is embodied by his con of a father only makes the choice he is confronted with more vivid: "Let go of him, John . . . As long as he's still breathing you'll still be that same sad pathetic little man that was kicked off his walkabout tour because you couldn't walk."

## "Free will is all we've really got, right?"

Rebirth is everywhere on the island, where the dead reappear (Christian Shepard, Yemi, Ana-Lucia, Boone), where the dying are cured (Rose, Charlie, Sawyer, Locke), and where Juliet's quest is to break the curse of the island's pregnant women. Moral rebirth is even more frequent, however, as each survivor is given a chance to reinvent themselves. When Libby confronts Hurley with his food problem ("Dave"), she asserts her faith in the force of free will:

> *Hurley:* When we first crashed here, I was like, this isn't all bad – it's, like, the all-mango diet. I wasn't turning any heads or nothing but I did drop a couple belt sizes. Then we found this hatch and it was full of food – tons of food. I tried giving it all away, but I guess I kind of kept some of it for myself. I wish I could just get rid of it.
> *Libby:* Then get rid of it. You want to change – then change.

Thus encouraged, Hurley dumps the food from his pantry in front of Libby.

> *Libby:* How do you feel?
> *Hurley:* I feel free.

Contradicting Libby's faith are the internal determinisms tying *Lost*'s heroes to their past: second nature, subconscious, and bad faith. The mere fact that each character's behavior seems predetermined by his or her name (Jack Shepard can't help but act as a leader, Sawyer seems always on the run) challenges his or her desire for autonomy of choice.

The description of *Lost*'s island as a narrative, physical, and philosophical device aimed at testing, on a fictional level, the thesis of free will and internal determinism is consistent with a striking feature of the show that puzzles so many of its fans: the inconsistencies between life before the crash and life on the island. A possible interpretation of these discrepancies would go as follows: if, as Locke keeps saying (corroborating what J. J Abrams and Damon Lindelof repeat in interviews), "the island is real," then it is tempting to consider that it is the past that is not real. Collective hallucinations, fake memories, artificially injected or dream-like sequences – the flashbacks would not present us with the actual past but with the character's illusory perception of a past that in fact never happened. The mere fact that it is conceivable to make such a hypothesis, which creates as many difficulties as it solves, is remarkable. If Jack didn't lose his father and Kate didn't kill hers, if Sayid didn't torture and Sawyer didn't betray, if they just think they did all these things, what they experience on the island is the difficulty to reinvent themselves, the weight of self-representation.

Are we truly free to reinvent ourselves? So far, *Lost*'s three seasons have offered contradictory answers, varying with the characters but also with the episodes. Caught between freedom of reinvention and failure to change, between second nature and subconscious, Jack, Kate, and their companions are truly lost. In season three, the character of Juliet embodies this tormenting doubt. When Adam criticizes her for picking a book that Ben wouldn't like ("A Tale of Two Cities"), she offers a sarcastic retort: "Here I am thinking that free will still actually exists." Later, the Others try to break Jack by playing with his inner tendencies (his obsessive need to fix everything) and his past traumas (Juliet looks like his ex-wife), in order to have him operate on Ben's spine ("The Cost of Living"). When invoking Jack's free will in order to convince him to accept, while at the same time asking him to kill Ben, Juliet adopts an unreadable tone, in one of *Lost*'s most ambiguous moments: "You probably feel like you don't have a choice, but you do, Jack. Free will is all we've really got, right?" She eventually leaves it to us to determine if she's sincere or not. More importantly, she leaves it to us to decide if free will is something we can believe in or only a foolish illusion masking the irresistible strength of internal determinism.

# 9

# *Lost*, *The Third Policeman*, and Guerilla Ontology

## *Jessica Engelking*

### "Orientation": A Brief Introduction

During the episode "Orientation," the novel *The Third Policeman* by Flann O'Brien is shown as Desmond David Hume rushes from the underground bunker. In an interview with the *Chicago Tribune*, *Lost* writer Craig Wright says *The Third Policeman* "was chosen very specifically for a reason" and "will be prominently featured at a key moment." Wright is also quoted as saying, "Whoever goes out and buys the book will have a lot more ammunition in their back pocket as they theorize about the show. They will have a lot more to speculate about – and, no small thing, they will have read a really great book."[1]

A character in *The Third Policeman*, the fictitious philosopher de Selby, also appears in *The Widow's Son*, the second of three novels in the *Historical Illuminatus! Trilogy* by Robert Anton Wilson. *Lost* creator/writer/producer Damon Lindelof has referred to Wilson in an interview, saying, "The only number [that] was always sort of a key number was 23, and anybody who knows anything about Robert Anton Wilson or any of his writing can read into that what they will."[2]

O'Brien's work influenced Wilson, and both in turn influenced the creative team behind *Lost*. Understanding the work of both O'Brien

---

[1] Patrick T. Reardon, "Another Clue: Literary Publisher Gets Mysterious Role on ABC's Lost," *Chicago Tribune*, September 21, 2005.

[2] From www.eonline.com/Gossip/Kristin/Trans/Lindelof/index2.html.

and Wilson is valuable not only in analyzing the show, but also because the ideas they present are relevant to contemporary philosophical debate. However, before delving into the philosophy, some (very) brief background information on *The Third Policeman*, O'Brien, and Wilson is required.

*The Third Policeman* was published posthumously in 1967, and quite fortunately so, for O'Brien had told friends the manuscript was "lost" after it had been rejected for publication.[3] The novel tells the story of an unnamed narrator who studies the fictitious philosopher de Selby. De Selby never actually appears in the novel, but is referenced via footnotes. In an attempt to finance his publication of the critical work on de Selby, the narrator commits robbery and murder. The narrator's partner in crime hides a black box believed to contain the stolen money. When sent to retrieve the box, the narrator discovers that it is missing. Oddly enough, the narrator encounters Mathers, the man he robbed and murdered, who tells him of three unusual policemen. The narrator decides to find the policemen and enlist their help in retrieving his missing box. He sets out to find the policemen's barracks, and what follows is a bizarre and fascinating series of events.

It's interesting to note the parallels between *Lost* and *The Third Policeman*. Like the Others, the policemen in *The Third Policeman* live in barracks. Both the novel and show take place, in part, in underground bunkers. The bunker is identified as "eternity" in *The Third Policeman*. In *The Third Policeman*, the policemen in the bunker are fanatical about taking readings (numbers read off instruments in "eternity"), much like the fanatical button-pushing on *Lost*. One of the policemen, the Sergeant, suggests that if readings are neglected, "there is bound to be a serious explosion."[4] On *Lost*, when the numbers are not entered and the counter reaches zero at the end of the second season, the system failure results in an electromagnetic force causing an implosion of the hatch. When the policemen take the narrator of *The Third Policeman* to "eternity," they show him a cabinet from which he can conjure anything he desires. However, he is unable to bring anything back with him. On *Lost*, Ben describes to

---

[3] From www.en.wikipedia.org/wiki/The_Third_Policeman.
[4] Flann O'Brien, *The Third Policeman* (Dublin: Dalkey Achive Press, 1967), p. 138.

Locke a box that could contain anything he imagined. When Locke goes to open the box, he opens a door to find his father, Anthony Cooper, bound and gagged in a wheelchair.[5] In *The Third Policeman*, the map to eternity is discovered in the cracks on the ceiling. On *Lost*, a map was discovered on the blast door by Locke. De Selby refers to human existence as a hallucination. In the episode "Dave," Hurley's imaginary friend Dave tries to convince him that everything that is happening is a hallucination, and that he is still in the mental institution. The narrator of *The Third Policeman* is a murderer (like Sawyer and Kate) who finds himself in a strange place from which there is no exit. These are just a few parallels between *Lost* and *The Third Policeman*, hinting at a connection between the two creative works and the influence of O'Brien on *Lost*'s writers.

Flann O'Brien (1911–1966) is the pseudonym of Irish author Brian O'Nolan. He is perhaps best known for his novel *At-Swim-Two-Birds*. O'Brien was heavily influenced by James Joyce and is considered to be a major figure in twentieth-century Irish literature. O'Brien is known for creating elaborate conspiracy theories in his novels.[6] As O'Brien himself made use of characters from the works of others, it's somewhat appropriate that Wilson used O'Brien's character, de Selby, in his own writing.

The recently departed Robert Anton Wilson (1932–2007) was a former *Playboy* editor, prolific author, and counter-culture philosopher, among other things. Wilson helped popularize the chaos-based religion Discordianism.[7] The *Principia Discordia*, the sacred text of Discordianism, is heavily referenced in Wilson's *The Illuminatus! Trilogy*. Wilson himself wrote an introduction to one addition of the *Principia Discordia*. Central to the *Principia Discordia* is the Law of Fives:

> The Law of Fives states simply that: ALL THINGS HAPPEN IN FIVES, OR ARE DIVISIBLE BY OR ARE MULTIPLES OF FIVE,

---

[5] According to Lostpedia, the box as described by Ben is similar to the black box in *The Third Policeman*. However, the black box in the *The Third Policeman* contained omnium. The box as described by Ben is much more similar to the cabinet in "eternity."

[6] From www.en.wikipedia.org/wiki/Flann_O%27Brien.

[7] www.en.wikipedia.org/wiki/Robert_Anton_Wilson.

OR ARE SOMEHOW DIRECTLY OR INDIRECTLY APPROPRIATE
TO 5.[8]

## "The 23rd Psalm": The 23 Enigma

Discordian numerology also holds sacred the number 23 (2 + 3 = 5). Wilson explicitly addresses the *23 Enigma* in his writings. The *23 Enigma* refers to the belief that all incidents and events are connected to the number 23. Wilson claims to have been introduced to the *23 Enigma* by William S. Burroughs while working as an editor at *Playboy*. As the story goes, Burroughs knew a certain Captain Clark, who ran a ferry from Tangier to Spain. One day, Captain Clark told Burroughs he had been running the ferry for 23 years without an accident. That same day, the ferry sank, killing everyone on board. That evening, Burroughs turned on the radio to hear of the crash of a plane, Flight 23, piloted by another Captain Clark.[9]

Instances of 23s can be found in *The Third Policeman*. The third policeman, Policeman Fox, went crazy on "a certain 23rd of June."[10] Also, without giving too much away, the narrator has an extremely important, life-altering experience on page 23. The number 23 features heavily in *Lost*: 23 is one of "the numbers"; Flight 815 leaves from Gate 23; there are 23 survivors from the tail end of the plane; Jack and Desmond meet when Jack hurts his ankle on the 23rd step of the stadium; there were 23 people on the deck that Hurley blamed himself for collapsing; the tenth episode of the second season is titled "The 23rd Psalm"; and Jack, Bernard, and Rose were seated in row 23; the slang expression "23 Skidoo" (which in general refers to leaving quickly) has suggested origins in both the Flatiron Building (located on 23rd Street in New York), which Michael cites as his architectural inspiration, and the stage adaptation of Dickens' *A Tale*

---

[8] Greg Hill and Kerry Thornley, *PRINCIPIA DISCORDIA or How I Found Goddess And What I Did To Her When I Found Her* (1965). Page numbers will not be provided due to unconventional pagination. Also, interestingly, an alternate title is *PRINCIPIA DISCORDIA or How the West Was* Lost.

[9] Robert Anton Wilson, *Cosmic Trigger (Volume 1) Final Secret of the Illuminati* (Tempe, AZ: New Falcon Publications, 1977), p. 43.

[10] O'Brien, p. 77.

*of Two Cities*, the title of the first episode of the third season; the season finale of the third season was aired May 23 (5/23); and perhaps the most interesting 23 occurs in the third season, when Karl is taken to Room 23 and is forced to watch a brainwashing video. More discussion of the Room 23 video will follow.[11]

## "The Greater Good": Guerilla Ontology

Robert Anton Wilson has described his writing as "guerilla ontology" and has referred to the *PRINCIPIA DISCORDIA* as an exercise in guerilla ontology.[12] Wilson picked up the term in the Physics Consciousness Research Group, though no one claims to remember who coined it. In philosophy, ontology is the study of existence. One who does ontology is concerned with the question, "What types of things exist?" In guerilla warfare, a smaller group uses its mobility and tactics of ambush and deception to combat a larger opponent. The practice of guerilla ontology involves introducing people to radically new ideas or concepts with the aim of evoking cognitive dissonance and discomfort by challenging their rigid belief systems. Ideally, guerilla ontology would lead to the replacement of old belief-systems with better, more positive ways of experiencing reality. Guerilla ontology is related to Wilson's assertion that "reality," in the commonsense way we speak of our lived experience, is almost entirely self-programmed.[13] This means that the individual plays a large role in determining what things he or she experiences. If the programming is changed, via guerilla ontology, perceived reality is changed as a result.

To better understand guerilla ontology, it may be helpful to consider an analogy. In screen-printing, a stencil is attached to a screen. Ink passes through the open areas of the stencil and creates an image. The stencil could be considered analogous to one's worldview, which shapes how the world appears. Like a properly prepared stencil, which is impermeable to water/ink and thus does not allow ink where it's

---

[11] Some examples taken from www.lostpedia.com/wiki/23.

[12] www.deepleafproductions.com/wilsonlibrary/texts/raw-inter-95.html; and Wilson, p. 59.

[13] Wilson, pp. 51–52.

not intended, a dogmatic worldview does not allow information in that does not conform to the worldview. Abuse or contact with certain chemicals can cause a stencil to break down, allowing ink to permeate.[14] Guerilla ontology can be thought of as abusing another's stencil/worldview, allowing in information that creates an image that does not match up to the images created by the rigid stencil/worldview.

Instances of guerilla ontology can be readily found on *Lost*. In the second episode of the third season (episode 2:3), Ben tells Jack that he wants him to change his perception. This is precisely the goal of guerilla ontology. Indeed, the Others claim to be the "good guys" and the aim of guerilla ontology is to create more positive models of reality. In Room 23, Karl is shown a brainwashing video with the phrases "EVERYTHING CHANGES" and "We are the causes of our own suffering" superimposed over images. The ideas that reality is in flux, and that the way the world appears is a product of the mind's imposing a certain interpretation of it, are central to guerilla ontology.

Another (potential) example of *Lost*-related guerilla ontology involves *The Lost Experience*. *The Lost Experience* reveals "the numbers" to be the core values of the Valenzetti Equation, a mathematical equation predicting the end of humanity. The six numbers represent the environmental and human factors in the equation. It is claimed that the purpose of the Dharma Initiative is to change at least one of these numerical factors so as to give humanity a chance for survival.[15] Here a change in a determinate factor that produces an undesirable reality would result in producing a better reality. Perhaps the human factor Dharma aims to change is the way in which we construct our reality.

In *The Illuminatus! Trilogy*, the term Operation Mindfuck (OM) is introduced as a key Discordian practice. OM involves activities such as pranks (called "Jakes" in Discordianism), hoaxes, etc., designed to disrupt and alter the perceived reality, in the same sense as guerilla ontology. On a related note, Mindfuck is a term being introduced as a concept in television and film as designating a narrative phenomenon which invokes tension and confusion in the viewer.[16]

---

[14] Much like certain chemicals alter mental states, as in Locke's hallucinogenic substance.
[15] www.lostpedia.com/wiki/The_Lost_Experience.
[16] www.lostpedia.com/wiki/Mindfuck.

Mindfucks have been baffling *Lost* viewers from the very beginning: tropical polar bears, a black cloud monster, and so on, right up through the introduction of the invisible Jacob and the reappearance of Walt. It is not being argued that the *Lost* writers are explicitly or intentionally engaging in acts of guerilla ontology. Mindfucks as narrative devices need not be employed with the aim of altering anyone's perceived reality. Tension and confusion, while potentially leading to cognitive dissonance and a challenged worldview, can also make for great ratings.

## "Man of Science, Man of Faith": Kuhn and the Purge

In 1962, Thomas Kuhn, an important historian and philosopher of science, wrote *The Structure of Scientific Revolutions*. In it, Kuhn argues against the notion that scientific knowledge progresses in a linear fashion, with new theories building upon old theories. Instead, Kuhn argues that science undergoes radical revolutions (much like social/political revolutions) in which new theories overthrow their predecessors. Such revolutions are called "paradigm shifts." Kuhn describes the process leading up to these paradigm shifts as an accumulation of anomalies (results that don't fit the theory). As the anomalies compound, science reaches a crisis, and a paradigm shift occurs, ushering in a new theory which accommodates the previous theory's anomalies. Kuhn also claims that competing paradigms are incommensurable – that is, it is impossible to interpret one paradigm through the conceptual framework or using the terminology of another paradigm. Paradigms are in a sense too radically different to compare. With a paradigm shift comes a radical alteration of ontology and worldview. By this it is meant that what exists does so relative to the paradigm in place. A paradigm shift ushers in a new reality.

A paradigm shift in science bears a similarity to the purging of the Dharma Initiative by the Hostiles (the name given by the Dharma Initiative to the people on the island before they arrived). Ben claimed that the Dharma Initiative was unable to coexist with the Hostiles. When it became evident that one of them had to go, Ben sided with the Hostiles. The Dharma Initiative was entirely wiped out, their bodies dumped into a mass grave. The Hostiles replaced the Dharma

Initiative and became the Others as we know them. The similarity to a paradigm shift lies in the inability of the two competing groups to coexist, much like the difficulty a theory has in coexisting with an accumulation of anomalies. As tensions increase, "crisis" is reached and something has to give, or as Ben put it, one side had to go. Like a paradigm shift in science, when a successor theory overthrows its predecessor, the Hostiles overthrew the Dharma Initiative. The history of the island, like the history of science as described by Kuhn, is marked by radical upheaval.

Furthermore, one can see a sort of similarity between the incommensurability of paradigms that Kuhn describes and the alleged inability of the "Losties" to understand what is really happening on the island. Perhaps the worldviews of the "Losties" and the Others are so radically different that the Others are unable to translate their knowledge in such a way that the "Losties" would understand. A prime example of such incommensurability would be John Locke's inability to see Jacob. Locke did, however, hear Jacob, which in addition to other hints, may indicate he is not entirely operating within the "Lostie" paradigm. Through the use of narrative devices, such as the flashbacks, one gets the sense that there are radical differences between the "Losties" and the Others. The "Losties" experience flashbacks of life before the crash; the Others, with the exception of Juliet and then later Ben, do not. When Locke experiences flashbacks to events on the island, it perhaps indicates that he has undergone a radical shift – that he is now operating in the paradigm of the Others.

To return to guerilla ontology, one can think of these tactics as a means of speeding up the process of accumulating anomalies in one's worldview, with the aim of revolution of the mind. In instilling cognitive dissonance, guerilla ontology practices put a person's worldview into a situation of crisis. The more confusion is induced, the less reality seems to fit with one's dogmatic worldview, the more likely the worldview is to be overthrown.

## "Further Instructions": Some Final Suggestions

If one theme can be thought to unite *Lost*, *The Third Policeman*, and guerilla ontology, it's the idea of not taking things too seriously.

Taking things too seriously means getting oneself locked into a rigid and dogmatic worldview. It means not acknowledging the contribution one's own belief system makes to one's experience of reality. It means resisting a radical shift in the way one perceives the world, when this shift could be for the better.

Strange places, events, coincidences, and other Mindfucks can leave one puzzled and perplexed. We seem to live in a world that is governed by certain laws of nature, where people and places stand in causal relation to one another, where time progresses in one direction. *Lost* and *The Third Policeman* call into question such assumptions. But such strangeness is not confined to the realm of fiction: the descriptions of the universe as put forth by the contemporary sciences of quantum mechanics and string theory might strike one as something cooked up by the *Lost* writers. Such theories purged the causally deterministic worldview and replaced it with a description of a probabilistic universe. Such theories are still rejected by many, for the oddities they entail (quantum entanglement, for instance) can leave one feeling a bit uneasy.

The "Further Instructions" suggested by *Lost*, *The Third Policeman*, and guerilla ontology are to keep an open mind, for an open mind is necessary to create a better reality. Start noticing 23s. As the 23s start to accumulate, and you start to feel a tension, begin to question. You may eventually come to acknowledge and appreciate the contribution you make to the reality you perceive.

In Wilson's *The Illuminatus! Trilogy*, the word "fnord" is introduced. In the trilogy, the children are brought up to be unable to consciously see the word "fnord." As adults, encounters with fnords instill a feeling of uneasiness or discomfort. Fnords are in the books and news, but not advertisements, encouraging a consumer society. For one to see the fnords involves breaking the spell of the word, of reprogramming, in a sense.

If you can find the fnords, what else can you find?

# 10

# *Lost* in Codes: Interpretation and Deconstruction in *Lost*'s Narrative

## *Tom Grimwood*

## *Lost* and the Postmodern

There are several reasons why one would view *Lost* as bearing the hallmarks of a "postmodern" show. In the telling of a seemingly familiar tale of survival after disaster, it employs non-linear narrative, conflicting viewpoints, disjunctive temporal schemas, and a pressing moral ambiguity over each character's situation. There is the absence of a clear "hero" or "heroine" – a point made in "Live Together, Die Alone (2)," and again in "Through the Looking Glass," when Ben declares to Jack that the Others are, contrary to what we've believed, "the good guys." Of course, since the birth of television, shows such as these have attempted to maintain the audience's interest with such seductive mysteries within the direction of the narrative. Where *Lost* breaks with this tradition is the various mediums of techno-communication through which the narrative is presented as a puzzle for the audience to solve. Various "codes" are dispersed and recur through characters' backgrounds and plot development, not only in the televised broadcasts but also through the internet, advertisements, and even telephone answer messages, which appear to stand in some relation to the "master narrative" – the "what's really going on" of it all.

The philosophy of interpretation, which is also known as "hermeneutics," deals with the problem of how we interpret meaning from a message – an utterance, a communication, a text – and what claims we can legitimately make over such meaning. The question that *Lost* poses for hermeneutics is whether such an apparently post-modern method of storytelling requires a postmodern interpretive practice, which would differ in some degree from the "traditional" or "commonsense" models of interpretation. But is this the case?

## What is a Code?

What do we mean by "code" here? Of course, part of the appeal of such codes is that they cannot be rigidly defined, so half of the fun is working out what is a meaningful code and what isn't. But some working definition is obviously necessary. A code, the *Oxford English Dictionary* tells us, is a "system of words, letters, figures, or symbols used to represent others, especially for the purposes of secrecy." Examples of this are not difficult to find. Road signs often use abstracted figures to convey their message (no overtaking, dead end ahead, etc.). These figures are set in a certain type of code (the Highway Code). The Highway Code is relatively simple to identify, because it is a commonly known code. The arrangement of language as "coded," so that the sign means one thing and not another, enables communication to project meaning.

The observant might notice that on this definition it's possible to see all forms of communication as coded in some way. Indeed, philosophers of language will often use the term "code" in a broad sense to indicate a framework within which individual "signs" – words, sounds, units of meaning – make sense.[1] But clearly, we're thinking about something more specific and recognizable than this. That is to say, the vast number of websites devoted to "decoding" *Lost*'s meaning are not, on the whole, grounded in obscure semiotic theories.

It is the "purposes of secrecy" element of the definition that simultaneously narrows our criteria for what a code is, and significantly complicates it, because it suggests that a code can often be used without openly identifying itself. A spy's coded message, for example, remains hidden from prying eyes because the appearance of the code will mean different things to different people. It is this very fact that

[1] See Daniel Chandler, *Semiotics: the Basics* (London: Routledge, 2004).

keeps the discussions over which elements of *Lost* are coded as intense as those over what such codes mean. So let's get more technical. A code is not just something that means something else, even if other mediums of communication that act similarly – metaphor, irony, etc. – might be considered certain types of code. What *Lost* attempts to do, I would argue, is use a more "mysterious" type of code, where we do not have – or at least, appear not to have – a ready-made handbook on how to interpret it. When I talk of "codes" here, I am referring to a specific arrangement of signs that *affects our ability* to interpret the meaning of that particular communication by separating the meaning of the communication from its immediate presentation.

It will be helpful to understand this with an example. Probably the most distinct "code" in *Lost* must be the mysteriously recurrent numbers. These are distinct from other elements of communication for several reasons. First, and most obviously, because they *look* like a code. They appear in unexpected and unrelated places, yet display enough consistency to suggest a relation. For example, the Flight number 815, Kate's deposit box no. 815, and Charlie's photocopier serial number 815, and so on. The presentation of ciphers rather than letters to contain meaning might make us think of historical uses of code such as the Enigma machine. However, without the suggestion that these numbers hold some significance to the master narrative – without the suggestion that they are, in fact, a code – the numbers are meaningless. In this way, the surface of the code is, initially at least, detached from its "original" or "intended" meaning. We see the tension involved with this in Hurley's struggle to convince the other characters that the numbers mean anything at all. Of course, just as the arrival of Hurley's imaginary friend in "Dave" threatens to undermine his belief in such a meaning, this detachment raises a problem of how we identify what an "original meaning" is, or even if there is one at all.

The discussion we have before us is thus centered on the following questions: How do we go about discovering and attributing meaning to such a dispersed network of signs and codes? What is it about the series that compels a belief that there is, in fact, a "master narrative" to be found? If such codes can only be found in certain places, how does one qualify the meaningfulness of a code? Does it make a difference if these codes are intended or not?

# The "Commonsense" Methods of Decoding Narrative

"But surely," you may well protest, "the meaning of these codes is obvious. The show is created by the writers, who then create the codes, in order that we trace our way back to them."

Friedrich Schleiermacher (1768–1834), the founder of modern hermeneutics, claimed that, *because* of the distance between the original meaning and the interpreter – a distance which necessitates a theory of interpretation in the first place – there can be no utter *certainty* that we have understood the original meaning of a communication. This is not a problem, on the whole, in everyday life. Imagine a typical way of understanding the "meaning" of a television series. We know from experience that the series has been "written" by somebody, for a particular viewing audience. We view the series with the assumption, therefore, that to "understand" it is to discover what the writers intended the meaning to be. To do this is no different from engaging in a conversation with somebody: we discern what the other person might be talking about by establishing the context in which the communication has meaning. The "codes" we encounter, when viewing *Lost*, are merely extensions of this process, slightly more "difficult" to piece together, but fundamentally operating under the same structure of communication.

This standpoint would agree with what I would term the "commonsense" or, more technically, the "intentionalist" account of meaning. For this approach to interpretation, the communicative act must possess "intentionality" to have any meaning. This view has been developed by John Searle (1936–). Searle distinguishes two "aspects" which we refer to when we assess the meaning of a conversation.[2] The "secondary" aspect refers to the meaning of the sentence (in a spoken conversation), or medium of expression (e.g., a code). The "primary" aspect determines the speaker's actual meaning, or in our case, the "master narrative" of *Lost*. When we engage in a conversation, the speaker employs the secondary aspect to express the primary meaning: we, as listeners, reverse this process by using the medium of expression in order to uncover the meaning which the

---

[2]  See John Searle (1979), "Referential and Attributive", in *The Monist* 62.

speaker intends us to hear. If we apply this "commonsense" account to *Lost*'s codes, we can see that it provides answers to two questions: (1) What is the original meaning of *Lost*? The intention of the *Lost* writers. (2) How we can tell if something on the show is meant as a code? It is a code if (a) it has an original meaning, and (b) this meaning is accessible by the viewer.

Searle denies that meaning can be construed independently of a context. By understanding the context of the intentional meaning, we will understand the references involved in the primary aspect of meaning. Let's illustrate this with an "illustration": the Dharma Initiative logo. This appears at various points both in and out of the show; but similarly to the general act of understanding we have just described, despite its fragmented appearances, the logo nevertheless has a context by which it can be "understood," and the more this context is detailed, the clearer the meaning of the logo becomes. Thus, when it first appeared, we saw only an amalgamation of images (on the hatch entrances, on websites, etc.), but as we contextualized and connected the various appearances, the logo began to "make sense." Just as Locke pieced together the roll of film that instructed him as to the meaning of the hatch, we piece together clues that build a bigger picture of the meaning of the Dharma Initiative to the show in general.

What if the viewer has access to multiple possible meanings, though? This problem was addressed by the literary critic E. D. Hirsch Jr. (1928–). In cases of ambiguity, Hirsch argues, there is rarely a case where *probability* cannot inform us of the most likely correct meaning. Any assessment of a communication's meaning – and any ambiguity that this might raise – is always grounded on the original intention of the communicator.[3] As Searle argues, a sentence cannot have *both* a literal *and* a figurative meaning, because "sentences and words have only the meanings that they have."[4] Thus, the fact that the Dharma logo might look like a swan from certain angles, for example, is only incidental to its final narrative meaning (unless, of course, Dharma happens to relate in a more direct way to the preservation of birdlife, or some such contextual reference).

---

[3]   See E. D. Hirsch Jr., *Validity in Interpretation* (New Haven, CT: Yale University Press, 1967), p. 161.

[4]   John Searle, "Metaphor," in Andrew Ortony, ed., *Metaphor and Thought* (Cambridge: Cambridge University Press, 1993), p. 84.

# Problems for Common Sense

With the intentionalist theory of meaning, we have certainly answered questions over the "original meaning" of the code. But how relevant is this answer?

The fact that *Lost* has not finished its arc – and nor, indeed, is it known how long this arc will be – might be considered a factor here. We cannot hope for a finality of understanding, at least not now in 2007, because there is no designated "closure" as yet. We presume that there is some coherent "intentionality" to the show. Given the context of the show – i.e., as a science fiction/mystery televisual narrative – we assume that there will be answers, that the "final" revelations will "make sense."

But is this account of *Lost*'s codes too general to deal with the problem we have set ourselves? Let's approach it via a different question: Why place something in a code? To make it more exciting, yes. But if one utilizes codes (rather than straightforward narratives) in order to make the show more mysterious and intriguing, could there be an argument that one is not utilizing the code as a medium of communication, but as a medium of *ambiguity*? This is a key point. The notion of ambiguity is, somewhat naturally, a tricky area for any interpretation theorist. There is a tendency, when claiming to "solve" the ambiguity of a message, to ignore the operative sense that ambiguity has. This is, one might note, something of a circular process: if we ask "why is this ambiguous?" we are looking for an unambiguous answer. But then we are still left with the original problem of why one should be ambiguous about it. Ambiguity being what it is, it is immensely difficult to "understand" something that exists as a confusion, distraction, and general obstacle to straightforward understanding. The reason is that, while being an obstacle to understanding, it is not an obstacle to meaning.

If we approach these codes in terms of this ambiguity, is the "commonsense" model of meaning of any use to us? Consider again the case of the numbers. In Hurley's quest to discover their meaning, he is frequently given answers, which are frequently straightforward. But a straightforward answer cannot explain the meaning that Hurley identifies with the numbers as a sort of mystical quality. Nothing can be less ambiguous than numbers – that $1 + 2 = 3$ is as sure as magnetic north and south – yet it is this fact that makes the link between them and the events surrounding them so ambiguous. Furthermore, could it not be the case that reducing a code to its "original meaning" is to miss something important about the effect of dispersing these codes across different mediums of techno-communication? Would this mean that understanding the meaning of a code – not just the meaning "behind" the code, but the meaning of the code as a medium in itself – involves the unpacking of our presumptions over what constitutes "meaning"?

## Deconstructing the Meaning of Codes

The challenge of "poststructural" or "deconstructive" practices, such as those of Jacques Derrida (1930–2004) or Michel Foucault (1926–1984), to the philosophy of interpretation (and the philosophical tradition in general) coincides with many of these problems with the "commonsense" model. While, for Searle, meaning was always tied to context, the first basic assumption of a poststructuralist approach to interpretation is that meaning is not "fixed" above and beyond the means of its *production*. Neither the "commonsense" approach nor deconstruction posits a "transcendental signifier" that will guarantee the meaning of a communication. But for the deconstructionist, the situation is worse: language does not map on to the "real world" as a direct reference, but rather, the meaning of each word is dependent on the meaning of other words, and they in turn on others. So the prospect of a "final" meaning, which the "commonsense" approach identified as "intention," is always suspended or deferred. What this entails for interpretation is that the means by which the intentionalist theories suggest we trace back to the original meaning are never "original" themselves but always reproductions of meaning, and reproductions of reproductions (poststructuralists will often use the term "simulacra"). Think here of the first time that Locke fails to press the button in the hatch. As we reach the end of the countdown, and expect some sort of explanatory climax (or, perhaps, "meaning"), the numbers are replaced by hieroglyphics, and the illumination of a map on the hatch's blast doors. Yet more codes! This is, at a very basic level, a deconstruction of the way in which the meaning of the numbers have themselves been constructed: not by a

117

direct reference to a qualifiable "meaning," but because – as we noted at the beginning – they look like a code. If one attempts to force one's way beyond this process of meaning, in the search for some sort of transcendental signifier that eliminated such tricks, risks, and insecurities, one may well find oneself like Sayid, opening the guarded doors of the Other's camp in "Live Together, Die Alone (1)" and discovering behind the constantly repeated image of the Dharma Initiative that the (literally) closely guarded secret is revealed as . . . a meaningless blank wall.

It's important to recognize that deconstruction is less something which is "done" to philosophy and more something that is "revealed" about its processes.[5] Recall that the code established a particular type of distance between us, as interpreters, and an original meaning. The intentionalist theory identified this distance as a medium through which we gained access to the original meaning. But there is a certain faith in the probability of discovering the original meaning. How stable is this assumption? Derrida points out the fact that such approaches are based on the idea that all communication is assumed to follow the same structure as a spoken conversation. In the act of speech, the listener must be present both spatially (in order to hear the words) and temporally (they must be there to hear those particular words at that particular time). Indeed, this proximity ensures that the *intention* of the communication is closer to the *medium*. On the other hand, acts of communication not based on immediate personal contact, acts that can traverse time and space – writing, television, internet, etc. – are based, conversely, on *absence*. I write this essay in order that my communication will remain in my absence. Because of the absence of the addresser, such writing is able to be read by any addressee. This is, of course, the benefit of writing and recording, because it enables you to listen to my argument without me having to travel to your living room every time you want to hear it (not, of course, that the spoken word guarantees a successful communication – as Nikki found to her cost in "Exposé").

However, if this is the case, it is questionable why a model based on "speaking" and "presence" is applicable to the problem of codes. Treating a fragmented code in the same way one would a conversation

---

[5]   See Arthur Bradley, *Negative Theology and Modern French Philosophy* (Routledge: London, 2004), p. 23.

does not enable us to understand the original meaning better: rather, it prefigures our notion of what an original meaning is, and how important it is to our understanding.[6] Derrida terms this the "metaphysics of presence," which renders all forms of non-spoken communication secondary to speech itself, a hierarchy which, Derrida argues, has dominated the spirit of western philosophy. Think of the first time the survivors pick up Rousseau's repeated message in the second "Pilot" episode: because they can hear a voice they wrongly presume the message is contemporary with them (as opposed to, say, the stack of notebooks ejected from the hatch in "Live Together, Die Alone (1)," which are presumed not to signify any other contemporary presence on the island).

By thinking of the notion of "original meaning" in terms of its absence, rather than its presence, a certain instability comes to light. For example, think of an "original intention" not as a mental act, but rather the physical reproduction of it, the written *signature*. Although the role of a signature seems straightforward, as an inscribed date that situates a piece of writing, Derrida argues that "For the attachment to the source to occur, the absolute singularity of an event of the signature and of a form of the signature must be retained: the pure reproducibility of a pure event."[7] This is a paradoxical situation: the original meaning must be purely *singular* in order to be "original" (there can only ever be one event where the signature is produced), yet it must be instantly *repeatable* in order to have meaning (it is written down so that the text can be read in the absence of the signer).

## Problems for Deconstruction

Deconstruction is dismissed by many to be an anarchic form of relativism. Relativism asserts that there is no such thing as truth, thereby rendering all meaning relative. Therefore, Derrida's interpretive strategy is little more than word-play and sophistry. In fact, the deconstructive approach to interpretation is more subtle: it is arguing that

---

6   See Jacques Derrida, *Of Grammatology*, trans. Gayatri Spivak (Baltimore: Johns Hopkins University Press, 1976).

7   Jacques Derrida, *Margins of Philosophy*, trans. Alan Bass (Englewood Cliffs, NJ: Prentice-Hall, 1982), p. 328.

the structure of meaning in western philosophy is never secure, but rather somewhere between collapse and completion: it relies on the presence and force of an "original meaning," but only in order to *postpone* the fulfillment of such a meaning. The writer's intention is only a "function" of our interpretive procedure.[8] The meaning of the codes lies not in a reduction of their ambiguity to an original intention, but rather in the investigation into how such codes suspend themselves as "codes" in our interpretive practice.

This still presents a problem for us, however, as *Lost* enthusiasts. The deconstructive approach might enable us to theorize better the ambiguity of the code, but has it done so at the expense of giving us a *direction* to which we can turn? Are we to conclude with Locke, after discovering in "Three Minutes" that the button-pressing is only part of an experiment, that *Lost*'s codes are only really "a joke": "Rats in a maze, with no cheese!" By dwelling on the absence of narrative within the codes is there not a sense in which we might be tempted – just as Locke projects his character's history onto the act of pressing the button – to look at every narrative structure (the back stories, the island, the temporal organization) and conclude: "It's meaningless"?

"We do it," Mr. Eko responds to Locke, "because we believe we are meant to."

## "Believing we are meant to?" More Questions . . .

Deconstruction celebrates the ambiguity of the code, through recourse to the "absence" within its medium. The "commonsense" intentionalist theory, in contrast, reduces the code to nothing but a delay in communication. In doing so, it fails to account for the ambiguity of the code as an effective quality of the medium. The deconstructive approach sees meaning as dispersed throughout the means of communication as well as the communication itself. Consequently, "common sense" oversimplifies. There could be no "single" meaning to a message, and, in fact, the imposition of a single meaning would defeat "meaning" in general.

---

[8] See Michel Foucault, "What is an Author?" in Paul Rabinow, ed., *The Foucault Reader* (Oxford: Blackwell, 1984), pp. 101–120.

But could it not be suggested that, in another sense, the appeal of the code as a medium is based on the possibility that ambiguity can be solved? In other words, does the code's use of concealment actually reinforce the notion of a "correct" or single "original" meaning? Even if the tension involved in the use of codes as forms of communication is grounded on the mystery of whether there is a meaning behind them or not, it seems this is still predicated on the notion of an original meaning.

Perhaps the understanding of *Lost*'s codes reflects the play of the presence and absence of meaning in the codes themselves. In which case, the viewer's interpretive approach would hinge on the answer to one particular question: Is the meaning of a code given in the excitement of knowing, or the excitement of not knowing?

# PART III

## S IS FOR SURVIVAL

# 11

# No Exit . . . from the Island: A Sartrean Analysis of *Lost*

## Sandra Bonetto

Hell is other people.
Jean-Paul Sartre

There are striking similarities between *Lost* and the existentialist philosopher Jean-Paul Sartre's (1905–1980) famous play *No Exit* (*Huis clos*, 1943). In *No Exit* Sartre examines the concepts of facticity, freedom, and "the other." Three people – two women (Inès and Estelle) and one man (Garcin) – find themselves "thrown together" in a room for all eternity. This is Sartre's representation of hell. Each person is there for a specific reason: Garcin because he cheated on and tormented his wife, Estelle because she killed her own child and her lover, then committed suicide, and Inès because she tormented her (female) lover until that lover killed both of them.

*Lost* offers a similar dramatic situation. The crash survivors, all of whom seem to have ended up stranded on the island for a reason, are confined there. They can neither escape from the island nor from each other (or, indeed, from the Others), just as Inès, Estelle, and Garcin are confined to the room and each other's company. And just as the audience learns very slowly the facts concerning the three characters in Sartre's play, the same applies to *Lost*. With each episode, we learn a little more about the individual characters and their pasts. Moreover, the characters in *No Exit* all have something to atone for, and this, again, applies to the survivors in *Lost*. While *Lost* is not to be interpreted, in my opinion, as set in purgatory or even hell (as has been suggested by some fans of the show) – the survivors are *not*

dead, unlike Sartre's characters in *No Exit* – its dramatic situation is nonetheless a form of "existentialist hell." It centers on the conscious, lived experiences of its central characters who find themselves in a situation – akin to the absurd and meaningless universe that forms the existentialist backdrop to human existence – that has not been entered into freely and from which there appears to be no escape. Moreover, consciousness – individual and collective – is largely determined and circumscribed by "the Other" and "the Others." The existentialist, and especially Sartrean, undertones of *Lost* are thus evident.

## At Least They're Not in Hell

In his monumental *Being and Nothingness* (*L'Etre et le Néant*),[1] Sartre distinguishes between two modes of existence. The first is consciousness, which he calls being-for-itself (*pour soi*). The second is things (for example, a plane, a raft, a hatch), which he calls being-in-itself (*en soi*). Things have their essence pre-given (for example, the essence of the raft is to float) and they exist not for themselves but for me or for others. By contrast, consciousness is not a thing, but an *activity*. Conscious existence is a *project*, not an established, let alone preestablished, essence. Sartre concludes, "Man is nothing else but what he makes of himself" – this is "the first principle of existentialism."[2]

Sartre further distinguishes two aspects of the human condition – *facticity* and *transcendence* – which, for him, are the essential components of being human. Facticity can be defined as the sum total of facts about us and the situations into which we have been "thrown" – the "given facts" of our existence and situations which we did not ourselves choose to be in (for example, the color of our eyes, our parents, when and where we were born, finding ourselves stranded on an island after a plane crash). One's facticity is, moreover, "one's

---

[1] Jean-Paul Sartre, *Being and Nothingness: An Essay on Phenomenological Ontology*, trans. Hazel E. Barnes (London: Routledge, 1998); subsequent citations will be given parenthically in the text as Sartre, B&N, followed by page number/s.

[2] Jean-Paul Sartre, *Existentialism and Humanism*, trans. Philip Maret (London: Methuen, 1994), p. 28; subsequent citations will be given parenthetically in the text as Sartre, E&H, followed by page number/s.

past, those deeds and events that are over and done with, but whose consequences largely determine the present circumstances and constitute a significant part of who or what we are."[3]

A man like Mr. Eko, for instance, who has murdered someone in the past, is, and in some sense always will be, a murderer. Someone who has been disabled from birth must live with his disability for the rest of his life. Once a criminal, like Kate and Sawyer, always a criminal, we might say. For Sartre, a person is, at least in part, his or her facticity. As Inès tells Garcin in *No Exit*: "You are nothing else but your life."[4] Man, in short, *is* what he *does* – "existence precedes essence" (Sartre, E&H, p. 28) because man makes himself what he is.

In *No Exit*, Sartre casts his characters into hell to judge for themselves what they have become. There are echoes of this in *Lost*. The central characters of the show, all of whom are cast onto the island, have to confront their past and redefine themselves in their present situation with a view to the future. Everybody seems to have something from their flashback lives for which they need to atone, like the characters in Sartre's play. However, unlike the characters in *No Exit*, who are all dead, the survivors in *Lost* still have possibilities. For example, they have the possibility to escape from the island, the possibility to become a different person, to atone for past misdeeds, and so forth. In short, they can *transcend* their present situation, unlike Inès, Garcin, and Estelle, who have nothing left but their facticity.

## Transcendence: A World of Possibilities

Transcendence consists of our various possibilities. But, for Sartre, such possibilities apply only to consciousness, not to things. For example, a tree has the potential of becoming part of a raft, but it does not have the possibilities that constitute transcendence. A tree can't anticipate becoming part of a raft. A human being, on the other hand, has the possibility of becoming whatever he or she chooses,

---

[3]  Robert C. Solomon, *Continental Philosophy since 1750: The Rise and Fall of the Self* (Oxford: Oxford University Press, 1988), p. 182; subsequent citations will be given parenthically in the text as Solomon, followed by page number/s.

[4]  Or, as Sartre put it in *Existentialism and Humanism* (p. 42): "You are nothing else but what you live."

within the given limits of his or her facticity. "Man is nothing else but what he makes of himself." Consciousness propels itself towards a future and is aware that it is doing so.

Facticity defines our situation and who we are up to that point. In *Lost*, the general situation we can regard as the survivor's facticity is the plane crash and the island. The past deeds and life-events of the individual characters define them as this or that person up to that point: Jack, the doctor with a bad conscience; Kate, the escaped criminal; Hurley, the mental patient and unlucky Lotto winner; Charlie, the musician and drug addict; Sayid, the Republican Guard; Ana Lucia, the trigger-happy cop; Mr. Eko, the drug-dealer; and so on.

Transcendence, on the other hand, opens up the world of possibilities – what we can make of the situation and ourselves, given who or what we are so far. Of course, "one rarely has a clean slate, an opportunity to establish oneself without baggage from the past" (Solomon, p. 183), and this becomes increasingly evident with each episode of *Lost* as we come to see who and what somebody *is* based on the flashback revelations about their past. One can certainly try to establish a new identity in a new town, or, in the case of *Lost*, on the island, but even when the situation is novel, one still carries the past with one – "in habits, expectations, memories, and in one's face" (Solomon, p. 183). It thus becomes apparent that facticity and transcendence, as Solomon points out, "are something in brute opposition, as when one tries to change an old habit or a way of life" – consider Charlie's struggle to stay drug-free – "but most of the time they fit together, transcendence 'gearing itself' to facticity and facticity being reinterpreted according to one's transcendence" (Solomon, p. 183). Mr. Eko is a case in point. He was a murderer and a drug-dealer but now seeks to redefine himself (in the image of his now-dead brother) as a priest. Being stranded on the island with other people who know nothing about his past affords him the possibility to do so. Our plans usually fit our circumstances. Indeed, it is the circumstances that circumscribe if not dictate (but do *not* determine) our plans.

## Bad Faith: No Excuses

Related to our discussion is another important Sartrean notion, *bad faith*. Bad faith is "not just a tendency to fall back into the routines of everyday life," the role one plays in society (for example, "the doctor," "the musician," "the salesman," "the cop," and so on) or the *persona* one has adopted, "but is nothing less than a betrayal of one's self, a lie in which one deceives oneself about oneself" (Solomon, p. 183). The most prevalent example of bad faith is "the denial of one's freedom in the form of an excuse, typically beginning with 'I couldn't help it'" (Solomon, p. 183). For Sartre, human beings are "condemned to be free" (Sartre, E&H, p. 34), and he insists that our freedom is absolute. In other words, Sartre does not accept the legitimacy of any such excuse. Sartre gives the example of the Nazi soldier who insists, "I was only following orders," "I could not do otherwise." But you can *always* do otherwise – there are *always* alternatives! Bad faith, then, amounts to "the denial of one's transcendence, by way of appealing to one's facticity" (Solomon, p. 183). Bad faith, to be more precise, is the lack of proper coordination of transcendence and facticity, either at an individual or an interpersonal level.

If we apply Sartre's arguments to *Lost*, we can say that the difficult and often hostile circumstances in which the survivors find themselves cannot serve as an excuse for them. They are, in short, not determined by those circumstances, as they are absolutely free to choose their own responses to that situation. Similarly, each individual survivor is not determined by the circumstances of their past. While they can't change the past, they are totally free to choose how they react to it – and also how they wish to project themselves into the future. For example, Hurley can continue to define himself as unlucky based on his past experiences, but he is free to choose otherwise; Charlie can continue taking drugs, but he is free to choose otherwise.

Indeed, Sartre maintains further (in opposition to Freud's view that much of our behavior is determined by unconscious desires) that our desires, emotions, and motives do *not* determine our behavior. No one is compelled to act as he or she does, and no one can appeal to his or her desires, emotions, or motives as an excuse. In the case of Sayid's torture of Sawyer, for instance, Sayid's desire to help Shannon and his desire for revenge (he believes that Sawyer had attacked him earlier) constitute the motives for the torture, but they do not determine – and are therefore no excuse for – his behavior. Sayid opted to give in to his desires, but he could have chosen differently. Sayid's motive cannot serve as an excuse for his subsequent action. His free choice was to choose *that* motive.

## Condemned to Freedom and Responsibility

For Sartre, man *is* total freedom. His whole life is one of choice, and even if he decides not to choose, that very decision is a choice.[5] Man must choose, and he is totally responsible for every choice. According to Sartre, man is condemned to be free. Condemned because he did not create himself, yet is nevertheless at liberty, and from the moment that he is thrown into this world he is responsible for everything he does (Sartre, E&H, p. 34). But, with the realization of our absolute freedom and responsibility, comes *dread*. Rather than living *authentically*, it is far easier and more comfortable to fall back into bad faith, into the past roles we've played, rather than redefining ourselves in the light of free choice and accepting responsibility for what we make of ourselves.

Sayid has no excuse for torturing Sawyer. He cannot appeal to the circumstances to offer excuses like "I had to do it to help Shannon" and "I thought Sawyer attacked me earlier." It was Sayid's free choice to torture Sawyer, and he alone is responsible for that choice. Moreover, Sayid acted in bad faith, for he fell back into his past role as Republican Guard – someone accustomed to "extracting" information from others. He could have acted differently. Similarly, Locke decided to donate his kidney to his father. It was his choice and he must take responsibility for that choice, regardless of the circumstances (his betrayal by both parents and subsequent paralysis). An excuse of the kind "I was tricked by my mother and father" will not do on Sartre's analysis. Locke can't change what happened in the past, but he is absolutely free to determine his response to it. And this is the case for the survivors in general.

## Stop Looking at Me

What happens when I, as a "being-for-itself" with absolute freedom of choice, encounter another "being-for-itself" with absolute freedom?

---

[5] According to Sartre (*Existentialism and Humanism*, p. 48) "what is not possible is not to choose. I can always choose, but I must know that if I do not choose, that is still a choice."

This brings us to the problem of the "Other" and "the Others" in *Lost*.

When others give us "the look" we find ourselves defining ourselves (and probably also resisting that definition) on *their* terms. You know all about the look if you're a smoker. Just recall "the look" some people give you when you light up. Their "look" reduces you to a thing, "a dirty smoker." This produces an ambivalent struggle or conflict with the other person. "The Other" is recognized as a consciousness, similar to myself. My consciousness resists becoming an object for another individual's consciousness, but such resistance is futile because this conflict is fundamental to all human interaction. One recognizes that "being with others" means "being-*for*-others." This, for Sartre, is the very nature of intersubjectivity, so that "hell is other people."

In *Lost*, this is dramatically highlighted by the survivors' confinement on the island and thus to each other's presence and "looks," as well as by the presence and "looks" of the mysterious Others. The conflict between the survivors themselves, and the survivors and the Others is, therefore, a struggle of opposing consciousnesses, that is to say, of opposing freedoms.

## Masochism, Sadism, and Indifference

Despite the inevitable conflicts with others, I have the need to feel confirmed or justified by another. In *Being and Nothingness*, Sartre outlines three basic ways in which we relate to others, and none of them is unproblematic.

To be acknowledged or confirmed by another, I must first attract his or her attention. This means, however, that I must become an *object* of interest or desire for the other and renounce my own desire for the sake of conforming to the other's desire. I must become a *thing* for the other. This is what Sartre calls *masochism*. In *Lost*, we might look on the relationship between Charlie and Claire in this light. Charlie tries to do everything possible for Claire because he fancies her and wants to be desired by her. Charlie thus turns himself into an object of interest and desire for Claire, for "the other." In a sense, he becomes her slave, so Claire becomes his master in the existentialist sense. We can also regard the relationship between the

131

survivors and the Others in this light. The survivors' presence on the island attracts the Others' attention; they become objects of interest *for* the Others. The survivors become things for the Others. They are slaves, the Others masters. While the survivors clearly do not want to renounce their own desires for the sake of the Others, their very attempts to find the Others can be interpreted as conforming to the Others' desire, as the latter seem to seek out the survivors to "act upon" them.

But the masochistic option is self-defeating. By becoming a desirable object for the other I actually confirm my subjectivity as free being-for-itself. With this realization, I might now want to recapture my former freedom from the other. This can only be done, however, by reversing the masochistic scenario, making the other into a slave and myself into the master. I have to reduce the other to *my* plans and projects. Of course, the other will most likely resist my efforts to deprive him or her of free subjectivity. It follows that I must now resort to coercion or even violence to achieve this reversal of fortune.

Consider again the Sayid/Sawyer torture scene. Sayid here reduces Sawyer to an object, a thing-in-itself in order to extract information from him. This Sartre calls *sadism*. But sadism is ultimately also self-defeating: "If someone declares 'I love you' only because I've tortured him or her to do so, I can take no comfort from this love."[6] The attempt by the survivors to find and confront the Others, largely driven by their desire to rescue Walt, can also be regarded as an attempt to reverse the current relationship in which they are slaves and the Others masters. Going after or acting against the Others in *Lost* is, however, a double-edged sword, for "every act performed against the Other can on principle be for the Other an instrument which will serve him against me" (Sartre, B&N, p. 265). So the very attempt to reverse the masochistic scenario could, in fact, lead to reinforcing the sadistic one. The same is of course true in reverse.

Another strategy Sartre considers is *indifference*. But indifference is no less doomed to failure than sadism and masochism. If we try to completely ignore others, we nevertheless remain perpetually obsessed with them. While I can try to persuade myself that I'm not

---

[6] Richard Kearny, *Modern Movements in European Philosophy* (Manchester: Manchester University Press, 1994), p. 65.

thinking of any other person, this is a sure way of thinking about them. (You can try this one yourself at home!) Consider how Rousseau's solitary existence is dominated by thoughts about the Others. Just think of her elaborate and extreme security measures to prevent the Others from coming near her. For the survivors, indifference is no escape from each other or from the Others. They are stuck on the island – the "hell" that is "other people."

In relation to *each other*, the survivors frequently deny their transcendence and act in bad faith. They often fall back into their past roles. In *No Exit*, each of the characters needs the other two in order to create some illusion about himself or herself. The same can be said about the various characters in *Lost*. Most of the characters have something to hide from others and try to present a particular front that is not true. Kate tries to hide her criminal past, as do Sawyer and Mr. Eko; Charlie tries to conceal his drug habit; Locke is not forthcoming about his disability, and so forth. In social or intersubjective situations we usually play a part that is not ourselves. We adopt a certain *persona* for others – how we think others *would like* us to be, or how others think we *should* be. If we passively become that part or *persona*, we are avoiding the important decisions and choices by which personality should be formed. None of the characters are determined by their past roles, but if they continue to define themselves in those terms, their existential project becomes "sandbanked" in bad faith. Of course, though, *redemption* is a key theme in *Lost*. And redemption in the Sartrean sense amounts to *transcendence*. It involves taking responsibility for our past and future choices, embracing new possibilities, and thus living authentically rather than in bad faith. The survivors, unlike the dead characters in *No Exit*, still have the possibility to become whatever they want to be.

In relation to the Others, the survivors adopt a collective identity. The Others are not *us*, we are not *them*. They reduce the Others to things and vice versa. The interplay between masochism and sadism between the two groups is evident in *Lost*. It follows that the survivors are individually and collectively hindered from choosing themselves and inventing themselves freely by each other *and* the Others because their actions are largely determined or circumscribed by the presence of the other and the Others. Their actions are therefore frequently products of bad faith.

133

## Blame the Others?

The Others, in a sense, also become a *scapegoat* for the survivors. And this, according to Sartre, always involves a flight from freedom and hence responsibility. As a group, the survivors have established a sense of intersubjective solidarity among themselves by attributing responsibility for all that is considered evil on the island to a collectively identified scapegoat, namely the Others. After all, was it not *them* who kidnapped Walt, who frequently assault *us* and prevent *us* from escaping the island? Are *they* not the cause of all that's wrong on the island? The survivors feel at one by virtue of their shared hatred of the Others.

For Sartre, however, this amounts to a collective flight from individual responsibility. The survivors as a group thus become a collective consciousness, which exists in bad faith, because they evade their own freedom and responsibility by making the Others responsible for all their problems. But they can always respond differently to the Others, or see them in a different light, despite some of the incidents that have occurred. Initially, for example, the survivors might have assumed that the Others are native islanders, who felt threatened by their presence. Indeed, perhaps the survivors are "the Others" for the Others?

For Sartre, scapegoating amounts to only one thing: fear of the human condition, that is, fear of one's own consciousness, freedom, and responsibility. Of course, the argument also applies to the Others as a group, if they, too, have made the survivors into *their* scapegoat. And we can't, as of yet, rule out the possibility that the Others are, in fact, on the island for the explicit purpose of "acting on" the survivors. But even if this is the case, the survivors are still free to respond *differently* to the Others, that is to say, in a way that does not entail the renunciation of their own freedom and responsibility.

## Hell is Other People

In *Lost* we are presented with the Sartrean reality that we cannot live with "the other" and we cannot live without him. For Sartre, in encounters with the other, there is always a conflict because consciousness posits the other consciousness as an object, while resisting being posited as an object itself by the other consciousness. This is the fundamental nature of human interaction, according to Sartre, and this, I believe, is highlighted in the depiction of inter-subjective relations in *Lost*, with regard to both the other and the Others. "Hell is other people" – nothing could be more evident in *Lost* than this Sartrean dictum.

# 12

# "The Others Are Coming": Ideology and Otherness in *Lost*

## Karen Gaffney

The early episodes of *Lost* feature a stereotypical conflict between a Korean man, Jin, and a black man, Michael. At first, it might seem that exploring such depictions could shed light on how the show constructs race. However, as the characters get to know each other, the tension along racial lines dissolves. As it turns out, *Lost* is not explicitly focused on race, but it does tackle a closely related issue that serves as a foundation for not only race but also all categories of difference, and that is the ideology of "otherness."

## Ideology

To say that something is socially constructed is to say that it is created by society; it is not inherent, natural, or the norm. However, what is socially constructed appears to be the norm because it is normalized, or taken for granted. No other way of looking at the world is even considered. This process is how ideology functions. An ideology is a belief system, but in order for it to be effective, it must be perceived as the truth, rather than seen as one of many possible belief systems. An ideology is like a pair of glasses you don't know you're wearing. You look through those lenses at the world as if that is the only way of seeing the world. Not only do you not know you're wearing glasses, but you also don't even realize that you might see the world differently through a different pair of glasses. Ideology ceases to function when it is seen as an ideology; to function properly, it must be subtly presented as "the truth" and taken for granted.[1] An ideology you're aware of loses its power to construct your worldview. Like a pair of glasses, such an ideology can be removed.

Philosopher Louis Althusser (1918–1990) calls the process of individuals becoming indoctrinated into an ideology "interpellation." For interpellation to work, an ideology must be presented as a given so that it will be believed and taken for granted. Althusser describes two different methods of controlling people: the Repressive State Apparatus (RSA) and the Ideological State Apparatus (ISA).[2] RSAs function by force, like the police or the military. RSAs can literally control people by placing them in jail. For example, in the first half of *Lost*'s third season, the Others imprison Kate and Sawyer in outdoor animal cages. This method of control is tangible and easy to see. ISAs, like religion, school, and the family, on the other hand, operate based on the power of ideology. People are interpellated into a particular ideology and then take that belief system for granted as the only way of thinking, without even realizing they were interpellated in the first place. Rather than being placed in a literal jail, they are placed in a figurative jail, an ideological jail, without knowing it. Continuing with the earlier example, not only is Sawyer imprisoned in a literal cage, but he is also tricked into believing that a device is monitoring his heart rate and will kill him if his heart beats too quickly ("Every Man for Himself"). The actual jail confines his movements to a certain degree, but then Sawyer himself contains his movements that much more for fear of triggering the device. He is taught to believe the device exists, when in fact it never did. He is interpellated into an ideology that controls his movements and makes him paranoid.

The notion of otherness works on this ideological basis. To identify someone else as an "other" is to identify that person as marked in some way, whether it is based on skin color, religion, language, gender, sexual orientation, or some other category of difference that

---

[1] Literary theorist Terry Eagleton explains that ideology "works much less by explicit concepts or formulated doctrines than by image, symbol, habit, ritual, and mythology." See *Literary Theory: An Introduction* (Minneapolis: University of Minnesota Press, 1983), p. 23.

[2] Louis Althusser, *Lenin and Philosophy and Other Essays* (New York: Monthly Review Press, 2001).

137

we use to divide people. Marking someone as "other" indicates a power relation because the one who has the power to identify someone else as "other" is by definition normative, not-other, and unmarked. Perceiving someone else as "other" then becomes a process of identifying that person as inferior. While the basis for otherness is often perceived as natural (like race), it, like all categories of difference, is socially constructed, and one must be interpellated into a certain ideology in order to identify "otherness."

## Ideology and the Dharma Initiative

The survivors from the front section of the plane come across a hatch in the jungle, and after considerable effort, they open it and find an extensive underground shelter, part of what's called the Dharma Initiative, complete with electricity, running water, food, weapons, and a social experiment that would make B. F. Skinner proud. They also find a man down there named Desmond who insists that a series of numbers must be entered into a computer every 108 minutes in order to prevent the end of the world.

Jack's initial skepticism reflects his resistance to the ideology of pushing the button ("Orientation"). He says to Desmond: "It says 'Quarantine' on the inside of the hatch to keep you down here, keep you scared. . . . Did you ever think that maybe they put you down here to push a button every 100 minutes just to see if you would? That all of this, the computer, the button, is just a mind game, an experiment?" Desmond responds, "Every single day." This conversation reveals that Desmond's skepticism still doesn't stop him from pushing the button and that Jack recognizes how fear plays a role in adopting a certain ideology.

Despite Jack's skepticism, when Desmond runs out of the hatch and disappears into the jungle, the survivors immediately begin to take shifts to make sure the numbers are entered and the button is pressed in time. But why? They have no clear evidence that anything bad will happen. If anything, the enterprise seems absurd and irrational, and yet they become immediately interpellated into its ideology. Despite some disagreement, the survivors collectively buy into the ideology of the hatch, and once they start doing so, it becomes incredibly difficult to stop. The show's representation of the Dharma

Initiative reveals how ideology operates. The audience does not take the ideology of the Dharma Initiative for granted as a given, which is how ideology must operate to maintain its power. Instead, the show forces us to be skeptical and constantly aware of the process and power of ideology.

Initially, Locke is passionate about "pushing the button," but when Mr. Eko and he discover another hatch in the jungle (underneath the question mark), Locke immediately replaces one ideology with another ("?"). They watch a videotape that explains this station's purpose, to "observe and record" the activities of the Dharma participants (via the multiple television screens). The tape instructs them:

> You and your partner will observe a psychological experiment in progress. . . . These team members are not aware that they are under surveillance or that they are the subjects of an experiment. . . . What is the nature of the experiment, you might ask? What do these subjects believe they are accomplishing? . . . You as the observer don't need to know. All you need to know is that the subjects believe their job is of the utmost importance.

Locke now believes they were tricked into believing that pushing the button mattered when in reality they are "rats in a maze." While Locke was initially interpellated into the ideology of pushing the button, he is now interpellated into an opposing ideology that pushing the button is, as he says, "meaningless." Interestingly, while Locke is critical of himself for having been so quick to believe the first ideology, he unquestionably immediately subscribes to the second ideology. Mr. Eko, on the other hand, finds his initial belief in pushing the button affirmed by their discovery in this station.

We witness yet another layer of the Dharma ideology when Michael, Sawyer, Jack, and Kate discover a giant pile of tubes with notebooks rolled up in them ("Live Together, Die Alone"). These are the notes that the observers in that station had written, notes that would have supposedly been opened and analyzed if that station were the final leg of an experiment. Instead, it seems that those taught to be observers were just another piece to this mysterious puzzle. When Locke substitutes one ideology for another, he thinks he is making the transition from a lie to the truth, when in fact he is just substituting one constructed ideology for another. The way the show reveals these multiple layers to us again illustrates how ideology operates.

Interestingly, even when Desmond attempts to abandon the ideology of the island, he cannot. He sets sail only to be pulled back to the island, and when he realizes where he is, he says: "This is it. This is all there is left. This ocean and this place here. We are stuck in a bloody snow globe. There's no outside world. There's no escape" ("Live Together, Die Alone"). His words neatly describe the insidious nature of ideology; one is trapped in a worldview. Theoretically, if one becomes aware of that worldview, then there is an opportunity to change it, but Desmond's experience reveals the difficulty of that change. Locke could easily change his worldview from finding meaning in pushing the button to finding it meaningless, but both of those ideologies still function within the larger ideology of the island, because Locke so passionately wants to believe in the island and discover its secrets. When Desmond, though, literally tries to extricate himself from this larger ideology of the island, by trying to leave, he cannot, signifying once again the ideology's power.

*Lost* invites us to examine the process of how ideology works, and how, in particular, people buy into an ideology that is socially constructed without thinking that it is socially constructed. Furthermore, because the show makes explicit the process of how ideology functions, that concept can be used as a theory for analyzing how the show depicts the socially constructed ideology of otherness.

## The Others

*Lost* makes the notion of otherness explicit. There is literally a group (albeit an amorphous, ill-defined group) referred to as "the Others." While we know they occupied the island before the plane crash, almost everything else that we know about them is based on conjecture, and the very idea of otherness is constantly evolving and morphing. That very slipperiness is what makes the idea of otherness so compelling. For otherness to function, it must be slippery, and it must adapt to new moments. If it is static, it will lose its power.

*Lost* reveals the multiple ways in which otherness operates, how it both creates fear and is created by fear, how it serves as a divide-and-conquer strategy, how it creates an "us vs. them," and how those who are associated with otherness are linked to savagery and to a lack of civilization.

## Fearing the Others

Consider how characters who have encountered the Others describe them to survivors who have not directly encountered them. Rousseau explains what happened to her when she was shipwrecked on the island 16 years ago, specifically being pregnant and delivering the baby herself:

> *Rousseau:* The baby and I were together for only one week when we saw black smoke. A pillar of black smoke 5 kilometers inland. That night, they came. They came and took her. Alex. They took my baby. And now, they're coming again. They're coming for all of you.
>
> *Jack:* Who's coming?
>
> *Rousseau:* The Others. You have only three choices: run, hide, or die. ("Exodus, Part 1")

The repetition of the word "they" is striking. That repetition focuses on a separation between "us" and "them," with "us" being the plane crash survivors and Rousseau and "them" being this anonymous group literally called "the Others."

When Ana Lucia, a survivor from the back of the plane, describes the Others to Michael, a survivor from the front of the plane, she reinforces that "us vs. them" mentality. When Michael demands to know what happened to Ana Lucia and the other survivors, she says, "They came the first night that we got here. They took three of us. Nothing happened for two weeks. Then they came back and took nine more. They're smart. And they're animals. And they can be anywhere at anytime. Now we're moving through the jungle, their jungle" ("Abandoned"). Like Rousseau, Ana Lucia repeats the word "they" in order to reveal a profound difference between "us" and "them." She also describes them as "animals," which is a conventional way of dehumanizing a group and constructing them as "other." Rousseau and Ana Lucia are incredibly fearful of the Others because the Others have posed a direct threat to them. This notion of the Others as a threat is important. Rousseau and Ana Lucia, though, are talking to fellow survivors who have not directly encountered the Others. Through their description, Rousseau and Ana Lucia's fear spreads to the other survivors, who become incredibly fearful as well, reinforcing the power of fear in the context of otherness.

141

Similarly, when Ana Lucia and her fellow survivors examine bodies of dead Others, she again reinforces the divide between "us" and "them." Ana Lucia says, "They're out here in the jungle with no shoes, nothing in their pockets, no labels on their clothes. These people were here before us" ("The Other 48 Days"). They have what might be interpreted as homemade clothing, since there are no labels, and the Others wear no shoes. In connection to Ana Lucia calling them "animals," this last scene depicts them in stereotypically native and uncivilized ways. The brutality of the Others' actions and their lack of predictability reinforce this perceived savagery and work together to build the fear that both Rousseau and Ana Lucia express. They successfully use fear in persuading the crash survivors from the front of the plane that the Others exist, and they are to be feared. Rousseau and Ana Lucia have already been interpellated into an ideology of fearing the Others based on their past experience, and they in turn share that fear so that it takes on legendary qualities. Ironically, while clothing may seem to mark the Others, the survivors' own clothes are ripped and dirty, and other-like, so it becomes very difficult for the survivors to determine who is an Other based on appearance, which just reinforces the slipperiness and socially constructed nature of the category.

## Recognizing the Others

Despite the fact that Michael, Sawyer, and Jin have been interpellated into the ideology of otherness by Rousseau, they still don't recognize the Others when they come face to face for the first time. Such a lack of recognition highlights the slipperiness of otherness. When the crash survivors leave the island on a raft, they soon encounter people in a motorboat and expect that these people will rescue them. Their hopes and expectations are dashed, however, as, to their horror, the Others shoot one of them, kidnap the child Walt, and blow up the raft ("Exodus, Part 2"). Perhaps because the survivors have temporarily left the island, they leave the ideology of the island behind. At first, it's as if the survivors on the raft have totally forgotten about fearing the Others; they seem naïve and innocent, perceiving anyone coming towards them in a boat as a potential rescuer. That perception quickly changes, however, and they realize their supposed rescuers are in fact the Others.

When Sawyer encounters the head Other again (who we know later as Tom), his innocence is lost ("The Hunting Party"). Sawyer, Jack, and Locke encounter Tom, knowing full well he is an Other. Interestingly, Tom expresses his feeling of ownership over the island, depicting the survivors at first as disrespectful guests. He asks, "You go over a man's house for the first time, do you take off your shoes? You put your feet up on his coffee table? You walk in the kitchen and take food that doesn't belong to you? Open the door to rooms you got no business opening?" This last reference is, of course, to the hatch that the survivors blew open, entered, and now occupy. That hatch revealed the Dharma Initiative, which helps the audience see the way ideology functions. Tom then says, "This is not your island. This is our island. And the only reason you're living on it is cuz we let you live on it." To the Others, the survivors are intruders, invaders, who are at the mercy of the Others. What is so interesting about this quote is in many ways its lack of context. One could interpret the Others' perspective as being that of indigenous peoples who are invaded by colonizers and are trying to protect their land. On the other hand, one could interpret the Others' perspective as that of a nativist, anti-immigrant group seeking to maintain racial purity. The only real difference in these two interpretations is the power dynamics, since the power lies with the colonizers in the first example but with the nativists in the second example. What Tom says is also important because it invokes the notion of privilege and entitlement, claiming something as "ours" and controlling access to it. Furthermore, while Jack, Sawyer, and Locke perceive Tom as savage and uncivilized, he is accusing them of not knowing their manners, of essentially being uncivilized.

In this scene, the power dynamic shifts from Jack, Sawyer, and Locke to the Others. Jack first tells Tom that he refuses to become interpellated into the Others' ideology. He doesn't believe that the Others rule the island. Instead, Jack says, "I think you got one guy up there with a gun. I think there are more of us than there are of you." Of course, Jack's perception is short-lived because Tom calls out "Light 'em up" and Jack, Sawyer, and Locke become surrounded by a circle of people with torches. They are outnumbered, and Tom was correct that the Others did have control of the situation. He takes this power further by demanding that Jack, Sawyer, and Locke return to their camp, never to enter this territory again. He says, "Right here, there's a line. You cross that line, and we go from misunderstanding to something else." He describes "a line," which is essentially a border. The notion of the border is key in creating, maintaining, controlling, and protecting that power. Jack and the other two survivors here are shocked when they realize how greatly the Others outnumber them. That sense of feeling outnumbered, and the way that the Others encircle the survivors, just fuels the fear that the survivors have, which in turn furthers their ideology of otherness.

A different variation of interaction with otherness occurs when the survivors who were on the raft make it to shore. By then, of course, they are incredibly fearful of the Others, so fearful of the Others, in fact, that when they see a group of people approach them on the beach, they assume they are the Others. Interestingly, this group of people assumes that the raft survivors are the Others ("Orientation"). The irony is that none of them are Others (they are all survivors of the plane crash); it's just that they were in different parts of the plane and have crashed on different sides of the island. In this scene, the men on the raft are approached by a group that appears other-like. After all, they have giant sticks that they carry like weapons, and they are dressed in torn clothing. In turn, the men who were on the raft also appear other-like; their clothing is ripped and dirty. Each group perceives the other group as the Others and therefore reacts with not only hostility but also sheer violence. Ultimately, though, the members of each group realize they are in fact fellow survivors of the crash, so they band together to fight against the "real" Others. This complex series of shifts in perception raises another key issue: the way that the ideology of otherness can divide and conquer those who could have potential alliances. This divide-and-conquer strategy is successful at pitting groups against each other and preventing them from working together to fight against the power structure. The two groups of survivors have been taught to believe that the Others are incredibly dangerous, so their suspicion of each other prevents their ability to create an alliance, at least initially.

What does the ideology of otherness attempt to accomplish? Ultimately, it naturalizes and normalizes what has been socially constructed. Returning to the Dharma Initiative, we are given an explicit way of understanding the very process of how ideology functions, how it is socially constructed, and how people are indoctrinated into that belief system. Fear fuels that indoctrination, a fear not only of losing one's status but even a fear based on pure survival.

Interestingly, later in the second season, Claire, Rousseau, and Kate come across another underground structure, and this time it seems to be a medical facility ("Maternity Leave"). Kate finds a locker with brown, ragged clothes and a cap, much like those worn by the Others. She even finds a bottle of theatrical glue and a fake beard. Later, in "Live Together, Die Alone," when kidnapped by the Others, Kate refers to the fake beard on one of the Others, and he removes it, confirming her suspicion. It seems as if the Others are dressing up in stereotypically "other-like" ways to perform and to be perceived as savage and uncivilized when in the presence of non-Others, but when they are not trying to manipulate any non-Others, they have an almost suburban, middle-class existence, complete with book clubs and football. If they must dress up to be perceived as savage, does that mean they aren't actually savage? Might this relate to them calling themselves "the good guys" ("Live Together, Die Alone")? To complicate matters further, one character mentions early in the series that the Others do not leave footprints, as if they don't really exist, as if they are social constructs. Their lack of footprints makes it seem like they're operating within a vacuum, without a trail, adding even further to the slippery nature of otherness.

## "Lost"

When one is interpellated into an ideology, one has an understanding of one's place; in a sense, one is not lost. Being lost seems to imply not having a clear worldview. Someone who is lost is aware of an ideology at work and so questions his or her perceptions. Even though *Lost* forces us to be skeptical and aware of the power and process of ideology, there have been a few fascinating moments where we, the viewers, are interpellated into a particular ideology because we are not aware of an alternative. In the opening episode of season two, we see a flashback to Locke, Jack, and Kate blowing up the hatch ("Man of Science, Man of Faith"). That scene is juxtaposed with the actual beginning of this episode, where we hear a beeping and see a man get up, type on an old computer, and play a record. Despite the juxtaposition of the hatch explosion and this scene, the viewer does not automatically assume that this latter scene is occurring inside the hatch. We then hear an explosion, and the record player skips, and some dust filters down from the ceiling. The camera winds its way through some passageways, up a long shaft and then turns 180 degrees. We see Locke and Jack staring down. We were in the hatch and didn't know it. We were interpellated into an ideology of believing we were off the island when in fact we were deep in the Dharma Initiative.

The show repeats this clever move in the opening of the third season, when we see a seemingly typical suburban scene of a woman baking muffins and hosting a book club meeting ("A Tale of Two Cities"). As in the first example, our notion that we are off the island is again disrupted when the survivors' world collides with this one. In this second example, we slowly realize we are very much on the island when we hear an explosion of some kind and realize a plane is crashing, Oceanic Flight 815. Instead of being in the midst of a far-off suburban book club, we are with the Others. While one might think that the audience couldn't be interpellated into the same belief system twice, it happens easily. Such is the power of ideology. Furthermore, *Lost* constantly makes this process explicit; it is always drawing attention to the very nature of how we know what we know and how we decide what to believe. The show explicitly engages with what it means to be "lost" in an ideological sense, of not feeling grounded in a particular worldview. What is so interesting about the third season's opening is that despite so many encounters with the Others throughout the second season, we still didn't recognize them in the opening moments of this episode. The notion that the Others are difficult to identify runs throughout the series and just reinforces the slippery nature of otherness and the constructed nature of ideology.

The second half of the third season takes the slippery nature of otherness even further. The character of Juliet completely disrupts our perception of the Others as monolithic. There are times when she seems unquestionably to be one of the Others and other times where she seems to resist them completely and side with the plane crash survivors. While the season finale probably left most viewers thinking she is more allied with the survivors than the Others, it's too soon to make that determination. What's more interesting, though, is the fact that the show reveals multiple layers of fragmentation within the previously unified Others. Ben is able to manipulate the Others and construct different worldviews for different Others in order to control their behavior. For example, in the past, Ben had told Mikhail that the two women in the Looking Glass Station were not there, but when he wants those women killed, he tells Mikhail that they are still in that station ("Through the Looking Glass"). The very name "Looking Glass Station" invokes the questioning of perception and worldview, as does the episode title, "The Man Behind the Curtain." In that episode, we learn how Ben came to the island as a child and finally killed all of the Dharma workers, including his own father. That episode's title refers to the Wizard of Oz, who, like Ben, is able to construct worldviews in order to manipulate people, which is exactly how ideology functions. Finally, in that same episode, we learn that Ben might not be in charge of the Others, but that he may actually defer to a mysterious man named Jacob. For otherness to retain its power as an ideology, it must retain a perception of being monolithic. The second half of the third season forced us to question this monolithic nature, thereby again revealing the process of ideology at work. The fact that we must change our assumptions from episode to episode draws attention to the socially constructed nature of an ideology like otherness and reveals how the process functions.

So, what conclusions can we draw? First of all, one could argue that the show's representation of "the other" as savage, primitive, and seemingly evil reinforces the negative connotation of otherness, thereby reinforcing the ideology of otherness. That's too simple a response, though. Instead, we should focus on the fact that the show makes the apparatus of ideology visible, thereby drawing explicit attention to the depiction of the Others. The fact that the Others are at some level performing otherness (using costumes) draws direct attention to the constructed nature of otherness. As viewers, we don't just blindly accept the otherness of the Others, as if we are unaware of our glasses. Instead, *Lost* forces us not only to realize we're wearing glasses and that we're being presented with something that is socially constructed, something that is an ideology, but also that there are a variety of glasses or ideologies out there. With every new episode, we get a new pair of glasses, and we know we're getting them because the show makes that explicit.

True to the experience of *Lost*, let's end with a question rather than an answer. What is it about our current historical moment that has produced a show that forces us to realize the socially constructed nature of otherness and see the apparatus of ideology?

# 13

# Tortured Souls

## *Scott Parker*

### Asthma

Every year far more people die of asthma than do in plane crashes. Shannon, as if to illustrate this fact, survives the latter only to have her life threatened by the former. For asthmatics, there are a number of triggers that can bring on an attack. These triggers can make the highly sensitive breathing passages contract, which can make breathing difficult, or in some cases impossible. One of these triggers (unfortunately for Shannon) is stress. She has survived a plane crash, and is living on a tropical island with a group of strangers (except for her contentious brother), not knowing if they will ever be rescued. Few scenarios could be more stressful. Perhaps if she also believed the island to be haunted and herself inadequate . . .

With medication, asthmatics can generally control attacks. Initially, when Shannon anticipates an attack, she is able to prevent it with her medication. But, given the level of stress in her environment, it's not surprising that she goes through her inhaler in the first several days. Without any more medication, there is a very real possibility that her asthma could kill her.[1] Luckily, Boone had packed more of her medicine in his checked baggage before they left Sydney. The problem is that Boone has lost his bag and believes Sawyer has it and her medicine ("Confidence Man"). The question is how to get the medicine from Sawyer.

---

[1] Sun will later treat Shannon with eucalyptus from the island, but in the meantime this natural remedy is unused.

If it were anyone else, Boone would just ask for the medicine. But Sawyer, who has made it quite clear that he is looking out for Sawyer only, will want to bargain for it. Boone, not thinking that his sister's life is the kind of thing that should be bargained, tries to steal the medicine. After Sawyer finds the would-be thief and whoops him for going through his stuff, Boone appeals to the authority figure on the island, Jack. As a doctor, Jack is particularly sensitive to Shannon's medical condition. This sensitivity coupled with his disdain for Sawyer leads Jack to approve Sayid's request to spend ten minutes alone with Sawyer, knowing the kind of torturous "alone time" Sayid has in mind.

For Jack to be complicit in such an explicit violation of the Hippocratic Oath, which shapes so much of what he does on the island, is surprising until we consider the circumstances. First, Jack believes that Shannon's life is more valuable than Sawyer's comfort. Second, that Sayid has experience in torture is reassuring for Jack. He knows what he's doing and will get the medicine. For Jack and Sayid, the end of saving Shannon's life justifies the means of torturing Sawyer. Are they right? Or at least excused?

On the island, where Shannon's next attack could take place soon, there might not be time for Jack and Sayid to fully consider the ethics of their plan. But philosophers, long accused of preferring the safety of opining from their ivory towers to the demands of acting on those opinions, do have time to make such considerations.

## The Ticking Time Bomb

The Ticking Time Bomb Case[2] is a hypothetical scenario originally presented by Niklas Luhmann (1927–1998) in which authorities have captured a suspect who, they believe, has information about a ticking time bomb. Typically, the scenario locates this time bomb in a large city, where its imminent detonation is expected to kill substantial numbers of innocent people. The thought experiment asks: Should the authorities torture the suspect?

---

[2] Niklas Luhmann, *Gibt es in unserer Gesellschaft noch unverzichtbare Normen?* (Heidelberg: C. F. Müller, 1993).

In order to say yes, there are some things we have to assume. First, we have to assume that the authorities have some proof that there is a time bomb that will kill innocent people if they do not prevent it. Second, the authorities must have reason to believe that this suspect knows something about the bomb. This part is troubling. Even if they have evidence that links the suspect to the bomb (say, he emailed the threat from an address with his personal information), they don't know if he knows what they want to know. Maybe he was involved, but doesn't know the location (or who does). In this scenario the authorities can't know *that* the suspect knows until they know *what* the suspect knows. And to find out *what* he knows they have to take a statement and then check it against the facts. This is called empirical knowledge; it is acquired experientially, through observation and can be contrasted with rational knowledge (like 2 + 2 = 4), which is known mentally, without observation. The location of the bomb can only be known empirically. Whatever the suspect says, the authorities will have to actively verify, which means that the suspect doesn't have to tell the authorities the truth (if he knows it).

Until they've found the bomb where the suspect said it would be, they can't be sure that he knows. What if the suspect is just boasting that he knows the bomb's location? He could be lying. If he is a terrorist, his goal might be the evacuation of the city and the chaos that would cause. He might be psychotic. He might be intentionally distracting the authorities from some other real threat. He might just want the notoriety. There are any number of reasons why even an admission of knowing would not mean that he actually knows. And without knowing *what*, the authorities can't know *that*.

So, how do they find out the *what*? How do they find out if the bomb is where the suspect's mouth is? This brings us to our third assumption, that by torturing him, the authorities will find out what they want to know. *Enough physical or psychological pain and he will reveal what he would otherwise conceal. The pain of enduring any more torture (or the pain of the thought of enduring more torture) will be greater than the suffering of a failed bomb detonation.* If this is true, the suspect will talk. But the suspect has another advantage (if he is the terrorist the authorities believe him to be): time; as long as it's ticking, is on his side. Because of the time-delay required for empirical verification, the suspect doesn't have to tell the authorities where the bomb is (if he knows), he just has to tell them something that will stall them until the detonation. "The bomb is attached to a red Honda Civic parked somewhere between the intersections of 3rd and Oak and 4th and Pine." By the time the bomb squad searches and discovers that there is no red Civic parked in that area, the real bomb on 2nd and Washington will have exploded.

## What Can I Know? What Should I Do?

Epistemology is the branch of philosophy that studies knowledge. It asks questions about what we can know, what we do know, how we know, and how we know that we know (and how we know that we know that we know). The first wave of trouble for would-be torturers is epistemological. How do they know that their suspect knows what they want to find out, or that he will tell them if they proceed with the torture? As we've seen, they do not. They are assuming (1) there is a bomb; (2) the suspect knows where it is; and (3) by torturing him, he will be forced to tell them where it is. It's a lot to assume. Even with proof of (1) they cannot know (2) or (3) with any degree of certainty.

There is a chance that the suspect does know. And if he does know, there's a chance that torture will get him to say where it is. Maybe those chances are worth taking. If the suffering caused by torturing a suspect is less than the suffering caused by not torturing him, it could be appropriate. We must consider the consequences. The consequence of torturing a suspect who doesn't know or won't squeal if he does, is the suffering caused to him. The consequence of not torturing him when he does know and will tell the truth is the total suffering of all the people who are killed or injured by the bomb plus their friends and families who suffer for them. Defenders of torture would say that if the number of people who might be saved is great enough, it is a chance worth taking. But what is the magic number that warrants this cruelty? Would it, for example, be acceptable to torture two people, one guilty and one innocent (not knowing which is which), to find the location of the bomb and save 10,000 lives?

This is a standard "end justifies the means" argument given by utilitarian ethicists. The end (saving lives) is important enough that we can excuse means (in this case, torture) that we would otherwise eschew. The original utilitarian ethic, as posed by Jeremy Bentham

(1748–1832), is that an action is right if it maximizes happiness for everyone.[3] But, in reality, when we weigh the consequences of our actions we rarely maximize our contribution to others' happiness. In Bentham's conception there would be no time for me to watch *Lost* (a sure indication of the failure of any ethical system), as doing so would be a selfish act that does not contribute as much to the general good as would, say, doing aid work in Darfur. In this case, I could (and should) be pulled from the TV and taken to Sudan to maximize collective happiness.

John Stuart Mill (1806–1873) amended utilitarianism with his injection of appreciation for individual rights. His "harm principle" says that "the only purpose for which power can be rightfully exercised over any member of a civilized community, against his will, is to prevent harm to others."[4] Accordingly, short of protecting people from harm, we have no right to use force in affecting behavior.

It is hard to argue against utilitarianism in the fictional scenario in which 10,000 innocent people will be saved if one innocent person is tortured. But what about one innocent person tortured versus zero innocent people saved? In this case, the expected consequences used in justifying the torture haven't changed – there was still a chance that he might have known and torturing might have made him talk – but it is considerably harder to justify the means without the ends to back it up. The reasonable expectation that a suspect might have and provide the information is lost in hindsight with the certainty that he didn't or wouldn't. The torture has failed both Mill's "harm principle" and its ethical edict of maximizing happiness, as the threat was either imagined or undisclosed.

## Sawyer as Time Bomb

> The strong will resist and the weak will say anything to end the pain.
>
> Ulpian (??–228 CE)

---

[3] Jeremy Bentham, *An Introduction to the Principles of Morals and Legislation* (London: T. Payne, 1789).

[4] John Stuart Mill, *On Liberty* (Peterborough, Canada: Broadview Press, 1999), pp. 51–52.

The ticking time bomb scenario, unlikely as it may be, has much in common with Sawyer's situation on the island. Everyone believes that he has Shannon's asthma medicine. Sawyer, in fact, all but confesses that he has it. Why he does this, when we later discover (or trust) that he doesn't have it, is difficult to fathom. It could be that Sawyer doesn't deny having the medicine because he seeks notoriety, or that he expects (rightly) that he wouldn't be believed, but Sayid reads selfishness and guilt into his defiance and proceeds accordingly. Immediately, this brings us to two pragmatic failings of torture, whether or not the act itself can be provisionally accepted on moral grounds:

Some people will think the torture is better suffered than the consequences.
Some people will say anything to stop the torture.

Before we turn to Sayid's failures with Sawyer, let's suppose, for the sake of strengthening Sayid's (and Jack's) case, that they genuinely believe that Sawyer has the medicine, and that there is no personal agenda in their willingness to tie him to a tree and shove bamboo shoots under his fingernails; Sayid has forgotten that Sawyer accused him of being a terrorist because of his ethnicity ("Pilot, Part 2") and that he may have smashed his transceiver; Jack has forgotten the disdain in Sawyer's voice when he mocks the "hero," as well as the euthanasia Sawyer botched and left for him ("Tabula Rasa"). And both are trying to bracket what they know him to be [an asshole] and do what is right, given the circumstances. Let's also assume that Shannon will certainly die in a matter of days without the medicine. And further, that Sawyer might have other medicines that could later save the lives of other survivors.

Applying utilitarian ethics, Sawyer is in trouble. Even with the caveat of the "harm principle," the ends of extracting Sawyer's information justify (demand!) his torture. That is, doing so will do the greatest good for the greatest number of survivors and protect them from the harm of not having medicine. Resigned to the fact that torture is the only way to save Shannon's life and possibly more lives, Jack and Sayid proceed into the jungle and tie Sawyer to a tree. Jack, subscribing to the above argument in the abstract, but not wanting to be confronted with the details – that torture isn't just the word *torture*; it's a guy tied to a tree, fearing that his enemy, in a consequence-free

153

environment, who has no reason not to kill him, except the sadistic pleasure of prolonging his suffering, as he slowly slides the bamboo further and further underneath his nails; it's a blood-curdling scream – is torn between assisting Sayid and leaving as he winces and turns away, as if out of sight can mean out of mind, even if it's still in earshot. A few feet away, remote in the jungle with all manners of inflicting pain accessible to his imagination, acceptable to his conscience, Sayid encounters the first obstacle of torture: Sawyer would rather be tortured than talk.

The frustration that Sawyer causes Sayid is worth the pain he suffers himself in the exchange. Being broken by Sayid is a concession that Sawyer will not easily make. This scenario is admittedly hard to imagine in the real world, but motives other than pride can be readily substituted. Imagine the suspected terrorist in the original ticking time bomb scenario is a religious fanatic and has credible links to various nefarious terrorist organizations. Further, let's imagine in this hypothetical situation, he actually knows where the bomb is and is capable of providing the appropriate information that could deactivate it. Will he talk if he's tortured? Maybe not if he doesn't respect his torturer. Likely he holds his torturer in the same regard as the people he is hoping to kill with his bomb. Some personal suffering is a small price to pay for doing what is right in God's eyes. In this case the person being tortured is as certain in his moral superiority as our torturer is in his. With eternal reward waiting, temporary physical pain, even severe pain, can be tolerated.

For Sawyer, like this religious terrorist, the psychological pain he gives his torturer outweighs what he suffers in his own physical pain. Winning a battle of wills with Sayid is worth more than the bamboo under his fingernails. But it isn't worth losing an eye. And this is how Sawyer differs from the terrorist. The terrorist can suffer *all* pain because he has God on his side. Sawyer, with only pride on his, has to weigh it against his vision. But, as Sayid brings the knife to Sawyer's eye, we come to the other failure of torture: all the tortured person has to say is what the torturer wants to hear.

Sawyer says he'll talk, but only to Kate. Sayid, thinking he's getting what he wants, accepts these conditions and goes to find Kate. When Kate comes for his confession, Sawyer finally admits that he doesn't even have the medicine. That is, he says that he doesn't have it and we believe him. Because Sun's eucalyptus remedy suffices and Shannon is killed before her next serious asthma attack, we don't find out if, in an attack, Sawyer would have suddenly remembered where the medicine was and gotten to it just in time to save her life. Telling Sayid he will talk is enough to keep his eye. And convincing Kate he doesn't have the medicine buys him enough time to free himself from Sayid's knot. Similarly, the terrorist has only to stall the torturer until the bomb explodes. A plausible story that diverts the torturer's attention will be as effective as not talking, and less painful. Once the bomb explodes, the torturer's moral defense is lost. Execution becomes a possibility, but no longer torture.

The terrorist no longer cares; his goals have been reached; the rest is up to God. Sawyer, his concerns more worldly, is lucky to free himself before Sayid returns to kill him. It seems that Sayid's method of finding the truth can be discredited if the truth it provides doesn't coincide with the truth he wants. Hearing from Kate that Sawyer doesn't have the medicine is unacceptable. What he believes to be true (that Sawyer has the medicine) can be confirmed (by finding it), but it cannot be refuted. As long as Sawyer denies having the medicine, Sayid can never know if he's telling the truth. There's no empirical proof of a negative. Sawyer can't win and Sayid doesn't.

## Torture of the Torturer

"If you do this . . ." ( . . . you'll be no different than him.) So Kate cautions Jack, and by association, Sayid, as well. She believes that resorting to torture cedes the moral authority that Jack and Sayid hold on the island. With her categorical rejection of torture, Kate is impugning the kind of utilitarian argument that Jack and Sayid are relying on. While it's true that Sawyer is an asshole, torture is wrong and that's that. Our hands are tied, she says, so to speak. We can't do what's wrong.

That Jack anticipates Kate with "This was Sawyer's choice. Not mine" affirms his view that torture is a last resort, but once resorted to, morally justified. That his participation in the torture is merely auxiliary suggests that he hasn't completely convinced himself of this argument. If he believes that torture is morally justified, it's hard to see why he wouldn't believe it to be morally required and take action.

155

By contrast, Sayid's actions reveal his confidence that what they are doing is right.

But when it turns out that Sawyer doesn't have the inhalers (if we are to believe him, as it seems we're meant to), Sayid flies into a rage. The answer he's getting from Sawyer isn't the one he wanted. It might be true, but it's not what he wanted. And, not getting what he wanted, and not knowing with any certainty if what he's getting is the truth, Sayid begins to recognize the failure of his actions, effectively and morally.

To Sayid's thinking, short of having the medicine in his hands at the end of the day, the torture fails. His primary motivation was to protect Shannon. Morally, he required the medicine (which he doesn't have) or certainty that Sawyer doesn't have it (which he can never have). He's lacking the ends that his means depended on. And without them, Sayid begins a rapid transformation from torturer to self-tormented. Insofar as Sayid believed the medicine would have justified the torture, he's finding out that these ends (not knowing much more than before) are not without their own moral: that torture might not work, and that if it doesn't, the torturer will suffer psychological consequences along with the tortured. Thanks to Sawyer (petty as his motivations may have been), we learn about the dangers of torture.

In his past, as a communications officer with the Iraqi Republican Guard, Sayid tortured people successfully on a regular basis ("Solitary"). Sayid was well respected in his role, but sometime between the end of the Gulf War and the plane crash he swore to himself that he'd never do what he learned again. Now that he has tortured, but with no good results, he suffers shame for what he has done to Sawyer and guilt for disappointing himself. As a punishment for his actions he leaves the group on a self-imposed exile. Expecting to be gone permanently, or at least until he can make peace with himself and face the group again, Sayid finds a cable that leads him into a trap set by the Frenchwoman, who captures him and holds him prisoner.

Believing Sayid to be one of those who made her team sick, the Frenchwoman (Danielle Rousseau) tortures him with electric shocks. The island, as is its way, seems to be forcing or allowing Sayid to face the source of his own psychological torment. Between electric pulses, Sayid cries out again and again that he doesn't know what she's talking about or who Alex (Rousseau's child) is. We know Sayid is telling the truth, but Rousseau does not, so Sayid finds himself in a very similar situation to the one he recently held Sawyer in. Short of getting Alex back to her, nothing Sayid does (even fixing her music box) can satisfy Rousseau and no amount of torture will make Sayid know where Alex is.

When Sayid eventually rejoins the group he has a showdown of sorts with Sawyer at the caves. Still weak from being tortured and languishing from his journey, Sayid is vulnerable to Sawyer, who doesn't take advantage of this opportunity for revenge (something we know is in his character) ("All the Best Cowboys Have Daddy Issues"). Indeed, Sayid virtually apologizes to Sawyer for what he did, saying that he is guilty for what he's done, but importantly, not saying that given the same opportunity he wouldn't do it again. This is important because later we will see Sayid is willing to torture Ethan before Charlie kills him ("Homecoming"). And in season two he will torture Ben ("Dave"), again failing; this time on two counts. He won't get the information he wants and (as we'll find out later) he won't get the truth. The question remains: Is it a mistake for Sayid to return to these methods despite their repeated failure?

## Acting without Knowing

*Jack:* What if he's telling the truth, John?
*John:* What if he's not?[5]

We have seen the epistemological obstacles to a defense of the kind of torture practiced on the island and in the ticking time bomb scenario. Until the torturers know *what* the tortured knows, they cannot know *that* he knows. And to find out *what* requires empirical evidence that might not exist or might not be found. These epistemological hurdles are the roots of the practical failure that besets torture: that it often doesn't work. It is all too possible to torture an innocent person (Sawyer, Sayid) or to never confirm guilt (Ben). In the first case the failure stems from the mistaken belief that the suspect knew. In the second case, it results from Ulpian's point that the strong can resist and the weak can lie.

---

[5]  "One of Them."

In any case, the possibilities for failure outnumber the one possible success: that the suspect knows and will talk. But, as unlikely as it might be, the fact is inescapable: it might work. There's a chance.

But the same epistemological problems that undermine torture's efficacy preclude the knowledge of when it will work. In the cases where it fails, we learn after the fact that it was wrong to do it. Mill's "harm principle" is violated and collective suffering is increased, rather than collective happiness. Fatally, we don't learn the torture was wrong until after the fact. We must act before we know (a philosopher's nightmare). And we must make the decision by considering the effects of the consequences along with their probabilities. There are a number of reasons why this kind of torture might not work and one way that it could work. From this disparity in likelihood, the initial reaction is to want to eschew torture in all forms. However – shocking as it is to say – the arguments against torture do not adequately counter the one valid argument for it, when we consider the outcomes alongside their likelihoods. While the effects of failed torture are unfortunate, the effects of not trying could be tragic. And it is this gap between unfortunate and tragic that makes torture, in these particular kinds of cases, necessary.

In Sayid's shoes, we must torture. The chance of not acting is too grave. If not, how could we console Shannon that Sawyer might have the medicine that could save her life, but there's nothing to be done? Or Sawyer, Jack, and Kate that Ben might have revealed himself, but that torturing him would not have been worth the chance that he would not? On the island, if the right suspect comes into Sayid's custody and under torture provides information that protects them from the Others or gets them off the island, Sayid will be a hero. If he tries again and fails, he should be respected.

# 14

# Friends and Enemies in the State of Nature: The Absence of Hobbes and the Presence of Schmitt

## *Peter S. Fosl*

Despite the sublime and beautiful physical landscape of the island onto which the survivors of Oceanic Airlines Flight 815 have fallen, one would be hard pressed to describe the setting of *Lost* as a Garden of Eden, a Xanadu, or a paradise – especially in light of inhabitants already living there, the ones that emerge from the jungle to assault, abduct, and kill them. In this chapter, I'd like to consider what the conflicted social landscape *Lost* constructs in this strange green world has to say about a number of topics that have vexed philosophers for thousands of years, in particular the nature of human beings and the way reason and passion play out in human society. In particular, I wish to argue that while *Lost* in many ways adopts the social vision developed by early modern liberal political philosophers, its conception of human beings and human societies is, perhaps despite its own intent, also deeply informed by one of the most influential political philosophies of National Socialism. To show you what I mean, let's start by unpacking the idea of "liberal political theory" and the way it's presented in the universe of *Lost*.

## Locke: Reason, Rights, and Torture

It's no accident that the names of a number of the most prominent characters on *Lost* allude to early modern philosophers who thought

159

about what people would be like in a "state of nature," like the island, beyond the reach of human civilization. I'm of course referring to French philosopher Jean-Jacques Rousseau (1712–1778) and to English philosopher John Locke (1632–1704). While the characters on *Lost* named after these philosophers don't precisely symbolize the philosophers' philosophical theories, their prominence does, I think, herald something of the show's interests.[1]

In order to understand human society and, in particular, the nature of legitimate power and authority, the second of Locke's *Two Treatises of Government* (1689) explores his vision of the "state of nature." In the Lockean vision, each person is naturally *free* – absolute lord over himself or herself, free from external authority. Each free individual is also *equal* to every other, with no artificial social hierarchies to establish privilege and subordination. Moreover, each is – and this is important – *rational*, born with innate, natural capacities to reason. One of the reasons that reason is important for Locke is that it allows people to apprehend a set of *natural rights* that also exist prior to society and therefore provide not only guidance for societies, when they come along, but also an independent standard by which any society can be judged. Among the most important natural rights Locke identifies are those of life (or security of one's person), liberty, and property.

Society comes along, according to Locke, as people realize that in the state of nature they're vulnerable and likely to have their rights trod upon. Recognizing this problem, people get together and, by mutual *consent*, set up a contingent authority over themselves to

---

[1] In addition, "Eko" seems to allude to Italian philosopher Umberto Ecco; "Sayid" to Palestinian political theorist Edward Said; character John Locke's father, "Anthony Cooper," to philosopher John Locke's patron, Anthony Ashley Cooper (aka Lord Shaftesbury); "Boone Carlyle" to Scottish historian Thomas Carlyle (and of course Daniel Boone); Other "Mikhail Bakunin" to the Russian anarchist of the same name; "Henry Gale" to Dorothy's uncle in *The Wizard of Oz* as well as to the wizard, who arrives in a fantastical green world via a balloon and becomes its leader – but who is a fraud nonetheless (not to mention that Henry Gale, bizarrely, as "Ben Linus," calls to mind Charlie Brown's friend or perhaps wooly scientific genius Linus Pauling; or does "Ben" refer to early modern Dutch philosopher, Benedict Spinoza?); "Sawyer," of course, names the wily but loveable Tom Sawyer; Irish "Colleen" and her "Danny" Boy "Pickett" renames the tragic Confederate charge at Gettysburg; and "Ethan Rom" hearkens to Edith Warton's tragic character, Etham Frome. There are many other allusions, as well.

secure the rights they possess naturally, as well as other new rights that might be conferred by government. By contrast, illegitimate governments derive their authority not from consent but by conquest and coercion. This distinction makes democracies legitimate forms of government and dictatorships illegitimate. The flip side to government by consent, of course, is the change of government by consent (the repudiation of authority). Characteristic of governments by consent is that they can be changed by the will of the people, and – what was especially radical to early modern thinkers – rebellion against them is legitimate when the government fails to secure natural rights or itself violates those rights.

Jack's rising to a position of authority among the survivors of Oceanic Airlines 815 in season one seems, at first, to follow the Lockean model in a fairly straightforward way.[2] While no formal vote is ever taken, Jack by no means acquires authority by conquest or domination. Jack's leadership receives acknowledgment and consent through his bringing security to the survivors' bodies with his medical care, through his issuing directives that are followed and that produce rational order as well as safe habitation. And, let's not forget, Jack organizes the group's defense against Ethan Rom (an anagram for "Other Man") and the Others when Ethan abducts the pregnant Claire (Jack's half-sister) and with her, Charlie.[3] Jack Shepard is, as his name implies, their shepherd.[4] Ana Lucia, the former cop and officer of state power, similarly rises to authority through her ability to provide (a bit of) security to the tail section survivors. Unlike the castaways of *Gilligan's Island*, the Oceanic survivors need real protection.

Now, to a remarkable degree people follow Jack's directives only because they consent to them. There is almost no coercion, and those

---

[2] Of course, who but a handsome, white, male physician could be leader in this universe? For what it's worth, I'd rather follow the early Locke (before he went around the bend and blew up the sub), Sayid, or Eko. The volatile, angry, arrogant, and shallow Jack seems less than an inspiring leader to this viewer. But, then again, why must there be a leader at all?

[3] Philosopher John Locke was himself a physician; he apparently cured his patron Lord Shaftesbury of a liver ailment. Similarly, character John Locke cures Anthony Cooper's kidney failure.

[4] Jack's surname also calls to mind the heroism and technological mastery of nature in Alan Shephard, the first American in space (May 5, 1961).

who wish to go their own way – for example, Sawyer, Kate, and Locke – are free do so. In fact, deviations from this principle of un-coerced authority seem shocking (such as when Locke ties up Boone to prevent him from telling the other castaways about the hatch). There are no police, no courts, no surveillance, no informants, and no prisons among the survivors, or at least among fuselage survivors. Indeed, on the whole, aside from the (as we'll see telling) position of Jack as "Leader," freedom and equality are maximal.

But this liberal edifice isn't without its cracks. In the first place there is the recurring issue of torture – in particular Sawyer's torture, which seems a decidedly serious violation of the liberal political idea of human rights, especially since he is not one of the Others. Like the American republic in the wake of September 11, 2001, *Lost* finds itself both endorsing and fretting about the use of torture. By implication, we might wonder if, like the American republic, *Lost* isn't fretting about how far it's willing to endorse liberal ideals. This anxiety unfolds on the show not only in the frequency with which torture is used. It also appears in the way the show almost simultan-eously regrets and excuses torture's application.[5] Here's the general template *Lost* follows: when those on the island resort to torture, they do so with clearly liberal justifications for its use; their use of torture, however, almost invariably fails in its objective, and those who engage in torture suffer the pangs of guilt afterwards. When, on the other hand, people besides the survivors, on and off the island, and in survivor flashbacks torture (e.g., Sayid's torture of a woman in Iraq) the conduct is more unambiguously wrong, though even then the show does its best to present mitigating circumstances when torture is administered by someone (like Sayid) who will become a survivor.

---

[5] Similarly, the same US government that has run programs of extraordinary rendition to states known to torture, secret abductions and secret prisons, and Guantanamo's notorious Camp X-Ray, has taken steps to stifle representations of torture in the media. The *Independent* (February 13, 2007) and *Democracy Now!* (February 22, 2007) report that in 2006 the Dean of West Point, Brigadier General Patrick Finnegan, along with military and FBI interrogators and representatives from the Prime Time Torture Project of Human Rights First, flew to Southern California to meet with the makers of the Fox television show *24*, in order to ask that the show stop using torture so frequently, this because American soldiers were copying what they had seen on the program.

When Sawyer, for example, is finally subjected to torture (at the hands of an American-trained Iraqi), he is (mistakenly) thought to be hoarding medicine that could save Shannon's life, medicine that arguably shouldn't belong to him in the first place.[6] Sayid tortures Ben because the survivors suspect him of being one of a group that has already assaulted them, threatened their lives and liberty, and, when the Others take the sailboat, taken their property, too. (The survivors' suspicions are, of course, correct; but Ben never cracks.)[7] Anna Lucia confines Sawyer, Jin, and Michael in a kind of prison and threatens Nathan with torture. She does so, however, only when she comes to believe that they also threaten fundamental Lockean rights to life and security. (It turns out she's wrong; none pose genuine threats, and her actions lead to Nathan's death.)

One might say, in fact, that Ana Lucia's challenge to the liberal social order of the survivors extends beyond her willingness to torture. In Ana Lucia's gun-wielding, physically abusive, interrogating, incarcerating, and threatening conduct we see a streak of the tyrant, particularly when she forces Libby at gun point to tie up Sayid ("The Other 48 Days"). Indeed, it's common for those who rise up in the name of the well-being of "the People" to become tyrannical.[8] But when her group insists on stopping in the jungle to camp at a water source, Ana Lucia, unlike a tyrant, yields to their will. Moreover, Ana Lucia's coercive behavior with Libby and the rest of the group occurs only after she killed Shannon and had reason to believe that she had placed herself outside of their society and perhaps even at war with it. After Eko convinces Jack and Locke that she is not their enemy and after Ana Lucia herself talks things through peacefully and honestly with Sayid, she is reincorporated into the survivors' society. Her violent, dictatorial, and illiberal conduct towards the survivors then

---

[6] Sayid's having been trained by an American and that American's later death suggest a recognition of American guilt for torturing detainees in Iraq. But then again that guilt is offset insofar as the officer Sayid tortures seems to be a "bad guy," and the information Sayid obtains seems important.

[7] Ben does produce information – the location of the balloon – that unintentionally exposes him as one of the Others. But given that he used the name "Henry Gale" all along, he may have been planning to disclose that information all along.

[8] Plato points this out in the *Republic*; and in fact the very name "tyrant" originated in ancient Greece to describe people who became leaders by currying the favor of the masses (usually in opposition to the aristocrats).

comes to an end. And, anyway, she pays for her violation of the liberal order with her leadership and with her life.[9]

## Rousseau and Hume: Friendship and Feeling

One might also, perhaps, point to Sawyer as an illiberal element of survivor society. But it's an accusation that's similarly limited. Sawyer does, yes, adopt a dictatorial posture after he cons the rest of the survivors into turning over their guns ("The Long Con"). But, then again, that posture is a reaction to Jack stealing the guns from him, violating his natural right to possessions. In any case, Sawyer's posture, like so much of Sawyer, is an act. He never really exercises dictatorial control over the group; and he gives up much of his weaponry and medicine quickly and willingly, partly in honor of a peaceable bargain he made with Jack while playing cards. But more importantly he gives the goods up as a result of the way his feelings and passions play upon him. His sexual desire allows Ana Lucia to acquire the gun that Michael will use to shoot Libby,[10] and through his consequent feelings of pity and guilt he turns over the medicine that might save Libby's life.[11] Sawyer's killing Anthony Cooper and Tom does show an illiberal willingness to violate the right to life,[12] but neither seem premeditated and rather show us how powerful Sawyer's emotions are. In any case, this recognition of the power of

---

[9] It's as if she has to pay with her life for killing Shannon, as if in the logic of their social order two leaders are too many. Leadership must be singular and strong, not divided among many in a democratic process; Nazi theorists called this requirement of good government *die Führerprinzip*.

[10] While Michael seems virtuous as a devoted father, it's troubling that the traitor of this story is a black man. Blacks (Michael, Eko, Rose, Walt) in fact appear as principally either violent or somehow mystical – in Eko's case, both. These characterizations reiterate time-worn stereotypes. Ana Lucia's, Sayid's, and Jin's violent capacities fit this pattern, as well.

[11] Perhaps out of similar feelings of remorse Sawyer initially refuses the same medicine when he is carried back to camp wounded ("Collision").

[12] Don't get me started on the stereotypes informing southern-man Sawyer's character – his violent, criminal, sexual, deceptive character. Let's just say that, like people of color, the liberalism of Southerners isn't entirely sure.

feeling to bind and separate people is no trivial matter. In fact, it's central to the way a number of other early modern thinkers justified their liberal political theories.

The feeling of pity that drives Sawyer, for example, illustrates an important element of the political theory of Jean-Jacques Rousseau, as well as Rousseau's sometime friend and contemporary, David Hume (1711–1776). For Rousseau (a thinker considered one of the seminal theorists of the French Revolution and associated with positive images of the "noble savage" leading a natural life uncorrupted by society), fellow feeling and the feeling of pity underwrite liberal society as much as reason does for Locke.[13] In the *Social Contract* (1762) and *Discourse on the Origin of Inequality* (1755), Rousseau describes a state of nature in which people enjoy the natural freedom to pursue the good and noble desires that Rousseau believed are natural to them.[14] The establishment of a government by consent, for Rousseau, like Locke, expands human freedom – but not simply by constructing a rational order that secures and elaborates natural rights. For Rousseau, the agreement that creates the state also creates an utterly new social being, something greater than the mere sum of the individual parts that compose it. It creates a collective thing that fuses individuals together into a larger whole, what Rousseau calls the "general will." We see the emergence of this collective in "White Rabbit" when Jack ends a fight that's broken out among them, gathers the group together, and lays down their founding principle: "If we can't live together, we're going to die alone." The collective is also evident whenever the survivors refer to themselves as "we" and "us," and when in Locke's emotional speech in season three he proclaims that he will retrieve those captive to the Others and bring them "home" ("I Do").

Scottish philosopher David Hume (*A Treatise of Human Nature*, Book III, 1740), although he thought the "state of nature" a pointless

---

[13] Perhaps that is in part why the character Rousseau has a "wild" personality, always carries a weapon, and lives in the jungle.

[14] Sadly, the survivors of the crash of Oceanic Airlines Flight 815 don't seem to exercise their natural freedom much in the enjoyment of their natural desires – Kate's swim with Sawyer ("Whatever the Case May Be") and the various references to lovemaking stand as notable exceptions.

fiction and didn't believe in the "general will," does share with Rousseau an important idea. Hume powerfully argues that what binds people together isn't just reason's calculation of personal interest or "self-love" (what Rousseau called *amor de soi*), but also various other-regarding feelings or sentiments. Human beings are "mirrors" to one another, writes Hume, in that through "sympathy" they take on the feelings of others – feeling, in a sense, their pains and pleasures. Rousseau, for his part, held that each human being in *pité*, which depends upon sympathy, finds something that will "mitigate, in certain circumstances, the ferocity of his egocentrism . . . by an innate repugnance to see his fellow suffer."[15] In the show's social dynamics the force of pity and sympathy are as prominent as they are powerful.

It is pity to which Juliet appeals when she asks Jack to help save Colleen. It is pity to which Ben appeals when he says he wants Jack "to want" to help him. Pity again when Eko carries wounded Sawyer through the forest. Even pity when Jack euthanizes US Marshall Edward Mars shortly after Sawyer's pity-driven attempt at a mercy killing fails ("Tabula Rasa"). Juliet's pity leads her to help Sun and contributes to her defection to the survivors. Alexandra's pity drives her to risk her beloved Karl, sending him to help the survivors. Kate's pity pierces the barrier of hostility separating her from Sawyer when she reads the letter she believes he wrote to the con man that destroyed his family ("Outlaws"). Kate also appeals to Jack's pity when she begs him to operate on Ben so that the Others won't kill Sawyer.

## Who Needs Hobbes?

Indeed, Kate becomes an especially important vehicle for a number of the liberal philosophical claims of *Lost*. Not only is Kate an erotic focus, evoking the desires of many of *Lost*'s central male characters (Sawyer, Jack, Ben) – especially through her distinctive proclivity for showering on screen. Her words and deeds also carry a specific kind

---

[15] Jean-Jacques Rousseau, *Discourse on the Origin of Inequality* Part I, in *The Basic Political Writings*, trans. Donald A. Cress (Indianapolis: Hackett, 1987), p. 53.

of philosophical freight. Kate advances the idea that people are not entirely selfish, that it's sentiment and feeling that bind people together, and that the collective surpasses the individual. The title of the episode "I Do," for example, doesn't just refer to Kate's failed marriage to police officer Kevin Callis and her choosing Sawyer. It also refers to the crystallization, in the face of her enemies and the adversity she now faces, of her fierce commitment to the survivors, even at the cost of her self-interest. But the dramatic scene in "I Do" where Jack's last minute intervention saves Sawyer from execution isn't the first time Austin has put others before herself.

Previously, in "Every Man for Himself" (note the title), Kate refuses to climb free of the Hydra Station cage, ignoring Sawyer's plea for her to look to her own interest and escape. By staying with Sawyer, Kate directly repudiates the selfish principle articulated by the episode title, embracing instead the principle Jack had established for the collective at its very founding moment (that's right, "live together, die alone"). As if having already made this point to Sawyer in "Every Man for Himself" wasn't enough, Kate in "I Do" literally screams her affirmation of the principle to Jack across the span of their separation, reminding him and us what the social order of the survivors is all about, or at least is supposed to be all about. (She does, of course, for the moment leave; but like General Macarthur, we know she will return.)

Again, Kate's stalwart refusal – like Pickett's fury, like Sawyer's defiant kiss at the work site, like Juliet's insubordinate enlistment of Jack's surgical skill for Colleen, like Michael's desperate efforts to save his son, like Charlie's wild attempt to baptize Aaron, and like many other events in the series – illustrates the ever-present power of passion to join people and to cause individuals to risk themselves for the sake of those to whom they are bound.

Kate's conduct, however, also repudiates the doctrines of an early modern philosopher tellingly not named on *Lost*, one whose striking absence among the characters is explained by this repudiation. Thomas Hobbes (1588–1679) preceded Locke and Rousseau as a philosopher of human nature, government by consent of the people, and the authority of the state. A giant of that period, Hobbes is nearly always mentioned in the same breath with the other two, so his absence from the highly literate nomenclature of *Lost* seems hardly accidental.

*Peter S. Fosl*

Like Locke and Rousseau, Hobbes in his *Leviathan* (1660) and *De Cive* (1651) imagines human beings existing in a state of nature without government. Unlike Rousseau, however, the condition Hobbes imagines is a pitiless one, a world without fellow feeling, populated by wholly selfish beings, where each is enemy to every other in what Hobbes describes as a "war of all against all" (*bellum omnium contra omnes*).[16] If Hobbes is different from Rousseau in attributing no pity to humans in the state of nature, he differs from Locke in rejecting the idea that the state of nature includes any natural rights or natural laws, except for the right of self-defense and the law of survival.

You see, for Locke, society is something like a farm or a garden – a methodized and corrected natural order. Lockean government, like a farmer, nurtures and cultivates the soil of human nature and natural rights in a way consistent with the laws of nature so that human beings will flourish peaceably and rationally. For Rousseau, the invention of society is more like the invention of human flight. Like an aircraft, according to Rousseau, society must honor nature and nature's rights (lest it crash in terrible corruption), but the delicate invention of society nevertheless allows us to transcend nature, to take a higher, enlarged view of our world and ourselves.

For Hobbes, by contrast, the state and society exist largely in order to limit, control, and oppose nature. People flee the state of nature because life there is, in Hobbes's famous phrase, "solitary, poor, nasty, brutish, and short."[17] Like wild beasts that must be broken and bridled, humans must, according to Hobbes, be coerced by threat of

---

[16] See, for example, *De Cive*, Chapter 1, Paragraph XII: "it cannot be deny'd but that the naturall state of men, before they entr'd into Society, was a meer War, and that not simply, but a War of all men, against all men."

[17] *Leviathan*, Chapter 13: "Whatsoever therefore is consequent to a time of war, where every man is enemy to every man, the same consequent to the time wherein men live without other security than what their own strength and their own invention shall furnish them withal. In such condition there is no place for industry, because the fruit thereof is uncertain: and consequently no culture of the earth; no navigation, nor use of the commodities that may be imported by sea; no commodious building; no instruments of moving and removing such things as require much force; no knowledge of the face of the earth; no account of time; no arts; no letters; no society; and which is worst of all, continual fear, and danger of violent death; and the life of man, solitary, poor, nasty, brutish, and short."

violence to recognize the rule of law and the rights of others. The social order satisfies more selfish desires than the state of nature (and that's why people choose it) but only as a consequence of limiting those desires. Like a caged animal in a zoo, the beast can remain well fed, peaceful, and long-lived only by being contained.

The state of things among the survivors themselves seems then, as Kate affirms, decidedly not Hobbesian. In the absence of the coercive powers of the state the survivors don't return to a war of all against all, where the strong take what they want when they want it from the weak. People on the island don't steal, rape, and murder as they please, acting strictly as individuals. They recognize the rights of others, but not from fear of punishment. And they don't devolve into the sort of savagery depicted in William Golding's *Lord of the Flies* (1954).[18] The survivors of Oceanic 815 are social beings through and through, woven together by bonds of reason and feeling.

On the other hand, at first blush there does seem to be something Hobbesian about the survivors' relationship with the Others. The survivors may not be Hobbesian among themselves, but their relationship with the Others is nothing if not struggle and conflict. This probably shouldn't be surprising, since many have argued that while Hobbesian theory may not describe human individuals very well, it does accurately describe the relations among nation-states. The Others, in particular, seem to take what they want from the survivors (notably, the survivors' children). Their gassing the people of the Dharma Project, their tossing their victims' bodies into an open pit, leaving them unburied, their taking over Dharma property, their ruthless disregard for the rational resolution of disputes, and the complete absence of pity and sympathy from them all exhibit their Hobbesian qualities.

But, despite these apparent indications, trying to see the relationship between the Others and the survivors through a Hobbesian lens doesn't entirely work. In the first place, the Others don't simply take because they can, and they don't assert their claims as matters of raw

---

[18] In *Lord of the Flies* a group of highly civilized British schoolboys finds itself, after a plane crash, castaway on a tropical island. In the absence of the forces that had until then constrained them, the formerly well-mannered children quickly revert to a life of extreme violence, cruelty, coercion, irrationality, and authoritarianism.

169

power and desire. They advance a moral justification for their actions, maintaining that they are the "good people."[19] Secondly, curiously, Ben honors the Others' agreement with Michael to provide him a means off the island with Walt if Michael will successfully lead a specified group of the survivors into a trap – and Ben does so in the absence of any coercion ("Live Together, Die Alone"). If this is so, then, perhaps no one on *Lost* is named Hobbes because the show rejects the Hobbesian vision. So, how should we understand the Others?

It's important to remember for the sake of my argument that, despite his differences with Locke and Rousseau, Hobbes is still a liberal philosopher. That's because even though he rejects the liberal idea of natural rights beyond self-defense, as well as the idea that people are bound together by feelings like pity and sympathy, Hobbes shares with the other liberals the same goal – namely, overcoming the conflict of the state of nature through a government founded upon the consent of the governed. For the early modern liberal philosophers, government and society are artifices, technologies, invented to put an end to conflict and war and to replace them with peace, reason, happiness, and order. Conflict, struggle, and war are, in short, for liberal political thinkers problems that can to be solved, problems that ought to be solved.

But recognizing this common trait among liberal philosophers is just what makes it possible to realize the persistently illiberal character of *Lost*, despite its pretensions, even its aspirations, to the contrary. In many ways, *Lost* pretends to defend a liberal, Rouseauian, and Lockean social order and to reject cynical Hobbesian ideas about human nature and political authority. But like the smoke monster that emerges from the island's idyllic forests, something even darker than Thomas Hobbes's philosophical vision slithers through the narrative of this popular American TV show.

---

[19] Ethan Rom, for example (who we first see in the opening of season three, like the Wicked Witch in *Oz*, under a house with his legs sticking out), tells Claire after he's abducted her that "We [the Others] are good people, Claire. Good family" ("Maternity Leave"). Ben tells Michael: "We're the good people, Michael" ("Live Together, Die Alone"). Furthermore, the Others are driven by need, as well as moral purpose. There are no children in Otherville because a disease kills pregnant women. The Others clearly see the acquisition of children as something necessary for their society's survival.

## About Schmitt

Rather than to Hobbes or any of the early modern liberal political philosophers, it's to a more recent intellectual that we should turn in order to understand the philosophical claim *Lost* makes about human societies. Carl Schmitt (1888–1985) was known as the "crown jewel" of the Nazi jurists. Despite his unapologetic service to Adolf Hitler's regime, Schmitt's philosophical work, especially *The Concept of the Political* (1927), has remained important, bizarrely enough enjoying a recent flurry of interest among leftwing philosophers like Chantal Mouffe.[20] Schmitt's central thesis is that an "enemy" is necessary to the formation and development of society. If liberal political theory is defined by its goal of eliminating conflict and securing a rational peace, Schmittian-Nazi theory is defined by its embracing conflict and war as not only desirable, but essential. This thesis becomes incarnate in the survivors' relationship with the Others.

Aristotle regarded friendship as crucial to the political order, and he characterized a friend as someone who (1) gives pleasure, who (2) is useful in helping with various projects, and who (3) makes one a morally better person (*Nicomachean Ethics*, Books VIII and IX). For Schmitt, by contrast, a friend is a member of one's own political group, an ally set against a common enemy. Whether anyone is an enemy or a friend is the most basic of political decisions, and to be a member of a polity is to be on one side of a struggle against people on one or more other sides – good guys vs. bad guys, Swiss Family Robinson vs. the Pirates, Americans vs. The Terrorists, US vs. USSR, the US vs. Iran, the US vs. Saddam Hussein, the US vs. al-Qaeda, Bloods vs. Crips, UKY Wildcats vs. Louisville Cardinals, Jason vs. Freddie, Republicans vs. Democrats, us vs. them. Subsequent political decisions turn upon the question of whether a course of action will help one's friends and harm one's enemies. Helping friends and harming enemies is, in fact, the fundamental project of the polity. Put in terms of early modern liberal theory, the state of nature, so far as it exists among social groups, should be preserved.

*Lost* seems to take a similar view. While the survivors among themselves, as we have seen, often operate according to many classically

---

[20] Chantal Mouffe, ed., *The Challenge of Carl Schmitt* (New York: Verso, 1999).

liberal conceptions of social order, if we look closer, especially at their relationship with the Others, we find that those liberal pretensions don't run very deep. The survivors of Oceanic Airlines 815 don't just form a society because of the infelicities of the state of nature, because of the difficulties of their relationships with each other, because of their struggles with the natural world, or even because of their fellow feelings. They bond together as a society *in opposition* to another society, to an *enemy*. Their strong, unifying leaders rise to authority as warrior chieftains. Jack isn't just the first among equals; he is their *Führer*. The enemy they face, moreover, seems hopelessly non-liberal. Ben, Jack's anti-*Führer*, seems to be feared as a ruthless dictatorial leader who, if Juliet is to be believed, can only be deposed by killing him.[21] Tom (whom Sawyer dubs "Zeke"), especially loyal to Ben, shows no willingness to negotiate when Jack and the search party sent to retrieve Walt confront the Others in the forest ("The Hunting Party").[22]

Season three of *Lost* begins by showing us things from the Others' point of view. This affords us more understanding of their conduct. But not much. And, more importantly, we see no efforts (perhaps no capacity) on the part of either group to embrace the other, to offer hospitality, to find ways of forging bonds of fellow feeling, friendship, and sympathy, to resolve conflicts peaceably and rationally, to solve problems collectively, to formulate a rule of law to regularize interactions, to share and cultivate the abundant resources that surround them, to join in defense against the black smoke monster and

---

[21] Juliet suggests that there may be a different social structure when she rebuffs Jack's attempt to play upon her evident discontent with Ben's authority in "Every Man for Himself." When Jack asks whether she takes orders from Ben, Juliet responds: "It doesn't work that way over here, Jack. We make decisions together." Curiously, Ben doesn't punish Juliet for showing Jack his x-rays or for allowing Jack to operate on Colleen. It does, however, seem that Karl is punished when he is caged next to Sawyer; later Alex suggests that he's been killed. Tom, speaking to Ethan after Claire's escape, seems to fear Ben's response, or some higher, still Other boss, "Him" ("Maternity Leave"). This elusive super-Other we later learn to be, in what may be the silliest and most disappointing of the series' scenes, the mysterious, semi-visible "Jacob" ("Man Behind the Curtain," another allusion to the *Wizard of Oz*). In the Bible, Jacob's youngest son is named "Ben." Genesis 49:27 describes Ben thus: "Benjamin is a ravenous wolf; In the morning he devours the prey, And in the evening he divides the spoil." Is Ben Jewish? Think of the otherness that would call upon.

[22] Could Tom by "Thomas Hobbes"?

the polar bear(s). Nothing of the sort is attempted. Nothing of the sort seems possible. But why don't the Others send a rescue party with medicine and food? Why don't they escort the survivors back to the safety of their compound and offer them help, care, shelter, and the chance to join their community? Because that sort of offer is impossible to imagine in a Schmittian political universe like *Lost*. Others are bad people, enemies, and like the cannibals Robinson Crusoe and Friday fight, the only language the enemy can understand is brute force.

Like the American republic, this television show has crash-landed upon the views of human nature and society current among Nazi intellectuals more than sixty years ago. If Frankenstein's monster symbolized the repudiation of early modern utopian dreams of reason and love,[23] the crumbling remains of the utopian Dharma Project and the monstrous Others who gas them symbolize the repudiation of the progressive politics of the 1950s, 1960s, and 1970s – even more philosophically of the progressive conception of *dharma* (which means natural law and higher truth).[24] So far as I can tell, however, progressive politics on this show hasn't been surpassed by something better. Instead, *Lost* argues that since *dharma* failed to stop the return of the repressed from the forest's heart of darkness, our best chance of surviving is to cast off utopian liberal naïveté and embrace the Schmittian law of the jungle.[25] In short, our best chance against the bad guys, the "evil ones," is to "blow them all to Hell," as *Führer*-Jack nakedly puts it in "Greatest Hits."[26] Even when the enemy

---

[23]  One way of reading Mary Shelly's *Frankenstein; or, The Modern Prometheus* (1818) is as a repudiation of her mother Mary Wollstonecraft's and her father William Godwin's progressive, optimistic politics.

[24]  Perhaps the black smoke monster should also call to mind the black smoke of the crematoria in the Nazi death camps, where like the members of the Dharma Project the Nazis' adversaries were gassed. The Dharma Project itself recalls the idealistic project of Jack Kerouac's 1958 novel, *Dharma Bums*, which has inspired beatniks, hippies, and other free spirits looking for a more meaningful life for decades. Our culture's come a long way from Jack Kerouac to Jack Shepard.

[25]  Americans, of course, first encountered others of the forest in Native Americans. Perhaps the lingering fears and prejudices of that era have made them especially receptive to the Schmittian views expressed in *Lost*.

[26]  President Bush famously referred to the Islamic *jihadis* who had attacked the United States as "the evil ones": "Our job now is to find the evil ones and bring them to justice" (October 29, 2001).

surrenders, they don't really surrender, as Sawyer opines after he blows Tom away. The only good Other is a dead other.

Americans flatter themselves as liberal and democratic in their political ideology. If at times they are given to violence, they see the violence as unfortunate but justifiable, justifiable invariably because it's somehow necessary to secure their Lockean rights to life, liberty, and property. Sure, sometimes they feel a pang of guilt afterwards, but as they see it, whatever wrongs they commit are anomalous and nowhere near as bad as the others'. More often, Americans find their conduct to have been animated by pity and compassion, saving the world from the "evil ones." Like the survivors, they see themselves as beautiful and sexy, racially diverse (to a point), superlatively technical and scientific (especially in medicine), and yet also deeply spiritual. On the whole, they bring good things to life.

This liberal self-image, however, periodically crashes for Americans when faced with some other. Classically liberal among themselves, Americans nevertheless have come to see others through National Socialist eyes. With an almost tiresome predictability, they imagine others to be dangerous, cunning, illiberal, and subhuman murderers, capable of understanding only force, sprinting to assault them even before they've crawled from the wreckage. If the *Body Snatchers* (1956), the *Creature from the Black Lagoon* (1954), and the giant insect movies of the 1950s incarnated American anxieties about communism, the Others of *Lost* incarnate American anxieties about the "enemies" the US faces today. While, however, the source of anxiety has changed, the response to it has not. Before problems posed by Islamic militant *jihadis*, the Palestinian resistance, Iraqi insurgents, Iran, North Korea, North Vietnam, communists, Black Power, Native Americans, Sith, or Mordor, the solution has so often been the same gruesome final solution: kill them all.

What's as astonishing, however, in the text of *Lost* as it is in American culture is that this dim view of "our" society's relationship to others persists even as we learn that the Others are in many ways – in their thoughts, in their reading, in their bodies, in their history and ideas, in their manner, in their emotional lives, and so on – not, in fact, terribly other. We find that the Others read Stephen King, speak English, share the same biological features, share the same histories, play the same sports, suffer the same sorts of needs and feelings and desires as those that characterize the survivors. As Shylock puts it so well in Shakespeare's *Merchant of Venice*, "If you prick us, do we not bleed? If you tickle us, do we not laugh? If you poison us, do we not die?" (Act III.1). So why, then, are the Others conceived as irredeemably other? Why do they remain others even after we discover they are not? Why does *Lost* chant with French philosopher Jacques Derrida (1930–2004), even in the face of its own evidence to the contrary, *tout autre est tout autre* ("every other is totally other")?[27]

There seems, then, in the logic of *Lost*, little to be hoped for besides continuing war between the Others and the survivors – and, if Ben is right about Naomi,[28] a possible new war with a possibly new group of others, let's call them other-Others, people from the ship that Charlie figured out isn't Penelope's, just before he (pointlessly?) died. Perhaps it will all end with another absurd showdown, a final confrontation, as it so often does in Hollywood, between the opposing Leaders (Ben and Jack), reestablishing the dominion of the really "good" people with an act of redemptive violence. Or perhaps we'll see the survivors escape the state of nature through an act of transcendence, by means of some *deus ex machina* like rescue helicopters, or a friendly ghost (Walt or Jacob or Jack's dad),[29] or an act of magic (like Locke's surviving the mass grave), without any real resolution to their conflict.

On the other hand, perhaps there is this: perhaps we may yet see the irruption of some sort of feeling or passion that will shatter the stony fascistic order under which *Lost* currently labors, consigning what in the show's future would perhaps be called the "Other War" to the rubbish heap of the three-toed colossus and other monstrosities. The unlikely appearance of erotic love between the beautiful, spoiled, blonde American (Shannon) and the swarthy, brooding Iraqi soldier (Sayid) signaled the possibility of reconciliation among enemies, of the overcoming of deep conflict through bonds of feeling. The attraction between Jack and Juliet (if it's genuine) promises something of the same. Might bonds of feeling, the desire for something besides war, and a recognition of all they share in common somehow appeal to what Abraham Lincoln called the "better angels"

---

[27] Jacques Derrida, *The Gift of Death*, trans. D. Wills (Chicago: University of Chicago Press, 1995), Chapter 4, "Tout autres est tout autre."

[28] I write this just after the end of season three and so don't know yet.

[29] Do you think he's still wandering around the island ("White Rabbit")?

of human nature and reconcile the survivors of Oceanic Airlines and the Others? Might the two groups then forge a democratic collective or federation of ordered liberty, or perhaps even an Eden-like green world of peace and harmony?[30] Might they somehow come to help each other to get off the island?

Or will any attempt to establish community with the Others die, like Shannon, in a hail of bullets, fear, and ignorance? Even worse, will the dream of peace among the island's inhabitants, like that between the US and its adversaries, asphyxiate in the gas chambers of Schmittian political philosophy and its terrible imperative to find in others not fellow human beings with whom one can sustain a common life, but an enemy to kill before that enemy kills us?

I confess to harboring some hope for the survivors, for the Others, and for us Americans. Given, however, the kind of political philosophy popular among us today, I also have my doubts.

---

[30] Lincoln used this famous phrase in his "First Inaugural Address" in 1861. His objective was to reconcile the North and the South in order to prevent the war that loomed on their horizon. Of course, Lincoln's appeal failed.

# 15

# *Lost*'s State of Nature

## *Richard Davies*

The phrase *state of nature* crops up frequently in comments on *Lost* for at least two reasons. The first is that two of the leading characters in the program (John Locke and Danielle Rousseau) bear the surnames of two philosophers who are famous for having used the phrase *state of nature* as a key term in their writings on political philosophy. These are the Englishman John Locke (1632–1704) and the Swiss-Frenchman Jean-Jacques Rousseau (1712–1788). The second, much better, reason why the phrase crops up so much in discussions of *Lost* is that the situation the survivors of Oceanic Flight 815 find themselves in after the crash can indeed be usefully described as a state of nature.

Before coming to some differences among the ways that Locke, Rousseau, and other philosophers have thought about the state of nature, let's consider a negative, and rather abstract, characterization of it that would be recognized by everyone working in the tradition of political philosophy that Locke and Rousseau consolidated. *In a pure state of nature, none of the codes and expectations, none of the rules and hierarchies, none of the roles and presumptions that make up the fabric of our social lives is operative, can be relied on or can be enforced.* Presented in this abstract way, a situation like this is very difficult to imagine. After all, very few of us have any experience of anything remotely similar.

The very difficulty of imagining something that fits the (negative) bill can help explain why Locke, Rousseau, and other philosophers have taken differing approaches to giving a more positive and concrete account of the dynamics of a supposed state of nature. Indeed, many philosophers, including another who gives his name to a character on *Lost*, the Scotsman David Hume (1711–1776), have thought that the difficulty of imagining a state of nature is a reason for not taking it as a key concept in theorizing about politics. If it is a hardly imaginable situation, it won't be of much help understanding the societies we actually participate in.

In what sense, then, can the situation of the survivors of 815 be described as a state of nature? Well, at the outset, most of the people (except the pairs Jin-Sun, Shannon-Boone, Michael-Walt and, to a small extent, Jack-Rose) are strangers to each other. They are individuals each with their own interests and aims, above all to survive in the face of the unfamiliar challenges of the island. They cannot be sure what the other castaways will be prepared to do to ensure their own survival, and they have no authority to turn to, either to tell them what to do or to protect them from harm. This, again, is a negative account of their situation, but I want to use ideas that have grown up within the tradition of state-of-nature theory to look at some of more positive factors in evidence in the early episodes of season one that the survivors can use to regenerate at least part of the social structure that has gone missing as a result of the crash.

## Lining up for Peace

Though in one sense (which Hume, the philosopher, was right about) the pure state of nature is just a philosopher's thought experiment, whose interest – if any – is only theoretical, there is also a sense (where Hume missed a trick) in which we do encounter partial, or as I shall say, "framed" states of nature all the time. Every time, in fact, the interests of various individuals are in potential conflict for some limited good.

Take, as a trivial example, the fact that, when I have filled my cart at the supermarket, my aim is to get out as quickly as I can. The same goes for all the other stressed-out cart-pushers. Each of us wants the immediate attention of the cashier, but there are only three cashiers open and fifteen loads of shopping to be paid for. In the words of Thomas Hobbes (1588–1679), one of the earliest modern theorists of states of nature, the fifteen shoppers are in a condition of "war, where every man is enemy to every man."[1] The surprising thing, then, is that, given the Hobbesian diagnosis, massacres at the supermarket checkout are fairly rare. What each of the fifteen normally relies on is the expectation that the other fourteen will follow the usual practice and form lines. This practice creates a "frame" within which the conflict among the shoppers isn't exactly resolved, but is at least kept under control. I still want to get out as quickly as I can and so do the others, but we all recognize a procedure for reducing the likelihood of violence. Somewhat less rare than supermarket massacres are those people who don't merely wish the others weren't there, but act as if they weren't (or ignore the item limit on the express lane). If anything, it is these people who might deserve just a splash of bloodshed.

With this trivial example, we can get a measure of the purity or severity of a state of nature. Because getting out of the supermarket in two minutes rather than ten doesn't make a great deal of difference to my life, the other shoppers are my "enemies" only to the value of eight minutes of mortality (which I'd set aside in the first place when I decided to go shopping). Hence, the principle: *the more vital or scarcer the good that is the object of conflict, the purer and more severe the state of nature.* And because I can be pretty confident that others will abide by the norms for forming lines, even the shoppers in front of me are in a sense also my allies because, by doing what's expected of them, they make shopping that bit less stressful for everyone. Hence, the principle: *the fewer or weaker (that is, the less likely to be observed) the frames, the purer and more severe the state of nature.*

In these terms, we can see that the survivors on *Lost* do find themselves in a pretty severe state of nature, because among the goods that they are no longer guaranteed by the society from which they are now isolated are the means of basic survival, and because it is hard for them to tell in advance what frames, if any, will apply to the distribution of those goods. The question, then, is: What can they do to reduce the severity of the state of nature? On the one hand, this is a question about the procurement of the means of survival; but perhaps more crucially it has to do with the way each of the survivors can come to trust the others not to make things worse.

---

[1] We modernize the spelling and cite in brackets the pages (here p. 89) of Richard Tuck's edition of Hobbes's *Leviathan* (1651) (Cambridge: Cambridge University Press, 1991).

Richard Davies

# Human Nature and Natural Man

One major question on which state-of-nature theorists have disagreed is whether, to understand the emergence of a society, we have to take a position on the very nature of mankind. Any effort to answer the question of "human nature" can easily lead to arguing in circles ("Man is by nature such-and-such because that's what he's like in a state of nature; so in a state of nature he's such-and-such"). But two sorts of stands have emerged about how to think of humanity in the raw.

Jean-Jacques Rousseau, for instance, is credited with thinking that, by nature, man is a compassionate and altruistic creature, and, hence, that the state of nature offers an ideal against which the corruptions of society can be measured.[2] In this direction, Rousseau – and with him others like David Hume – would say that humans are actuated by benevolent passions, while, for instance, Locke (the philosopher) would say that reason guides our behavior.[3] Let's call Rousseau's attitude "Innocence" (a key term in his *Discourse*; see p. 91).

On the other hand, Hobbes is generally interpreted as regarding man as wholly egoistical and suspicious of his fellows.[4] This, as we shall see, is not a necessary part of his theory. Instead of referring to the historical Hobbes, we can say that the view opposed to Rousseau's would be one according to which people always operate on the motto adopted by Special Agent Fox Mulder: "Trust no one" or, rather, "Trust No. 1," which phrase we may use as a summary of the attitude in question. This is the attitude that I would quickly

---

[2]  Generally, this attribution is made on the basis of his *Discourse on the Origin of Inequality* (1755), trans. G. D. H. Cole and others, in *Social Contract and Discourses* (London: Dent, 1973).

[3]  See his second *Treatise on Government* (1690) of which the standard critical text was edited by Peter Laslett (Cambridge: Cambridge University Press, 1960); we give in brackets the paragraph numbers that are common to every edition (here §§4–15).

[4]  Hobbes argues most explicitly against Aristotle's view that man is by nature a social animal (*zoon politikon*: *Politics*, I, ii, 1253a3) in the first chapter of *De Cive* (first published 1642), ed. Howard Warrender (Oxford: Oxford University Press, 1983) and especially in the footnotes added to the second edition (1647).

adopt in a state of nature like the one we can see in Danny Boyle's 2003 film *28 Days Later*, where everyone we meet should be suspected of being infected with aggressive rabies.

"Innocence" and "Trust No. 1" are labels for what are claimed to be the basic orientations of human beings, which would be given free rein in a situation where the norms of communal living have come unstuck. It may be that one or the other is a true description of what *would* happen in those circumstances (of which, as I've said, we have little direct knowledge). Perhaps Innocence is not a wildly inaccurate description of how Hurley and Jack behave, and Trust No. 1 is not a wildly inaccurate description of how Sawyer and Locke (the outdoorsman, not the philosopher) behave. But I, at least, don't claim to know that either is true of human beings in general and I think we can get on perfectly well without them in understanding the interactions on the island. Indeed, I think that we can understand the state of nature *better* if we are not hampered by a speculative theory about the "nature" of the people in it, beyond recognizing that, as animals, they need such things as food, drink, and protection.

## Amid the Wreckage

In the immediate aftermath of the crash, the plane is the survivors' source of food and drink. So long as they believe that they will be rescued soon, they can consume these without second thoughts.

After about a week, though, Hurley discovers that someone has taken some bottles of fresh water leaving only 18 for the rest. Hurley's intuitive – and accurate – analysis is that the others would "freak out" if they knew ("White Rabbit"). They would freak out because each individual wants for himself as much of the limited good (water) as he can get, while knowing that the more he takes, the less there will be in the long run for everybody, himself included.

Unlike the supermarket, where my access to a limited good (the attention of the cashier) doesn't reduce the total amount of that good available to all (at least until closing time), water is a good precisely when it is consumed: every drop I drink is a drop less to go round all the others who have some claim on it. Situations of this sort are a special case of the state of nature, and are known as "tragedies of the commons."[5]

Charlie suggests rationing as a resolution to the water tragedy. That is, each survivor must reduce their own consumption to allow all to have at least a minimum. But this requires everyone to subordinate their own interests to that of a group that is only just forming. Each can ask: "Why should I give up my water to people I don't know or care about?" The tragedy here is that it is very hard to answer that question, which would only be put by someone who doesn't recognize group survival as a good over and above their own.

Jack refuses to decide anything about how to distribute the water, because he too is in the same situation as the others and – quite apart from his "daddy issues" – has no authority to impose rationing. In a fit of optimism to minimize the theft from the group's common property, Sawyer tells Kate that "water has no value, Freckles; it's gonna rain sooner or later" ("White Rabbit"). He's surely right that when there is enough water to go round, no one needs to privatize it. But it's the possibility of a "later" that comes after the castaways have all died of thirst that makes the tragedy urgent.

When Jack is led to discover the stream of fresh water later in the same episode, and the survivors get the knack of hunting and fishing, they are no longer in tragic conflict with each other for vital goods. Because none of the other survivors is a threat to the survival of each of them, there is no reason not to group together. Because his immediate needs can be met, even Locke (the outdoorsman) can socialize with the others, though this is a matter of preference or temperament; if Sawyer shuns the company of the others on the beach, that does nobody any harm. And because each can look after himself, there is no need to plan for more than the time being, and no need for any of them to make any sacrifice for a common purpose, for instance in making an effort to get off the island.

This condition of minimal bodily security corresponds to the core of what Locke (the philosopher) had in mind in talking about a state of nature. There is no constituted government; all humans are equal and independent (second *Treatise*, §4); and everyone has the right not

---

[5] The label is due to Garrett Hardin; see his 'The Tragedy of the Commons," *Science* 162 (1968), pp. 1243–1248. Situations of similar sorts have been envisaged ever since Plato; see *Protagoras*, 321C–323C.

only not to be harmed "in his life, health, liberty or possessions" (§6), but also to take and use the things they find around them so long as there is "enough and as good" left for the others (§27).

## The Longer Haul

While the survivors of Flight 815 have been lucky in the climate and the availability of food and drink, there are several categories of goods that, like, for instance, clothing, they don't have the means or skill to make for themselves, but that, unlike clothing, are in short supply. One case here would be Sawyer's cigarettes. If he is the only smoker, then the fact that he cannot renew his supply is a problem only for him (apart from Charlie, who also has a problem getting his drugs). Likewise with Shannon's toenail varnish: no one else wants a pedicure ("1st Pilot"), so her using it causes no one else any upset (apart from the irritation factor for Boone).

Things are a bit different when it comes to medicine. We have here the making of a tragedy of the commons that the survivors are not in a position to resolve.

In the first days on the beach, Jack takes it for granted that he is authorized to use all the antibiotics he can find on the plane to treat Marshal Mars. Here, he must be supposing that their stay on the island is temporary and that the immediate use of the drugs is the only reasonable course of action to try and save a life. If, however, he had thought that they were going to be stranded indefinitely, it is not clear that using up what there is in trying (and failing) to heal one severely injured man would be the best line to take in the long run. After all, the drugs could be of more benefit to more people if spread over more, and more curable, cases. As Sawyer says, Jack may not be "looking at the Big Picture, Doc" ("Tabula Rasa"). We can keep that problem of medical ethics on hold, while allowing that Jack did well to go through the luggage of the other passengers and take all the stuff ending in "-myacin" and "-cillin" ("2nd Pilot"). That is, even if the antibiotics count as the common property of all the survivors, because only Jack knows how to use them, he should be given control of them for the benefit of those who need them.

Unlike her varnish, Shannon is not the only one who lays a claim to her anti-asthma inhalers. Her claim is twofold. One, that she (or rather Boone on her behalf) brought the refills with her; presumably, she paid for them and thus has what we might call a legal property right to them. Two, that her health depends on them; she is the only asthmatic on the island and thus has what we might call a moral priority in their proper use. The trouble arises from Sawyer's having taken some of the contents of Boone's suitcase, such as his copy of *Watership Down* ("Moth"). If the luggage of those who died can be rifled for clothes and for antibiotics without injustice (when Kate takes the walking shoes off the corpse to make the expedition to find the plane's cockpit in "1st Pilot," she isn't *stealing*), why not also that of the survivors? Isn't it all just luggage and so fair game?

When Jack confronts him, Sawyer brazens it out saying that, on the beach, "possession is nine tenths," meaning "of the law," where the law is "finders keepers" ("Confidence Man"). And this explains why he brushes off Jack's accusation of "looting" the fuselage in "Tabula Rasa." Though he doesn't say what the other tenth of the law is, Sawyer is standing up for the idea that, in a state of nature, it's every man for himself, a clear instance of his Trust No. 1 attitude. As Hobbes puts it, "if any two men desire the same thing, which nevertheless they cannot both enjoy, they become enemies" (*Leviathan*, p. 87). This means that the past property relation that Shannon enjoyed towards the inhalers is nullified by the new circumstances. Her legal right no longer counts because there is no constituted authority (like the police or law courts) to enforce it; and Sawyer is not obliged to recognize her moral claim, any more than in "1st Pilot" Hurley is *obliged* to give an extra portion of food to Claire because she is eating for two (though he does so out of Innocence).

Faced with Sawyer's refusal to "do the right thing" (and assuming, rightly or wrongly, that he has the inhalers), Sayid and Jack take it upon themselves to defend Shannon's cause by capturing and torturing Sawyer ("Confidence Man"). In so doing, they are beginning to move away from the Lockean state of nature towards a position in which legal and moral claims can be enforced and the use of violence (an infringement of the right not to be harmed in one's health) can be justified. Jack and Sayid are not acting in *self*-defense, but are seeking to defend the rights of others, which is a different concept altogether: that of punishment. In doing so, they are on the way to constituting what Locke calls "a civil society" (*Treatise*, §§77ff.) – of sorts.

## Over or Under the Language Barrier

Neither Sayid nor Jack is stronger than Sawyer, but together and using stealth (they attack him while he is napping) they can get the better of him. This is what Hobbes calls the "equality of ability": "the weakest has strength enough to kill the strongest, either by secret machination, or by confederacy with others" (*Leviathan*, p. 87). The association between Sayid and Jack requires them to trust each other for the purposes of getting information out of Sawyer about where the inhalers are hidden.

There are two obvious conditions for their being able to reach such an agreement. One is that they already agree on Shannon's claim – legal or moral or both – to the inhalers. And the other is that they understand each other, that they share a language. This is also a condition for their being able to get information out of Sawyer: Sayid would be a useless torturer if he couldn't put the questions and get the answers. The fact that the overwhelming majority of the passengers on Flight 815 are speakers of English, as a first or second language, means both that they can share information and that they can lie to each other.

Jin is the exception: he can communicate only with Sun. As soon as they arrive on the island, Jin reaffirms their previous asymmetrical relationship (marriage), with him giving the orders and her taking them, because, at that point, he believes that she is not in a position to talk to the others ("1st Pilot"). The pair keeps a distance from the wreckage, so Jin is the first to seek food from the sea. There are two possible interpretations of what he does after filleting the strange orange creature he has fished out of the water ("2nd Pilot").

On one interpretation, rather than try the food himself, Jin seeks guinea pigs for their edibility. On this account, he doesn't care what happens to them because they are not a part of any association that he recognizes as binding on him. Jin would thus be applying Trust No. 1. Even though Hurley tends towards the accepting attitude of Innocence, he declines the offer not just because he prefers airline snacks – or even hunger – to "natural" food, but also perhaps because he's not sure of Jin's motives.

On the other interpretation – taking into account the fishing community he comes from – Jin can be understood as trying to overcome

185

the language barrier by making a move that is universally recognized as a peace overture. Indeed, the offer of food convinces Claire of Jin's inclination towards Innocence.

## Confidence and the Con Men

Even if a shared language is *necessary* for generating the higher grades of trust and cooperation, it is not *sufficient*.

On the one hand, we might think about the suspicions got up by Walt's discovery in "2nd Pilot" of the handcuffs in the jungle. The cuffs mean there is at least one person on the island who was regarded as a criminal and who, therefore, might still be dangerous. When, later in the same episode, Sawyer accuses Sayid of being a terrorist, he backs it up with the allegation that Sayid was sitting with his arms covered at the back of Business Class and never moved out of his seat. The others present at the scene can't tell whether Sawyer really saw what he says he did, but they are given some reason for thinking that it was Sayid who was wearing the handcuffs. What they don't know – but we do – is that Sawyer is a professional liar and, as we have already seen, motivated by Trust No. 1.

On the other hand, there is Marshal Mars's warning to Jack that he should not trust Kate ("Tabula Rasa"). Jack can be pretty sure that a man – and a US marshal at that – on his deathbed will be speaking the truth; but he still does not heed his words. We can distinguish two aspects of this. One is that he trusts his own feelings more than Mars's information. For sure, Jack recognizes that he doesn't know whatever it is that the Marshal knows about Kate's past, but he doesn't want to think the worse of a person who has so far behaved with fortitude and in the interests of all (not only in helping him sew up his own wound on their first meeting ("1st Pilot"), but in dismantling and distributing the parts of the pistol, making a monopoly on its use impossible for any one individual ("2nd Pilot")). The other point – and this is a crucial feature of a situation in which people don't have background knowledge of one another – is that it is the "island of second chances." As far as Jack is concerned, Kate is free to wipe the slate clean: there is a presumption of Innocence. In "Tabula Rasa," he repeatedly says things like "it doesn't matter who we were" and "it's none of our business."

We might pick up a hint of uncertainty here about the relations between "before" and "after" the crash. If, in addition to her moral claim in virtue of being asthmatic, Jack defends Shannon's property right as a leftover from the society from which the survivors have been isolated, he seems not to think that Kate's criminal record has any value without the criminal system that keeps it.

## Roles and Rules

What Jack himself undoubtedly carries over from his life before the downing of 815 is the fact of being a medical doctor. Equally obviously, he doesn't carry with him his degree certificates, and there is no authority on the island to license his practice of the Hippocratic art. By contrast, Arzt asks the others to address him as "Doctor," though he is in reality a schoolteacher. (The apparent title may be regarded as no more than a nickname understandable to someone who knows a bit of German.) It is the fact that Jack has acquired skills that makes him a doctor and, so, as Sawyer ironically puts it, "a hero" ("2nd Pilot") or, in Boone's challenge, "our savior" ("White Rabbit").

As we saw with the antibiotics, Jack's expertise confers rights; but it also carries with it the duties of a doctor and it is up to him more than to anyone else to do what he can for the injured. When Sawyer fails to put Mars out of his misery with his one bullet ("Tabula Rasa"), Jack must act, as he had refused to act before, and put an end to his patient. In this case, his role as doctor means that he must break the rules that apply off the island and save Mars from an agonizing death that could not otherwise be avoided with the resources available. Another nice dilemma for the medical ethicists, but a clear case of the special responsibility of doctors to decide.

Though the previous occupations of most of those on the island have little bearing on how they interact, the crash itself produces a category to which they all belong: that of "survivor." As Hurley says in "2nd Pilot," "we're all in this together." To get a bit clearer who "we" are, he sets himself to compile his census, trying to find out from each of them where they come from and what they were doing on the flight. When he and Boone compare the resulting list with the flight manifest, they discover that the man who calls himself Ethan Rom was not on 815. This is clear confirmation that the island is not as deserted as it at first seemed, and means that the 46 who have been trying to get to know each other now face a potential external threat: there's an "us" and a "them," the Others.

The immediate effect of this discovery is to bind the survivors together, and Locke (the outdoorsman), who had previously stuck to his motto "you can't tell me what I can't do" (first announced in "Walkabout"), now becomes a defender of the group's integrity, organizing a search party to rescue Claire from the man who has abducted her and who is now definitely not one of us. Here, his knowledge of the jungle gives him the right to give orders to his comrades. As Locke (the philosopher) puts it, the survivors determine to "act as one body" (§96). This is the moment at which we witness the birth of what can properly be called a "commonwealth" (§§122ff.), in which, by the consent of its members, roles can be established and rules can be laid down for the good of all those included.

## Tit-for-Tat

So far, we have been running a counterpoint between the causes of conflict in a state of nature and the means of its resolution. I want to conclude by illustrating briefly a general ground for thinking that it is the condition of initial conflict that really matters to how a state of nature turns out.

Take any situation in which two people can either cooperate with each other or not in some enterprise, and suppose (1) that, if they each cooperate with the other, then they will both get the optimum result; (2) that, if they both refuse to cooperate, they will go without the full benefit but are not much worse off; and (3) that, if one cooperates and the other doesn't, the non-cooperator gets a less than optimum result, but still better than if they had both refused, and the cooperator gets the worst outcome.

This sort of situation is easily illustrated, for instance in Sandra Bullock's 2002 film *Murder by Numbers*, by the case of two suspects in a crime, to each of whom the police offer a deal so long as he is the only one to denounce the other, though the police don't have evidence enough to convict either unless at least one suspect sings. For this reason, the choice between cooperating or not is called a "prisoners' dilemma." It's worth stressing both that the "cooperating" is as between the suspects (that is, not squealing), not a matter of their helping the police; and that there is no limit to the number of players who can be involved in such situations – even 46, as on the island.

What makes the prisoners' dilemma a dilemma is that the suspects don't know for sure what the other one has done or is going to do. While Trust No. 1 would indicate non-cooperation to avoid the worst case for me (that in which I cooperate and the other doesn't), Innocence would go for cooperation out of fellow feeling at the risk of coming off worst. But neither option is particularly convincing as it stands, and it would be crazy to rely on some theory of "human nature" to decide what to do if you might go without the basics of survival or go to jail for twenty years rather than walk free. The craziness is most obvious when the dilemma is repeated more than once and involves the same people over again. In that case, the thing to do is consider what the other did last time and act accordingly.

What does *accordingly* mean here? Well, there is a strategy that has been shown to do better than any other over the long run and that has been called "tit-for-tat," which, as its name suggests, says that you begin by offering cooperation and, after that, you should do whatever the other did last time round: if she didn't cooperate, you shouldn't; if she did, you should too. If she, too, is running tit-for-tat then, given that you both begin by cooperating, you should both continue getting optimum results.

## Gaining Trust from the Past

The reason why I didn't want to attribute Trust No. 1 to Hobbes is that I think that chapter 13 of *Leviathan* – the one from which I've been quoting – envisages a situation in which a previous society has fallen apart by violence (for instance, the plague of *28 Days Later* or a civil war), and the first move everyone makes is to withdraw co-operation. In this sense, a Hobbesian state of nature begins at the second round of a repeated prisoners' dilemma. Because the first round was non-cooperative, it is not a winning strategy for people to start cooperating.

For this reason, I suggest that everything in *Leviathan* that comes after chapter 13 – with all the famous stuff about natural laws, social contracts, sovereign "leviathans" and the rest – is wildly misleading:

once you're in a Hobbesian state of nature, you're a goner. Hobbes might have half-seen the problem, which is why, at the end of chapter 14, he puts in the idea of an "oath," sworn before God to reinforce the contract (*Leviathan*, pp. 99–100). But this is no solution at all; among other things, why should God be so bothered about having his name taken in vain, when there's so much other mayhem in the state of nature and all the other Commandments (except perhaps the one about graven images) have been broken? Though I know that this is not a popular interpretation of the book, it might explain why virtually no one can be bothered to read all the remaining 400 pages of text.

With the same people in it and with the same tendencies to diffidence or to trust as in a Hobbesian state of nature (second round), a Lockean state of nature has to begin with a first round of tit-for-tat and can only explain a breakdown of cooperation by the unreasonableness of some of the people some of the time. If the difference between Hobbes and Locke on the state of nature can be seen in the light of the point reached in a repeated prisoners' dilemma, then the relations among the survivors in *Lost* can be understood in terms of how closely their behavior is modeled on tit-for-tat.

In short, if the survivors can begin trusting each other, they can reasonably adopt more successful strategies than those that might be based on some merely suppositious theory of human nature, whether Innocence or Trust No. 1. By doing so, they can get a community off the ground so as to handle the shortages of some goods (tragedies of the commons) and to coordinate the security of all (Lockean on the inside and Hobbesian towards the outside) against the Others and whatever else is out there.

# PART IV

## T IS FOR TRANSFORMATION

# 16

# The Tao of John Locke

## *Shai Biderman and William J. Devlin*

### "Two players, two sides. One is light, one is dark"

*Lost* is an appropriate title for the series for several reasons. From the opening episode, we find that the characters themselves are lost – they don't know where they are, they don't know why exactly they are where they are, and they don't know where they're going. Furthermore, as we are introduced to over a dozen characters on the island, we find that they aren't simply lost while being on the island. Whether we are learning about Jack's relationship with his father, Sayid's confrontation with torture, Charlie's drug addiction, Claire's dilemma over single motherhood, Ana Lucia's struggle with revenge, or Desmond's fight for love, the flashbacks into the characters' earlier lives tell us that they were lost before they even arrived on the island. We the audience share this "lost anxiety" as we are left confused and baffled after each episode. Each episode reveals new information that leaves us with new questions: Why are there so many "happenstance" encounters between the passengers prior to the crash, and what does it mean? What is the significance of the numbers? Who are the Others? Why are they obsessed with children? The task of getting answers to these questions is a demanding process and becomes all the more frustrating when, like Desmond sailing west away from the island, we find ourselves moving in circles.

The main characters in the series are lost. That is, the characters feel a bit out of place – they are unaware of where they're going or where they should be; they may not understand what is going on. In short, they are lost insofar as there is a lack of complete order: whether it's Jack getting lost on the island, or Sun discovering that her wedding ring is lost, there is something that disorganizes one's systematic order. Prior to the crash of Oceanic Flight 815, the survivors are lost as they struggle with making sense of their lives. After the crash, of course, they all continue to find themselves lost in a further sense, as they are not where they are supposed to be.

When we are "found," the sense of order and coherency is restored. This order and coherency applies to the survivors, not only in the sense of being rescued, but also in the deeper sense of finding meaning in their lives. The survivors are confused in their personal lives, and so seek to "be found" insofar as they want order and coherency, and understanding of their personal lives. Among all the survivors, it is John Locke who stands out as someone who wants to move from "being lost" to "being found." He helps Jack to deal with his role as leader, Charlie to overcome addiction, Michael to be a good father, etc. In short, Locke is the central figure who uses philosophy to make sense of what is going on and help others. He seeks explanations to help him understand their situation so that he can restore the picture of coherency and order that is currently disorganized. As Charlie puts it, "if there was one person on this island that I would put my absolute faith in to save us all, it would be John Locke."

Given Locke's use of philosophy to understand the events on the island, it's no wonder that Locke is named after a philosopher – John Locke (1632–1704). Locke's relation to this philosopher may suggest that his philosophy towards explaining and understanding his presence on the island, how to survive, how to be found, is rooted in Lockean philosophy. However, we will show in this chapter that as the character John Locke engages the problem of being lost on the island, his philosophical approach widens to include the Lockean empirical tradition on the one hand, and the eastern spiritual tradition of Taoism on the other. Ultimately, Locke undergoes a transformation where he becomes both a man of science and a man of faith. Let's see what this combination entails as we look at Locke's journey towards being found.

## "I'm good at putting bits and pieces together"

As with the other characters, at first we know nothing about "Mr. Locke." But we are slowly introduced to his character through his behavior and mannerisms early in the first season. The survivors get their first real introduction to Locke in "Walkabout." When the survivors run out of food from the plane and a mild panic sets in at the camp, Locke takes the initiative to hunt the wild boars on the island. With his suitcase full of hunting knives, he explains to his fellow survivors that the boars they saw were piglets and lays out a plan to capture one by distracting the mother. This suggests that Locke is someone who has an expertise in dealing with the wild and survival. Our first impressions of Locke thus tell us that he is someone who knows his way around nature – he can hunt, he can track, he can create items with materials from nature, etc.

At the same time, we can see that Locke has a close relation to his philosophical twin, the philosopher John Locke, a relation that is deeper than name only. The philosopher John Locke maintained that at birth, the human mind is empty – it is a sheet of "white paper, void of all characters, without any ideas" and without any furnishings. That is, at birth, the human mind is a *tabula rasa*, or a "blank slate" or an empty mind. The human being initially has no inherent ideas, whether it is the idea of God, the idea that $2 + 2 = 4$, or anything else. But if we are born without any ideas or concepts, where do we get them: how does our mind "come to be furnished"? The answer, for Locke, is experience – the mind begins to accumulate ideas and concepts through our interactions with the world around us. How we come to know and understand the world is thus through our perceptions. Meanwhile, other methods, such as intuition or divine revelation, are not suitable sources for deriving knowledge and understanding of the world. We call this philosophical position, that knowledge and understanding are derived primarily through experience, sensations, and perceptions, *empiricism*.[1]

The scientific method is essentially an empirical method, because it uses observation and sensations to explain phenomena, or the world

---

[1]  See John Locke, *An Essay Concerning Human Understanding* (London: Penguin, 1997), Book II.

around us. This can be seen through the steps of the scientific method, where the scientist observes and describes phenomena in the world, formulates a hypothesis to explain the phenomena, uses that hypothesis to predict the behavior of the phenomena, and tests the hypothesis through the use of experiments. Scientists thus come to understand and explain the world by formulating and testing scientific hypotheses through observation and experience.

Locke's process of explaining and understanding the world around him employs the scientific and empirical method. His know-how for using knives, hunting, tracking, hiking, and even predicting the weather, are all forms of knowledge that are derivative from experience. Locke's overall depth of knowledge in these fields comes through empirical observation and action, and the scientific rules of hypothesis, testing, and deduction. For instance, he demonstrates the scientific method when hunting the boars, since he begins with a series of observations and descriptions (of the boars' size) and hypotheses (mother boars remain close to their piglets; a boar's method of attack is to attack from behind), to deduce a plan of action (distracting the mother boar, and flanking a piglet). Locke, Michael, and Kate perform an experiment that tests this method, as they try to capture a boar. Even though this experiment fails, we can see that, like the scientist, John Locke, the castaway, adopts Lockean empiricism. Thus, whether he is hunting boars, tracking fellow castaways, or discovering the cave for shelter, Locke's emphasis on observing nature and testing hypotheses to learn about the island through his perceptual experiences employs the scientific and empirical method.

## "This is destiny. This is my destiny"

As consistent as Locke may be in utilizing the Lockean empirical methods of scientific investigation, one should remember that his life on the island began with a phenomenon most foreign to science: a miracle. After the crash, Locke, who had been in a wheelchair for the past four years, wakens to find that he now has full control of his legs and feet. We find that Locke doesn't try to (or is unable to successfully) explain this occurrence through empirical methods. One of the reasons why Locke dismisses the Lockean method of explanation for such an event is because this method, as the scientific method, addresses *how* something occurred. That is, scientific explanation reveals the mechanism behind the events that occur, allowing us to understand the causal steps that led to the event. But the scientific method can never tell us *why* something occurred – it doesn't explain the *purpose* or *meaning* of the event. So, when Locke discovers that his legs are now healed, he is not concerned with how this recuperation came to be, but he is concerned with why it came to be. Thus, he confides to Walt his "secret" that a "miracle happened on the island" ("2nd Pilot").

In order to understand this miracle, as well as other miracles (such as their miraculous survival of the plane crash), Locke utilizes another method of explanation, which he begins to use in "White Rabbit." When Locke encourages Jack to become the leader of the camp, Jack reveals that he has been seeing someone who's "not there." Locke's initial explanation follows Jack's medical (and so empirical) analysis: it is "a hallucination. The result of dehydration, posttraumatic stress, not getting more than two hours of sleep a night for the past week – all the above." But Locke provides another method for explaining this hallucination, as well as for other strange occurrences on the island:

> I'm an ordinary man, Jack. Meat and potatoes. I live in the real world. I'm not a big believer in . . . magic. But this place is different. It's special. The others don't want to talk about it because it scares them. But we all know it, and we all feel it. Is your White Rabbit a hallucination? Probably. But what if everything that happened here happened for a reason? What if this person that you're chasing is really here? ("White Rabbit")

Though Locke is a "meat and potatoes" guy who "lives in the real world" and so adopts the scientific method, he entertains the possibility that there are "special" powers, which are noticeable on the island. Whether it is Jack's hallucination or Locke's physical recovery, these phenomena cannot be fully explained by science. It may be the case that one should refer to a different method – one that allows for miracles, special powers, and occurrences which are meant to be – to provide a full and adequate explanation of such phenomena that occurs on the island. Locke is the one to provide this method, as he tells Jack: "I've looked into the eye of this island, and what I saw . . . was beautiful."

197

Locke's new method to explain the phenomena on the island follows the eastern philosophy of Taoism. This religious and philosophical view, which stems from Lao Tzu's *Tao Te Ching*, holds that there is a special force, or power, in nature called the "Tao," which can be understood by looking at it in three ways. First, the Tao is said to be that which is "unnamable" – "The Tao that is named is not the real Tao."[2] Here, the Tao is something intangible insofar as it is beyond names and conceptual distinctions. The Tao is the origination of all things, both natural and "super-natural." As the unnamable, we may have seen the Tao represented by the "Yin-Yang" symbol – a circular symbol that unites one light side (the Yang) and one dark side (the Yin). The Yang represents specific attributes of the universe, such as light, activity, and the masculine, while the Yin represents the polar opposite of the Yang, darkness, passivity, and the feminine. Even though these two sides are said to be opposites, the Yin-Yang symbol presents them as being complementary. Neither side can exist without the other. The two are interdependent and so not only need one another, but exist within one another. This interdependence captures the holistic aspect of the Tao, as what may appear to be opposites, or logically contradictory to one another, is united by the Tao.

It is interesting to note that the dichotomy (but interrelationship) between black and white in the Yin-Yang symbol is also prominent as a visual element in *Lost*. For instance, we see that the backgammon pieces and Sawyer's glasses embody the duality of black and white. Even in Claire's dream, Locke appears with one eye black and one eye white, signifying not only that this dichotomy is in Locke's eyes, but also that Locke sees the world through such a complementary disjunction.

Second, the Tao is understood to be the "Way" of nature. When we see that the world is made up of many different objects, we can notice that these objects are dynamic – they are moving, they are changing, they are interacting with one another, etc. According to Taoism, all objects in nature follow the Tao as the path, so that nature flows in the direction of the Tao. This claim that nature is flowing with the Tao thus enables the Taoist to explain *why* events in nature occur.

---

[2]  See Lao Tzu, *The Tao Te Ching*, trans. J. C. H. Wu (Boston: Shambhala Publications, 1991), chapter 1.

Since the direction of the dynamic motions of nature is following the Tao, the Tao serves as the purpose to the events that occur.

Finally, the Tao is understood as the proper direction for human beings. When we confront the world – facing challenges, events, decisions, and questions – we should apply the holistic picture of the Tao to help understand what we should do. Once we realize that nature flows with the Tao, and that the Tao helps to explain why events unfolded they way they did, we can then use this understanding to direct ourselves. That is, Taoism maintains that we should follow the flow of nature, as it is following the Tao. Our lives, then, too, should also follow the path of the Tao.

When Locke looks into the "eye of the island" and sees its beauty, Locke takes the first step in becoming aware of the Tao. He recognizes a beauty that he cannot explain – something that is inexpressible – in the island. That is, he becomes aware of the Tao as the "unnamable." This awareness allows Locke to begin to shift his method of explaining the events that occur on the island. Everything that occurs on the island – all the events of nature – follow the Way of the Tao. Locke accordingly begins to suppose that "everything that happened here happened for a reason." From Locke's miracle, to their survival of the crash, to the splitting and reuniting of the two tribes (as well as uniting the two parts of the Dharma Initiative film), to the various "hallucinations" and dreams of the castaways – everything that occurs on the island is happening for a reason. That is, there is a reason *why* these events have unfolded the way they've unfolded. For Locke, the explanation lies in the "Way" of the island. As he tells Jack, "Do you really think all this is an accident? That we, a group of strangers, survived, merely with superficial injuries? Do you think we crashed on this place by coincidence? Especially this place? We were brought here! For a purpose! For a reason! All of us! *Each one of us was brought here for a reason*" ("Exodus: Part Two"). For Locke, what brought everyone here is "the island," or the Tao.

Locke's appeal to the Tao as a way of explaining what occurs on the island, and his application of this understanding as a guide for how human beings should act, can be seen in his sage-like advice to his fellow castaways. Locke uses a moth that must break out of its cocoon on its own as an analogy to Charlie overcoming his addiction to heroine ("The Moth"). Here, the moth's struggle of becoming free and surviving in nature is an example of nature following the Tao. Locke – who sees that it is best for human beings to follow the Tao – believes that Charlie should struggle to free himself using his own will power. Likewise, when Locke teaches Walt how to throw knives, he advises him to picture the knife hitting the mark in "his mind's eye" where he can "visualize the path" ("Special"). Here, Locke is helping Walt to see where the knife should be – its proper place as a result of its proper path and motion – in order to succeed. Such picturing is a process of seeing and following the path of the Tao. Furthermore, when Sun loses her wedding ring and is frantic about finding it, Locke explains how he found what he was looking for: "By finding it the way everything gets found . . . I stopped looking" (". . . And Found"). Aware of the flow of the Tao, Locke has realized that he should not struggle *against* it. Instead, he allows nature and the Tao to take their course, and, as one follows this flow, what was once lost will be found.

In short, Locke is one who follows the Tao, and finds Taoism as a way to understand *why* the events in both nature and human beings occur the way they do. Locke has a growing *faith* in the Tao as he is on the island, and uses that faith to understand his "destiny" and the destiny of those around him.

## Man of Science, Man of Faith

In addition to the implicit Taoism we have just traced, the show makes an explicit allusion to eastern philosophy with the Dharma Initiative. Dharma is a concept in Hinduism and Buddhism which can be understood as the cosmic "law of nature" or "reality" which one should follow to free oneself from the chains of reincarnation.

Locke's eastern consciousness slowly develops throughout the first season of *Lost*. While we are given indications of Locke's transformation early in the season, a single event proves that Locke is not just using Taoism along with the scientific method, but that the scientific method is giving way to Taoism for Locke. This event is the discovery of the hatch ("All the Best Cowboys Have Daddy Issues").

When Locke and Boone discover the hatch, their top priority is to figure out how to open it. Boone becomes skeptical of Locke's "obsession," reminding Locke that their role in the tribe is to hunt boars. Locke, however, dismisses this role, a role that, as we saw, was a solid indication of Locke's appeal to the Lockean-empirical method: "There's plenty of fruit and fish to go around . . . What we're doing here is far more important . . . Right now, this is our priority." Locke is thus beginning to change priorities from a role that has an empirical basis to a role that has a spiritual basis. The reality of the island forces him to confront and acknowledge the limits of science, so that he turns to the Taoist method to complete his understanding of what is really going on. The hatch is Locke's "calling," as it were: "We didn't find this by accident. We're supposed to."

Guided by the spiritual power of the island, Locke redirects his attention to opening the hatch. To accomplish this new challenge, however, he returns to what he knows best, the scientific method of trial and error. As if an "engineer," he constructs a trebuchet, with the hope that it will provide enough force to break the glass of the hatch. Like a true empiricist, when this experiment fails, he suggests to Boone that they should "build another one . . . and hope it works this time." But the Lockean approach to determining how to open the hatch only goes so far. When Boone questions what will happen if the next experiment fails, Locke turns to the Taoist approach and the appeal to the powers of the island: "the island will tell us what to do . . . The island will send us a sign." Locke thus turns to the spiritual method for explaining and understanding their role of opening the hatch. Their discovery of the hatch is explained by the power of the Tao that is most obvious to Locke on the island. Locke and Boone were meant to find and open the hatch since the Tao was directing them towards this role. Likewise, when they initially fail to open the hatch, Locke doesn't appeal to scientific reasons for their failure; rather, their failure and their future direction is still explained by the Taoist approach: "All that's happening now is our faith is being tested – our commitment. But we will open it. The island will show us how."

Just as Locke's advice to Charlie, Walt, and Sun is successful in producing the desired results, so too Locke's decision to "ask for a sign" from the island is fruitful as he has "a dream [that] was the most real thing he's ever experienced" that lets him "know where to go now." The dream points him to find the Beechcraft 18 that crashed years ago on the island. This triggers a sequence of events – the discovery of the plane, the death of Boone, the revelation of the hatch to Sayid and Jack – which ultimately ends with the explosive destruction of the hatch. In short, from Locke's appeal to the Taoist method of listening to and following the path of the Tao, Locke is able to fulfill what he was meant to do.

Locke's adoption of the Taoist method over the Lockean method, and so his full transformation, is completed when Locke realizes what is in the hatch. Through the chaotic events surrounding meeting Desmond, Locke learns that the purpose of the bunker sealed by the hatch is to type a specific series of numbers into a computer every 108 minutes to prevent "the end of the world" from occurring. Locke decides that, even when Desmond leaves, the numbers still need to be entered. He employs the scientific method to explain and understand *how* he is to succeed in "entering the numbers" properly as he follows the rules of "executing" the numbers at the appropriate time, which is indicated by the movement of a flip card timer and the sound of an alarm. He will know that he is successful when the timer returns to 108. But while the scientific method is employed to determine how to succeed, the question of *how* to do it is secondary to *why* Locke is pushing the button. The "why" question is the ultimate question for Locke, and it is answered by the Taoist method. Locke comes to understand that this is not only the purpose of the hatch, but it is *his* purpose. It is his destiny to make sure that the numbers are entered on time. That is, he follows the Way of the Tao by entering the numbers: all prior events in Locke's life on the island – events that are guided by the Tao – have led him to this point, and so he was meant to be here making sure the numbers are entered.

Locke thus completes his transformation by completing the leap of faith to the Tao. This completion of the leap is made clear as Locke discusses the number-entering with Jack. Locke encourages Jack to make that leap of faith and believe that they were brought here to enter the numbers. While Jack is skeptical and accuses Locke of falling into faith too easily, Locke protests that it has not been easy. Locke has slowly moved from a strict "man of science" to a man who includes its opposite and contradictory aspect, the "man of faith." As he explains to Jack, "That's why we sometimes don't see eye to eye, you and me. You're a man of science and I'm a man of faith" ("Orientation"). While Locke can understand Jack's scientific approach to understanding the world around him, since Locke does utilize the empirical method to explain *how* things occur on the island, Locke has made a "leap of faith" and so now is transforming his approach to understanding by using the Taoist method of explaining *why* things occur the way they do through his leap of faith in the Way of the Tao.

## "I was looking for something . . . it found me"

Locke's transformation to include the spiritual Taoist method of explaining and understanding the world around him, as well as his own life, is a transformation that completes him. Locke acknowledges this transformation as he tells Boone, "this island . . . it changed me. It made me whole" ("Deus Ex Machina"). Locke is now someone who not only adopts the Taoist method, but also uses this method to understand that he is someone who employs *both* the Taoist and Lockean methods to help him answer the questions of why and how things occur the way they do. This understanding is rooted in the Taoist picture of the universe, as the Taoist method and Lockean methods, like the Yin and Yang, appear to be direct opposites, but are ultimately complementary and interdependent. Furthermore, through his own spiritual and empirical journey on the island, Locke is no longer lost. The completion of his journey is made clear as Locke gives his compass to Sayid, telling him that he doesn't "need it anymore" ("Hearts and Minds"). That is, empirically, Locke no longer has a need for this "scientific instrument" because he knows *how* to move around the island – he has found the direction he needs. He doesn't need the compass anymore, as he now knows who he is, where he should be, and *why* he is going where he is going. In short, through both the Taoist and Lockean methods, Locke is now found.

# 17

# Of Moths and Men:
# Paths of Redemption on the
# Island of Second Chances[1]

## Brett Chandler Patterson

During the broadcast of the first season of ABC's television show *Lost*, viewers offered all sorts of speculation about what kind of place the mysterious island represented. One theory presented in *TV Guide*, on the internet, and elsewhere was that the island symbolized purgatory, the place of purification described in the teachings of Catholic Christianity. The *Catechism of the Catholic Church* identifies purgatory as that place where the elect who are "imperfectly purified" must undergo a form of cleansing "so as to achieve the holiness necessary to enter the joy of Heaven."[2] For Catholics, this purification is not something that can be earned, but comes through the grace of God in Christ. Yet there needs to be a point when sins can be confessed and penance can be worked out.[3] Those who enter

---

[1] I wrote the first draft of this essay, with its current title, in the summer of 2006 before the start of season three. I found validation in my allusion to John Steinbeck's *Of Mice and Men* in the third season episode "Every Man for Himself," when Ben (Henry) and Sawyer have a quoting match from the novel.

[2] Part One, Section Two, Chapter Three, Article 12, III: "The Final Purification, or Purgatory." www.vatican.va/archive/eng0015/__p2n.htm.

[3] Catholics further make a distinction between serious sins, mortal sins (which are outright rebellion against God – for they are about serious matters, done with full knowledge and without coercion), and lesser sins, venial sins (which hold us back from full communion with God). Those entering purgatory have unconfessed venial sins; once

purgatory are destined to heaven, but need to be cleansed before entering into the presence of God. As more of *Lost* unfolded and as rumors spread that the writers had denied such theories, it became more obvious that the show was not such a direct allegory. But what was it about the first-season episodes that would have suggested such a theory to begin with? The episodes consistently show characters who have failed in numerous ways in the past attempting to make a better life for themselves on the island; they feel that they have a second chance, that they, in certain ways, can "make up for" their pasts. The *Lost* writing team has shaped conversations among characters, musical cues, and the structure of most episodes around images of "redemption." One of the show's central writers, Carleton Cuse, has even voiced that *Lost* is "all about redemption."[4] These are the elements that suggested purgatory to Catholic viewers, but redemption is a concept that is larger than just this Catholic doctrine. It is a central tenant in Christian theology, whether Catholic, Orthodox, or Protestant; Christian theology draws from its Jewish origins in stating that humanity has fallen away from God and our intended roles in the world. The Jewish sacrificial system provided, after confession of sin, a second chance because the priest had made reparation for the sin. Christian theology then rooted salvation in the ministry, sacrificial death, and resurrection of Jesus Christ. As Christians receive forgiveness from God in the Christian community, they find transformation and new life. Salvation is a journey, where we grow in ways to prevent the same mistakes we made in the past; echoes of (and direct references to) this process appear in several episodes of *Lost*. In philosophical terms, we are in the realm of metaphysics and may be able to suggest some things about the nature of human existence in general. So, finally, what does *Lost* tell us about failure and redemption? How might we interpret Cuse's cryptic, yet enticing, statement?

---

sins are confessed and the person purified, that person enters heaven. On the other side, according to Catholic doctrine, those dying with unconfessed mortal sins head to punishment in hell.

4   Cuse offers this thematic analysis in his commentary on "The 23rd Psalm" on the second season DVD set (Buena Vista Home Entertainment, 2006) and suggests it again in season three's "Lost: The Answers."

### "I once was lost . . ."[5]

If we examine the structure of most of the episodes, we see that the writers juxtapose images from the past (of a particular character) with images of the present struggle on the island. Each episode highlights a character's life: the story from the past most often revolves around failure and loss while the story in the present represents a new, yet familiar struggle that offers the character a "second chance." This style of narration, rare in television, though often appearing in modern and postmodern novels, raises a series of interesting questions about identity, memory, time, faith, and redemption. Who are we? Does our past still claim us? How do present, past, and future shape us? Is life a cruel joke, blind chance, or an ongoing plan with a benevolent purpose? Can we find redemption, new success, when we are haunted by past failures?

All these questions find urgency in an environment that requires these characters to fight for their survival against each other, against the creatures on the island, and against the eerily inscrutable "Others." Pulled out of a technologically oriented society and placed in the midst of the wild, these characters find that their decisions have more immediate life-and-death consequences. As Desmond observes to Jack in "Orientation," in a little while he is going to be "either very right or very wrong." The environment magnifies their choices. It becomes that much more necessary to try to get to the bottom of crucial existential questions, from which we in society often let ourselves be distracted. The setting forces characters to commit to something; they must place their faith in something. The placement of faith is never easy; it always involves a struggle. But in the struggles to find faith, many characters encounter certain crucial moments, in their lives on the island, that become revelatory. A character's particular experience, typically in the heart of the island's jungle, opens up new possibilities, even as new questions also arise.

Frequently, throughout the episodes, we see characters, though, reminding each other that they are not alone. The suggestion is that if

---

[5] The sentence in the hymn "Amazing Grace" runs "I once was lost, but now am found." See John Newton, "Amazing Grace," in *The Baptist Hymnal* (Nashville: Convention Press, 1991), #330.

the characters are to find healing in this hostile environment, it is in becoming a member of the new community of the survivors of Oceanic Flight 815; in season three's "Lost: The Answers," Damon Lindelof stated that characters are most noble when they are acting in the interests of the community. Characters frequently talk about starting afresh, having a "clean slate." For the community that is forming, in many ways (though there are some notable exceptions), it does not really matter what lives the survivors had before they crashed on the island. However, for the viewers and the individual characters, it does matter what happened before. All characters seem to be haunted by past failures that motivate them to make sure that "things won't turn out that way again." They seek a second chance, and in choosing differently they hope to taste of redemption.

Thus, *Lost* gives us a portrait that includes past failures, existential questions, individual searches for faith, revelatory experiences, and the possibilities of communal redemption. Since philosophy and theology have been preoccupied with these questions over the centuries in different forms, we should not be surprised to see *Lost* as the object of this current study. Two important twentieth-century moral philosophers, in particular, will help to illumine our study of *Lost*. H. Richard Niebuhr offers an extensive study of faith, revelation, redemption, and community, while Emmanuel Levinas provides an emphasis on responsibility in our encounters with "others" and a suggestion of the importance of community.

## *Tabula Rasa*? The Flashbacks, or the Past Is Not So Easily Forgotten

Episodes of *Lost* on the whole follow a consistent pattern: one member of the large cast is highlighted in a series of flashbacks that are interspersed through an ongoing story about the survivors' struggle on the island. As we put the pieces together, the better episodes show distinct connections between the past and the present. We typically see images of past failures that affect how a character is interacting with new challenges on the island. Thus, in the first episodes, Kate's past running from a US marshal is juxtaposed against the present challenge of handling the marshal's death; Locke's past struggle against a company supervisor and a walkabout guide

207

who put parameters on what he could do runs against Locke's leading of the hunt for a boar; Jack's past perfectionism, his inability to let go, contrasts with his failure to save a drowning woman and his quest to find the vision of his dad in the jungle.

The pattern continues as we learn about the past mistakes of other characters: Charlie's struggle with his brother Liam as they both succumbed to the temptations of being a rock star and his feeling sorry for having betrayed Lucy to feed his drug habit; Sawyer's deep-seated hatred toward the confidence man who took advantage of his parents and toward himself for adopting the same lifestyle and for killing the wrong man; Sayid's regret that he allowed himself to be transformed into a torturer and that he cannot get away from that identity despite vows to the contrary; Claire's struggle to be a single mother and her guilt over contemplating giving the child up for adoption; Jack's remorse over holding his father accountable and for letting his marriage fall apart; Boone's feeling of guilt for being attracted to Shannon and for allowing her to take advantage of him; Shannon's search for self-worth when her stepmother disowns her and cuts her off from her inheritance; Michael's ongoing lament that he allowed Susan to coerce him into giving up custody of Walt; Sun's regret at how her father's influence infected her marriage to Jin and how she sought solace in an adulterous relationship; Jin's struggle to be a man of integrity as he seeks to advance himself socially (involving himself in violence and intimidation at Sun's father's request) for the sake of his wife; Hurley's feelings of insecurity manifested in the curse of the numbers and in the legacy of the lottery and in the tragic accident of the balcony that fell and in his hallucinations of Dave; Locke's regret that he was taken in by a father who tricked him out of a kidney and that his obsession with his father spelled the ruin of his relationship with Helen; Ana Lucia's fear of being a victim again; Kate's lament that she became estranged from her mother when she killed her abusive "stepfather" (who was really her biological father) and lament that her actions led to the death of her friend and high-school sweetheart Tom; Eko's search to be a priest to honor his brother Yemi's sacrifice; Bernard and Rose's separate struggles over her terminal disease; and Desmond's search to reclaim his dignity after a dishonorable discharge from the Royal Scots Regiment and the apparent loss of his love Penny.

It is a list that lengthens with each new episode. The flashbacks drive home to the viewers at least two major points: that the past haunts each of these characters and that they each hunger for a second chance, some more obviously than others. It is ironic that in "Tabula Rasa" Jack so adamantly argues to Kate that it does not matter what happened before their time on the island because they all essentially "died" in the plane crash and should each be given a chance to start over. In one sense they are given new chances in the new environment and will find new roles in the new community, but they do not exactly have "clean slates." Melodramatic baggage weighs down all of them, but most characters are not lost in their pasts; they are actively seeking a new start on the island. We might even say that they are trying to atone for past failures. What is it about the island, though, that might suggest such possibilities at a new start? How does the island create a scenario where these characters would confront their pasts and move on to a new way of life?

## "Guys, where are we?" The Questions

The setting or atmosphere of *Lost* is crucial; we could not have the show without it. This is more than just saying that without the island all the passengers would have drowned in the ocean – it is more than saying that a survivor plot requires an island. There is something about this particular island that demands that the survivors face some basic questions about the nature of human existence. (It is this questioning that has made *Lost* an excellent resource for the essays in the book in your very hands.) The situation on the island raises metaphysical problems, queries into the nature of reality itself: Why are we here? Where are we? Who are we? Where have we been? Where are we going? *Lost* heightens all these questions by ripping the characters out of their routines and placing them in a situation where there are no easily accessible answers to (and no advertisement jingles to distract us from) those questions. As Sawyer tells Jack, "I'm in the wild!" ("Tabula Rasa").[6] And as Charlie

---

[6]  Readers of Joseph Conrad will draw parallels to "Outpost of Progress" and *Heart of Darkness*. The show itself has made several allusions to the latter. Of course, there are further parallels to William Golding's *Lord of the Flies*, which is another conscious source for allusions.

intones for all the characters, at the end of the first episode: "Guys, where are we?" ("2nd Pilot").

The episodes revolve around how quickly each of the characters is adjusting to the situation on the island. Some characters, of course, adjust more quickly than others. Characters like Locke, Rose, and Walt have come to prefer life on the island, but a number of others, particularly those involved in the raft project in season one and those in the march to the radio tower in season three, are preoccupied with escaping the island and returning to civilization. The first major dispute between Jack and Kate centers on this issue (when Jack suggests that the community set up home in the newly discovered caves) ("House of the Rising Sun"). But they all question whether they will be rescued and whether they should form a new community on the island. In a crucial conversation between Locke and Michael over Walt's activities, Locke argues that as long as they are on the island then Walt should be allowed to reach his potential; Michael adamantly resists Locke's suggestion ("Special"). There is an ongoing struggle with each of the characters to discover what the new community is and what their roles within in it are going to be. By the end of "Tabula Rasa" the characters dramatically must face the issue of identifying who is the "fugitive" who was handcuffed on the plane and whether that former title holds any weight in their new situation. It is just one of a number of examples showing that characters, at varying speeds, acknowledge that life on the island is different.

The presence of the inscrutable and antagonistic Others also furthers the questions. How do we live in the midst of a world where there are other people whom we do not understand? How do we survive when the plans of others undermine, or directly challenge, our own survival? What are our rights and responsibilities in these encounters? These tensions clearly appear in season three when Juliet comes to live with the plane-crash survivors; no one knows where her loyalties lie ("One of Us"). Although the survivors themselves are a multicultural microcosm, embodying multiple conflicts of their own (from Sawyer and Sayid's first brawl onward), the threat of the Others magnifies questions about how we form and understand our identities in relation and opposition to other people. This important galvanizing effect appears in Locke's first-season reminder, when the community is turning on Jin, who the group's true enemies are. The overall story also dramatizes the misunderstandings and often-incoherent fears that we place upon those we do not understand. This is perhaps no more starkly illustrated than in the second-season scene where Jin and Eko study each other, each thinking that the other is one of "them" ("The Other 48 Days").

Above all, though, characters discover that one of the most significant parts to adjusting and finding at least a temporary home on the island comes in facing a central question, that they each confront in their own ways: Is there a purpose to their struggles on the island? Is God or fate somehow directing the events of their lives? Or is this just the way life is, according to our choices and to random chance? Are we masters of our lives or not? Several characters contemplate this question, but the meditation reaches its most extensive treatment in the relationship between Jack Shepard and John Locke. Carleton Cuse and Damon Lindelof, the two dominant writers for the series, have revealed that they based this relationship at least partially on their own relationship: Cuse is a Catholic who emphasizes taking a leap of faith and Lindelof is a Jew who grounds his understanding of reality in empiricist philosophy.[7] On first look, Jack, "the man of science," emphasizes that there is no such thing as fate, that we all stand or fall based upon our choices, and John, "the man of faith," emphasizes that there is a greater purpose, a plan that shapes their lives. However, on second look, as Lindelof and Cuse prompt us, Jack at times is a "man of faith" and Locke becomes more of an empiricist in his crisis of faith.[8] The duality is what interests them as writers, and it is what interests many viewers. Both Jack and John, and the other surviving passengers sharing the island, come back to these questions at crucial points in the story.[9] Though we get tentative answers along the way, the questions always remain.

---

7  "The Best of 2005," *Entertainment Weekly* (January 6, 2006).

8  Lindelof's and Cuse's commentary on "Man of Science, Man of Faith" on the second season DVD set.

9  Season three's finale, "Through the Looking Glass," presents another crucial confrontation between John and Jack, over whether they should trust Naomi and try to get off the island; the apparent flash-forwards in this episode suggest that Jack's life completely falls apart when he does leave the island. Jack never trusted in the island; in these scenes he now apparently sees this as a mistake and wants to find a way back to the island. We have yet to learn John's fate, but it is most likely that he never does leave the island.

## "It has never been easy": The Struggle to Faith

The conflict between Jack and John reaches an important climax early in season two: while arguing over whether they should continue Desmond's practice of entering the numbers every 108 minutes, John asks why Jack has such a difficult time believing that this is what they are supposed to do. Jack returns the question, asking John why it is so easy for him to believe. John's final comment is that it has never been easy. Viewers know that faith has never been easy for John; in this very episode, flashbacks tell us of a past time when John struggled with Helen's request that he take a leap of faith ("Orientation"). Observant viewers will also remember the notable first-season episode "The Moth," which portrays Charlie's wrestling with his drug addiction. John, who has already found his own revelatory moment about life on the island, seeks to test Charlie. Holding on to Charlie's heroin, John gives Charlie an ultimatum: he will give Charlie three chances, if Charlie requests the drugs three times, then he will give them to Charlie. Upon the second request, John turns Charlie's attention to the silk cocoon of a moth. John, opening his pocketknife, tells Charlie that he could open the cocoon to help the moth escape, but that it would not be strong enough to survive. It is the digging, the work that enables the moth to survive. Charlie must fight against his addiction to regain faith in himself, in his place in the new community of survivors, and in the ultimate meaning of his life. John has orchestrated events so that Charlie can have his "cocoon" to work through to the other side, to emerge the beautiful moth. But the struggle is not easy, and Charlie, as we see in season two, does fall back; he has not fully emerged. The struggle is ongoing, up to his "sacrificial death" at the end of season three.

The metaphor applies not only to Charlie's quest, but it also seems to apply to each character on the island. Guilt over past failures and the existential questioning brought about by the struggle to survive meet in each character's search to find faith in themselves, faith in others, and faith in the fundamental purpose of life. Rose, who along with Eko offers a Christian spin on "faith," says to Charlie, "there is a fine line between denial and faith" ("Whatever the Case May Be"). The moral philosopher and theologian H. Richard Niebuhr reminds us that we all fundamentally place our faith in something that gives life meaning, something that keeps us going on. We all have some center of value that helps us to organize our lives. But we must overcome suspicion and "broken faith" in our lives in our ongoing journey of faith.[10] We have all experienced or contributed to promises broken and trusts violated. From the Christian perspective Niebuhr represents, we live in a state of alienation from God, from each other, and from the world around us; we are free "to become faithless, an adulterer, a corrupt politician, a traitor." Treason is the opposite of fidelity, and its presence undermines our ability to claim trust and loyalty (FE 49). But we also live with our past failures and are highly suspicious that we could ever be trustworthy or that we could ever trust others. Thus, "treason begets distrust, distrust treason" (FE 81). The characters on *Lost*, as they discover experiences on the island that recall their pasts and suggest possible supernatural forces, must consistently engage whether they are going to live a life of trust or a life of suspicion. (Ana Lucia, who admits that she has "trust issues," is one of the more blatant examples of a life of suspicion.) What might be the difference between these two paths? We see the difference most clearly when characters have a mystical experience in the heart of the island.

## "I have looked into the eye of this island and what I saw was beautiful": Revelation and Faith

H. Richard Niebuhr also reminds us that faith often is rooted in revelation. Though some readers may find difficulty relating to the explicit Christian language of Niebuhr's discussion, I do think that it is appropriate to bring Christian concepts into conversation with the vision within *Lost*, because a number of characters make reference to Christianity and because one of the central writers, Carleton Cuse, has argued that his Catholic Christian faith has shaped his influence on the show.[11] Also, Niebuhr offers some suggestions that the categories of faith and revelation may also say some things about human

---

[10]  H. Richard Niebuhr, *Faith on Earth* (New Haven, CT: Yale University Press, 1989), ps. 48–51. Hereafter abbreviated as FE.

[11]  Cuse has expressed that he hopes that he can accomplish in the show what C. S. Lewis achieved in *The Chronicles of Narnia* (*Entertainment Weekly*, January 6, 2006).

existence in general. In *The Meaning of Revelation*, Niebuhr argues that revelation provides the context for understanding our experiences: revelation becomes the interpretive key that illumines our understanding of the rest of our lives, our history.[12] Certain principles guide our minds, and it is revelation that makes possible such understanding of order and meaning in personal history. Revelation makes the past intelligible, allowing us to appropriate what previously seemed strange to us and to remember what we have tried to forget. Particularly for Christians, revelation demands that we confess our sins (MR 80–84). Revelation in Jesus Christ's call of "Father" should mark the radical reconstruction of our knowledge of duty. Through Christ, we see our lack of unity, and the oneness of the Triune God demands our singleness of mind and purity of heart. The image of a powerful God manifested in the weakness of Christ revamps our notions of power and politics and humbles us in the face of our religious pretensions. God's love transforms our understandings of what is valuable. The revelation of Jesus Christ calls us to conversion and permanent revolution (MR 132–139).

For Niebuhr, revelation is also ongoing, for the reconstruction that it enables is not something easily accomplished, but is instead a permanent revolutionary orientation that involves a lifetime of participation in the Christian community (MR 86). Because there are failures in the application of it, revelation must be subject to "progressive validation." Revelation is moving, not static, for God continues to reveal Godself: revelation's "meaning is realized only by being brought to bear upon the interpretation and reconstruction of every new human situation in an enduring movement, a single drama of divine and human action." Niebuhr reminds us that the "revelation of God is not a possession but an event, which happens over and over again when we remember the illuminating center of our history." At no point in history will this project be complete; the Christian heart is engaged in a "never-ending pilgrim's progress" (MR 97–100).

The Christian vision within *Lost* particularly arises when discussing the central figures of faith in the series: Rose, Eko, Desmond, and John Locke. Rose and Eko make overt references to having faith

---

[12]  H. Richard Niebuhr, *The Meaning of Revelation* (New York: Collier Books, 1960), p. 68. Hereafter abbreviated as MR.

that God is directing their lives on the island. Rose prays for healing for Charlie, and Eko carves scripture references into his staff/ stick, baptizes (however unorthodoxly) Claire and Aaron, recites (an imperfect) 23rd Psalm over the burning plane wreckage, and starts to build a church before feeling led to take John's place as pusher of the hatch button. Revelatory moments for these characters largely have already occurred by the time they arrive on the island, but the longing for her husband and his quest for the plane and his brother's body do offer moments for the ongoing revelation that Niebuhr describes.

Desmond has had direct contact with the Christian community in a Catholic monastic form (as we see in "Catch 22"), but he also under-goes a revelatory moment at the end of season two. He feels that he has found his "purpose" in laying down his life for the others, by turning the failsafe key, but his survival and apparent ability to receive visions of the future present new possibilities in season three. Desmond at this point resembles a first-season John Locke, offer-ing guidance to members of the community, particularly Charlie. Desmond has been affected by a revelatory encounter with the island and has been gifted, in a similar way as the healing of Rose and John, but in a bizarre way that adds to the questions about the nature of the island.

Locke, though, offers a more ambiguous connection to this Christian concept of revelation, suggesting that the writers them-selves may be thinking more in terms of pantheism or transcend-entalism or a New Age perspective, influenced by Native American spirituality (as referenced by the sweat lodge) – but even here, under Cuse's influence, we see in a flashback in "Further Instructions" that Locke has at least tried a Christian worldview.[13] Locke does find "beauty" by looking into the "eye" of the island. Locke grounds the revelatory experience in the island: "This place is different." He believes that the other survivors are not willing to talk about the changes brought by the island because they are scared with the possibilities. The most significant area where Locke could represent a theological commitment, as Carleton Cuse has hinted, is in his

---

[13] In the flashbacks revealing his involvement in a commune, Locke offers up a very Christian prayer of thanksgiving. One might speculate that now with Eko's exit from the show Cuse might focus more of his Christian themes through Locke.

insistent commitment to the notion that everything happens for a reason. Revelation grounds faith that our existence contributes to an overall benevolent purpose. It is this message which makes Locke a priest of sorts to a number of others on the island: he guides Jack in "White Rabbit," challenges Charlie in "The Moth," tests Boone in "Hearts and Minds," confronts Michael over Walt in "Special," calls Shannon to a new start and reorients the entire community that is mistakenly punishing Jin in "In Translation," quietly helps Claire with motherhood in "Numbers," diverts Sayid's anger in "The Greater Good," and promotes the community's entrance into the hatch in "Exodus" and the assumption of the hatch duties in "Orientation." Locke more than any other character embodies the transformative power of revelation; thus, it is that much more important when he has his crises of faith: in season one, surrounding Boone's death, and in season two, following the discovery of the Pearl hatch. Even Locke, though, is not without setbacks, as we see in season three in his encouraging of Sawyer's killing instinct ("The Brig"), contributing to the devolution of Sawyer's character, who earlier had made quite a bit of progress in becoming part of the community under Hurley's tutelage ("Left Behind"). Locke still is struggling on his journey as well, as we see in his third-season destructiveness and in his wrestling with Ben and company. Revelation-inspired transformation is an ongoing process.

## "Live together, die alone": Faith, Community, and Redemption

Finally, *Lost* shows us that once characters have faced their past failures, asked the crucial existential questions, engaged the struggle to faith, and found some revelatory experience on the island, they may find "redemption." But this opportunity for a new start, for a second chance, arrives primarily in becoming a part of the community of survivors. The story reminds us that our identities largely arise in our relationships with those around us. The survivors on the island define themselves according to a common experience, those who have survived a plane crash and who must continue to fight to survive on an island of numerous dangers. The moral philosopher Emmanuel Levinas reminds us in *Totality and Infinity* of the primacy of relationship; we do not live as discrete individuals, but as beings in relationship to "others." When we encounter another face to face, we are bound to the other in a relationship of responsibility.[14] In *Otherwise Than Being*, Levinas argues that we understand ourselves only in transcending ourselves in encounters with others. These encounters occur through the use of language and through the proximities of our bodies. We find ourselves in situations that we did not create, in connection with other beings; we have a responsibility toward those others.[15]

H. Richard Niebuhr, once again, also calls us to see revelation as a social event, rooted in relationships rather than ideas. Revelation is composed of persons, not concepts; knowledge runs between people: "we cannot know here save as we are known." Thus, overall, the Christian life consists of becoming a person in relationship with Jesus Christ and his followers, rather than solely in accepting certain laws and beliefs (MR 105–108). Revelation alone does not accomplish conversion; there must also be a reasoning heart, a participating self, no longer oriented around itself (MR 88–90). Niebuhr further reminds us that our identities arise in communities, that our "knowledge" of the world is always in dialogue with the "knowledge" of those around us. All of our knowledge fundamentally rests upon the trust we place in certain persons within that social setting. We seldom seek to verify the language we inherit from our society and are not usually aware of our language's effect on our knowledge until we are challenged by another set of beliefs. In addition, knowledge from direct experience can move toward certainty when it is "verified" by observations from others, particularly those with social authority (FE 35–37). Not only do we have individual memories, but we also have communal memories. Faith is communal.

Niebuhr argues that faith, one of the most crucial categories for understanding human existence, expresses itself in social situations in two movements: as trust and as loyalty. Here Niebuhr argues that all "believing" (*fides*) depends upon the interaction of "trust" (*fiducia*)

---

[14] Emmanuel Levinas, *Totality and Infinity* (Pittsburgh: Duquesne University Press, 2002).

[15] Emmanuel Levinas, *Otherwise Than Being* (Pittsburgh: Duquesne University Press, 2002).

and "loyalty" (*fidelitas*): "On the one hand, it is trust in that which gives value to the self; on the other hand it is loyalty to what the self values."[16] Trust and loyalty reveal reciprocal movements between people, and since human beings have the freedom to be suspicious and disloyal, many relationships are distorted or broken (FE 48–51). Human knowledge is fundamentally based upon relationships of trust and loyalty, because we usually come to believe something because of tradition, authority, self-evidence, persuasion, or reasoning – all of which depend upon having faith in some source as the foundation for our believing (FE 33). Then, we express our knowledge in remaining loyal to that foundation, which is most often socially constructed. Not all groups are "communities," but only those that are grounded in faith commitments (FE 55–58).

The survivors of Flight 815 do seem in many ways to be such a community, though trust is a difficult thing for a number of the survivors. Suspicion or broken faith guide many of the characters, but the search for redemption is also a search for community. That is why the single most dangerous or pernicious communal sin is deception. Sun asks Shannon whether they are being punished on the island for lies that they have kept ("Exodus"). It is why the accusation that John is not telling the truth, that he is holding something back, is so damaging that he seeks to reveal his secrets first to Sayid, then to Jack and the others. It is why the "villains" on *Lost* are almost always involved in deception and lies. Lies are counter to the truth, to revelation, because they propagate suspicion, leaving no room for loyalty to the community. Thus, it is no accident that Ana Lucia, who has trust issues, is responsible for the death of Shannon, that "Henry Gale" provides such a masterful nemesis in season two, that Sawyer poses such a threat in stealing the guns, and Michael, the betrayer, kills Ana Lucia and Libby.

But those who find faith are community-builders. Locke, who at first seems to be an outsider, leads a number of them through their struggles, allowing them to become part of the developing community. Jack becomes their early leader, in many ways because his profession of physician is clearly oriented around the community. He

---

16  H. Richard Niebuhr, *Radical Monotheism and Western Culture* (Louisville, KY: Westminster/John Knox Press, 1970), p. 16.

struggles with this calling, but assumes the mantle adeptly when he argues to the community that they cannot function on "every man for himself," that they need to organize to survive. If they cannot "live together," then they will "die alone" ("White Rabbit"). Hurley builds a golf course to help the community relieve the tension that they are perpetually under as survivors. One of the many scenes revealing the nature of the new community is the send-off at the end of season one for Walt, Michael, Jin, and Sawyer; the raft and the bottle of letters carry the hopes of the entire community, and the four on the raft are the community's representatives. The community develops with the ongoing story, and each survivor represents a different level of commitment to it. Not everyone warmly embraces the community. Sawyer, Charlie, and Michael obviously, to different degrees, rebel against it, but they too long for the community, even as they betray it. (Think of Ben's assessment of Sawyer at the end of "Every Man for Himself." In quoting from *Of Mice and Men*, he argues that Sawyer too needs companionship.[17] Charlie struggles with his place in season two, but there is a suggestion that he has healed that brokenness by the end of that season. We are still waiting to see how Michael will fully handle his betrayal of Hurley, Jack, Sawyer, and Kate.)

Their betrayals heighten their alienation and do nothing to alleviate the pasts that haunt them. The characters who seem the most content and well adjusted appear to have found peace on the island and in the new community. This is not to say that there are no disagreements in the community – there will always be differences – but it is to say that the members seek to work these problems out for their mutual survival. Survivors learn more about themselves, and "atone" for their pasts, as they serve their new community.

The island on *Lost* distinctly challenges the "worldviews" and the sense of "identity" of the various characters; they find themselves in new relationships, with new responsibilities and new challenges. They all come with baggage, with memories of past failures. The selection of passengers is a multicultural mix, a microcosm of the

---

17  Ben quotes, "A guy goes nuts if he ain't got nobody. It don't make no difference who the guy is, long as he's with you. I tell you, I tell you a guy gets too lonely and he gets sick." Sawyer is the one who has the most difficulty finding redemption in terms of community, as described in the last section of this essay, but even he longs for it.

world; and the encounters among them bring both violence and healing. Not everyone embraces responsibility and community; not everyone has faith in a good order. Many of the most notable of *Lost* episodes do show characters who find new realization in their new community. They have faced the existential questions; they have wrestled with faith and found new reasons for it in their revelatory encounters on the island; and they have started to develop into a community where they can trust one another in their struggle to survive. Jews and Christians should see parallels to their respective concepts of redemption, and just about everyone should be able to relate to the stories of failure and the longing for second chances. The characters on *Lost* are pushing out of their cocoons – we have yet to see whether they will be able to emerge vibrant and redeemed moths on the other side.

# 18

# Everything Happens for a Reason

## *David Werther*

### No Rhyme, No Reason?

John Locke – the guy with the shiny head who likes to play with knives, not the philosopher (1632–1704) – believes "everything happens for a reason."[1] So when he considers the fact that he has survived a plane crash and regained the use of his legs, Locke concludes he has a destiny to fulfill.

---

[1]  There are two key episodes in the first season. In "White Rabbit" Locke says: "I'm an ordinary man Jack, meat and potatoes, I live in the real world. I'm not a big believer in magic. But this place is different. It's special. The others don't want to talk about it because it scares them. But we all know it. We all feel it. Is your white rabbit a hallucination? Probably. But what if everything that happened here, happened for a reason? What if this person that you're chasing is really here?" Addressing Jack in "Exodus III" Locke states: "Me, well, I'm a man of faith. Do you really think all this is an accident that we, a group of strangers survived, many of us with just superficial injuries? Do you think we crashed on this place by coincidence . . . especially, this place? We were brought here for a purpose, for a reason, all of us. Each one of us was brought here for a reason."

In the second season, Locke has a crisis of faith and in "?", addressing Eko, he says: "I was never meant to do anything. Every single second of my pathetic little life is as useless as that button! You think it's important? You think it's necessary? It's nothing. It's nothing! It's meaningless! And who are you to tell me that it's not?" However, in the third season in "I Do," Locke's faith is at least partially restored. In response to Sayid's question, "So, you think that this Monster decided that Eko was meant to die?" Locke replies, "I believe that Eko died for a reason. I just don't know what it is yet." And, in the final episode of the third season, "Through the Looking Glass," Locke implies that Jack is not supposed to leave the island.

Some of Locke's companions see things differently. Kate believes that "some things just happen, no rhyme, no reason" ("The Moth"). There may be no deeper meaning to a plane crash than that a certain combination of physical forces happened to come together. Jack, "the man of science" ("Exodus: Part III"), might be inclined to agree with her. After all, he calls the cave-in "a fluke" ("The Moth").

Among the survivors who would agree with Locke, that their circumstances are somehow directed or purposeful, there is no agreement as to how to explain that direction or purpose. Rose, a Christian of considerable faith, would no doubt look to God's sovereignty. Claire, who consults a psychic and looks to astrology, may suppose that the stars are calling the shots. If the word on his band-aids is any indication, Charlie, at least initially, is ready to attribute the accident to fate, an explanation that pops up on more than one occasion.

## Could Hurley Have Lost the Lottery?

Our initial glance at the beliefs of the survivors raises at least three important questions:

1  Does everything happen for a reason?
2  If everything happens for a reason, are our lives purposefully directed?
3  If our lives are somehow purposefully directed, who or what is responsible for the direction?

We can begin to address these questions by looking at the various ways philosophers have understood Locke's phrase "everything happens for a reason." Philosophers call this phrase the *principle of sufficient reason* and have offered different versions of it. Here are three:

1  "There can be no fact real or existing, no statement true, unless there be a sufficient reason, why it should be so and not otherwise" (G. W. Leibniz, 1646–1716).[2]

---

[2]  G. W. Leibniz, *Monadology* 32 in *Discourse on Metaphysics: Correspondence with Arnauld, Monadology*, trans. George Montgomery (La Salle, IL: Open Court, 1902), p. 258.

2  "For everything that exists there is a reason for its existence either due to the causal efficacy of other beings or due to the necessity of its own nature."[3]

3  For everything that exists there is a reason for its existence *if* its existence is due to the causal efficacy of other beings or due to the necessity of its own nature.

The first version of the principle of sufficient reason is the strongest. It requires that there be an explanation for every fact, including, for example, Charlie's decision to stay in DriveShaft, Hurley's winning the lottery, and Jack's tattoo. The phrase "and not otherwise" requires that this explanation rule out alternative possibilities: Charlie's leaving the band, Jack's lacking a tattoo, and Hurley's losing the lottery.

The principle of sufficient reason doesn't just apply to things like Jack's tattoo, the DriveShaft saga, and Hurley's departure from Mr. Cluck's Chicken Shack. It also applies to the universe itself. Why does the universe exist? According to the first and second versions of the principle, since the universe need not have existed, the reason for its existence must lie in something outside of it. And that something must exist by its very nature; it must be something whose nonexistence is an impossibility. By contrast, the third version allows for the possibility that something exists for which there is no explanation. Philosophers call a fact like this, for which there is no explanation, a *brute fact*.

## Fatalism and Flukes

Suppose that the existence of our universe is not a fluke, as it might be, given the third version of the principle of sufficient reason. Instead, let's allow that its existence is, as in the first version, due to an action that "should be so and not otherwise." Since this action comes from something that must exist, and alternative actions are ruled out, it follows that our universe must exist. In short, given that

---

[3]  This principle comes from Charles Taliaferro's list of principles of explanation that have been used in cosmological arguments. See *Contemporary Philosophy of Religion* (Oxford: Blackwell, 1998), p. 355.

every fact is such that it "should be so and not otherwise," everything is a matter of necessity.

To say that everything is a matter of necessity, is to say that nothing could have been other than it is. Charlie could not have failed to be a heroin addict, Sawyer (the obnoxious beachcomber, not the friend of Huckleberry) could not have failed to be a con man, the numbers on the hatch could not have differed by a single digit, and likewise for absolutely *everything* that ever happens. Philosophers call this view *fatalism*.

What are we to make of the implied message on Charlie's band-aids, "FATE"?

Is it true that everything is a matter of necessity? Let's begin by thinking about it in terms of Claire's confidence in astrology, Sayid's Moslem background, and Rose's Christianity. If Claire is correct, our lives follow the configurations of the stars. If Sayid takes a typical Moslem approach, then our lives are determined by God.[4] Presumably for Rose, and most Christians, God knows the future and whatever God knows must come to pass.

One might think that so long as one of these perspectives is correct (astrology or divine power or divine foreknowledge), fatalism is true: all that happens is a matter of necessity. This, however, is not so. Even if we allow that what happens to Claire, or anyone else, is determined by configurations of the heavenly bodies, we cannot rightly conclude that there must have been a world that includes a pregnant Claire, a heroin-addicted Charlie, and the like. There is no reason to think that the stars had to exist, and good reason to think that they might not have. And, if the stars need not have existed, then insofar as events occur because they are dictated by the stars, these events need not have happened either.

---

[4] "Orthodox Islam teaches the absolute predestination of both good and evil, that all our thoughts, words and deeds, whether good or evil, were foreseen, foreordained, determined and decreed from all eternity, and that everything that happens takes place according to what was written for it. There was great discussion among early Muslim theologians as to free will and predestination, but the free-will (*al-qadariyya*) were ultimately defeated . . . The favorite solution is a doctrine of *iktisab*, according to which, though each individual action is foreordained, the individual 'acquires' it by identifying himself with it in action and so becomes responsible." Arthur Jeffery, ed., *Islam: Muhammad and His Religion* (New York: Liberal Arts Press, 1958), pp. 147–148.

Suppose that, in keeping with the Moslem perspective, God determines all that happens. If so, then we must attribute the plane crash
and the subsequent survival to God's all-powerful will. But, even if
this were true, the crash and survival would not be a matter of necessity. Only if God's will were itself a matter of necessity, so that it
would have been impossible for God to do other than will the crash
and survival, would these things have had to occur. However, there
is nothing about the Moslem belief that requires God's will to be a
matter of necessity. Thus, attributing all that happens to God's will
does not result in fatalism.

Furthermore, what goes for God's power, goes for God's knowledge. Suppose that, in keeping with Christianity and other
traditional theistic views, God has foreknowledge. Since God is all-
knowing, if God knows that Rose and Bernard will be reunited after
the plane splits apart, then that's what will happen. However, just as
we cannot infer "God could not have willed other than X" from
"God wills X," so we cannot infer "God could not have foreknown
other than X" from "God foreknows X."

There remains at least one more consideration in favor of fatalism
and that is the first version of the principle of sufficient reason by
itself. Given this view, "God wills X" is equivalent to "God could not
have willed other than X" and "God foreknows X" is equivalent to
"God could not have foreknown other than X." And, if God's existence
is a matter of necessity, then so are all of God's beliefs and actions.

If then, God, as an all-knowing being, believes that I am now
typing this sentence, then I could not have done otherwise. Given this
implication of the first version of the principle of sufficient reason,
insofar as I think that I could have decided instead to take a walk,
then I have good reasons for thinking that the first version of the
principle of sufficient reason is false. And, in fact, I have excellent
reasons for thinking that I could have done otherwise a moment ago.
For, apart from such truths as "I now exist," nothing seems more
plainly true to me than the fact that I might have chosen to do any
number of other things. It is then eminently reasonable for me to
reject the first version of the principle of sufficient reason. If you
disagree, keep in mind that one of the implications of your view is
that you could not have done otherwise. Also, remember that considerations that might seem to point to fatalism (astrology, God's
power, and God's will) in fact do not.

*David Werther*

# The *Black Rock*

In contrast to the first version of the principle of sufficient reason, according to the third version there might be no explanation whatsoever for something's existence. If the first version is unacceptable because it does not allow for a brute fact, the third is unacceptable because it allows existence to be a brute fact. To see why the third version of the principle of sufficient reason is unacceptable, let's think about the good ship *Black Rock*, a ship that is aground a mile or so inland. Hurley's question to Rousseau – the mother of Alex and alleged husband-killer, not the author of *Emile* (1712–1778) – "How exactly does something like this happen?" is appropriate if we suppose that there must be some explanation for the whereabouts of the *Black Rock*, and indeed for its very existence. The assumption that there is an explanation for the ship's existence has far-reaching philosophical implications. We can see this by adapting a passage from Richard Taylor to suit our *Lost* scenario:

> Consider again the [ship *Black Rock*] that we imagine we have found in the forest. Now, we can hardly doubt that there must be an explanation for the existence of such a thing, though we may have no notion what that explanation is. . . . If we in our imagination annihilate the forest, leaving only [the *Black Rock* and the ground it sits on] our conviction that [it does not exist by its own nature] and owes its existence to something else is not reduced in the least. If we now imagine [the ground the *Black Rock* sits on] to be annihilated, and in fact everything else as well to vanish into nothingness, leaving only [the *Black Rock*] to constitute the entire physical universe, then we cannot for a moment suppose that its existence has thereby been explained, or the need for any explanation eliminated, or that its existence is suddenly rendered self-explanatory. If we now carry this thought one step further and suppose that no other reality ever has existed or ever will exist, that [the *Black Rock*] constitutes the entire physical universe, then we must still insist on there being some reason independent of itself why it should exist . . . it matters not at all what the thing in question is, whether it be large and complex . . . or whether it be something small, simple, and insignificant, such as a ball, a bacterium, or the merest grain of sand. . . . And it would, in any event, seem quite plainly absurd to say that if the world were composed entirely of . . . [the *Black Rock*] then it would be contingent and there would have to be some explanation other than itself why such a thing exists, but that, since the actual world is vastly

more complex than this, there is no need for an explanation of its existence, independent of itself.[5]

The moral of this story is that the universe owes its existence to a being that must exist.

## A Con?

If Sawyer were on the scene, he would no doubt respond with skepticism. As a con man, he would be especially suspicious of an apparently simple argument with such a significant conclusion. And he would be good at identifying unjustified assumptions. In this case, he might rightly note that the Taylor argument supposes that the explanation for the existence of the universe must come from outside the universe and he might challenge that:

> Look man, I can explain the existence of the universe without going outside it. The universe is just a big collection of things: planets, people, polar bears, particles, and all the other stuff that smart people like our man Jack talk about. If I tell you why each of these things exists, I've told you why the universe exists. I can't tell you exactly why every itty-bitty thing exists but I know that my existence depends upon oxygen and water for starters. I owe my existence to other things; they owe their existence to other things and on and on. Hell, it's all tied together; it's a kinda cosmic support group.

Sawyer's folksy logic might appear, initially, to make sense, but we can illustrate the inadequacy of this cosmic-support suggestion with a pay-off scenario, modeled after an example from Richard Purtill.[6] Suppose Sawyer grabs Jones by the collar, throws him up against the wall, and asks, "Do you have my ten grand?" Between gasps for breath, Jones assures Sawyer that Brown has the ten grand and Jones will get it from Brown. And so Jones puts a gun to Brown's head and demands the money. Brown, sweating profusely and muttering profanities, convinces Jones that he can get the ten grand from Black and

---

[5] Richard Taylor, *Metaphysics*, 3rd edn. (Englewood Cliffs, NJ: Prentice-Hall, 1983), pp. 93–94.

[6] See Taliaferro, pp. 358–359.

makes his request with a blade to Black's jugular. And so it goes, and goes, and goes, and . . . Question: Will Sawyer ever see his ten grand? Answer: No. No matter how many people are threatened to pay up we never come to an individual who has the ten grand.

If the relevance of the pay-off scenario is not yet apparent, these remarks from Richard Purtill should help to clarify the matter:

> Now take any existing thing. It received its existence from some other thing or things, which in turn received its or their existence from other things and so on. . . . If the process of everything getting its existence from something else went on to infinity, then the thing in question would never come into existence. [In terms of the analogy, Sawyer would never receive the ten grand.] And if the thing in question has come into existence then the process hasn't gone on to infinity. There was something that had existence without having to receive it from something else.[7]

If the pay-off scenario did not satisfy Sawyer's skepticism, he might challenge the principle of sufficient reason itself and demand a proof of it. Why accept "For everything that exists, there is a reason for its existence, either due to the causal efficacy of other beings or due to the necessity of its own nature" unless it can be proven? In response, note that we could argue in favor of this principle only if we could appeal to claims more obviously true than the principle, itself – that could be offered as evidence in favor of its truth. But there don't seem to be any candidates for such claims, as the second version of the principle of sufficient reason appears to be a foundational or bedrock principle. Leibniz, while wrongly endorsing the first version of the principle, rightly noted that the principle of sufficient reason is one of the two great principles (the other being the law of non-contradiction) upon which all of our reasoning is based.[8] And, as Aristotle (384–322 BCE) noted, if our reasoning must be based upon a principle, proving the principle is an impossibility.[9] The moral to draw from this is not that this unproven principle is somehow suspect, but rather that those who ask for a proof are confused.

---

[7]  Taliaferro, p. 359.
[8]  Leibniz, *Monadology*, 31–32, p. 258.
[9]  Aristotle, *Metaphysics* 1006a.

## John Locke's Destiny

Suppose that the second version of the principle of sufficient reason is true. If so, then, given the fact that the universe exists but does not exist by its very nature, its existence depends upon a necessarily existing being. Since such a being cannot cease to exist, it must have whatever qualities are required to rule out its death. If this being were not perfectly good, it might commit suicide; if it lacked perfect power and the perfect knowledge needed to apply that power, then it might be destroyed by some other being. It follows that this being is, by its very nature, perfectly good, powerful, and knowledgeable.[10]

A perfectly good being might well wish to restore Locke's ability to walk and, with perfect power, could do so. Such a being could do so directly or through the agency of other persons and things subject to its sovereignty. With this in mind, let's return to our three original questions:

1   Does everything happen for a reason?
2   If everything happens for a reason, are our lives purposefully directed?
3   If our lives are purposely directed, who or what is responsible for the direction?

I've suggested that, if the phrase "everything happens for a reason" is understood in terms of the second version of the principle of sufficient reason, the answer to the first question is "yes." I've argued that from this version of the principle of sufficient reason and the fact that the universe does not exist through itself, we can conclude that there is a self-existent being that is perfectly good, powerful, and knowledgeable. A perfectly good being would care about dependently existing beings and want to provide them with direction, and a perfectly powerful and knowledgeable being would be able to do so. We can say then that, in response to question 2, our lives are purposefully directed, and in answer to question 3, that the

---

[10]   In this paragraph, I am deeply influenced by the work of Keith E. Yandell. See his *Christianity and Philosophy* (Grand Rapids, MI: Eerdmans, 1984), pp. 56–57.

one responsible for this direction is a perfectly powerful, good, and knowing being.

It appears, then, that there is good reason to think that John Locke has a destiny and that it lies with one beyond the bounds of the island and the universe itself. That one might choose to communicate with Locke through events on the island, just as the God of Sayid and Rose might communicate through a burning bush in the Sinai desert. In fact, given that the one in question is all-powerful, all-knowing, and all-good, it might just be the God of Sayid and Rose, a being with a reputation for seeking out the lost.[11]

[11] See Doc Jensen's "Desert Island Dish" in *Entertainment Weekly*, www.ew.com/ew/article/0,,20006484,00.html, for a theory relating John Newton's hymn "Amazing Grace," with the line "I once was lost but now I'm found," to the seasons of *Lost*. I am very grateful to Richard Davies, William Irwin, Mark Linville, and Susan Werther for their comments and corrections. I am deeply indebted to Richard Taylor's discussion of the principle of sufficient reason in his *Metaphysics* cited in note 5 and Charles Taliaferro's discussion of the cosmological argument in his *Contemporary Philosophy of Religion* cited in notes 3, 6, and 7. I also found the work of William Rowe, *Philosophy of Religion: An Introduction* (Belmont, CA: Wadsworth, 1993), pp. 1–28; William Wainwright, *Philosophy of Religion* (Belmont, CA: Wadsworth, 1988), pp. 38–48; and Douglas Groothuis, "Metaphysical Implications of Cosmological Arguments," in *In Defense of Natural Theology*, ed. James F. Sennett and Douglas Groothuis (Downers Grove, IL: Intervarsity Press, 2005), pp. 107–122, to be very helpful.

# 19

# "Don't mistake coincidence for fate": *Lost* Theories and Coincidence

## Briony Addey

The flashback sequences of *Lost* are littered with apparently coincidental connections between the characters' lives. In season one, for example, we see Sawyer and Boone cross paths in an Australian police station as Sawyer is arrested (in "Exodus") while Boone is making a complaint against Shannon's boyfriend ("Hearts and Minds"). But what exactly is a coincidence? To answer this question we'll explore the related concepts of randomness, determinism, freedom, and fate. We'll also discuss attributions of improbability and look at their role in thinking about coincidence. Finally, we'll look at "Coincidence Theory" and conspiracy theory as applied to viewers' theories about what is happening in *Lost*, the Dharma Initiative, and the Hanso Foundation.

## What is a Coincidence?

The *Oxford English Dictionary* defines coincidence as "A remarkable concurrence of events or circumstances without apparent causal connection."[1] Digging a little deeper, we can say that a concurrence of events or entities, say, A and B, must fulfill three criteria to qualify as a coincidence:

---

[1]   *The Oxford English Reference Dictionary*, 2nd edn., ed. Judy Pearsall and Bill Trumble (Oxford: Oxford University Press, 1996).

231

1   Those events or entities, A and B, must have been previously connected in some way X.
2   The events or entities, A and B, now concur, not because of that previous connection X, but seemingly randomly.
3   The concurrence is improbable and therefore surprising or unexpected.

A good example from *Lost* is Jack meeting Desmond in the hatch. The two men have a previous connection – their conversation in the stadium in LA; their meeting in the hatch doesn't seem to be causally connected to that previous connection; and the meeting in the hatch seems highly improbable. Therefore, the meeting in the hatch is a genuine coincidence.

## Coincidence: Fate, Freedom, and Chance

Whether or not the various connections between characters (the "Losties") are genuine coincidences makes a huge difference to the type of answers viewers of *Lost* give to the question "What the hell is going on?" Of course, the viewers are not the only ones trying to figure this out. The Losties themselves have been literally crashed into a situation that becomes more puzzling with each passing day. There have been many questions. What is the "sickness"? What was the Dharma Initiative up to? Who are the Others, and what do they want? What is the black smoke? What was the monster/security system? The structure of the show, alternating between thematically linked scenes of life on the island and flashbacks to life before the crash, suggests there is some kind of real connection between the Losties and the island. Just think of Locke and his belief that it is his destiny to go on a "walkabout."

Some viewers think all of the connections are pure coincidence. Consider this post to a major *Lost* internet forum, *The Tailsection*: "I think the losties have unwittingly stumbled upon all of this. The connections and flashbacks might all be a coincidence. The real story is what was already happening and what continues to happen on the island."[2]

---

[2]   Kloos78, The Tailsection, www.buddytv.com/forum/showthread.php?p=39215#post39215, posted on 06/05/06 at 05:45p.m., accessed on 10/04/06.

Another forum member replies: "Interesting theory, but seeing that ALL of the losties are all connected in some way, I don't think it is all coincidence. I think they were somehow meant to be on the island too."[3] In a thread entitled "Not just a coincidence" on the ABC *Lost* message board, one forum member comments: "I find it funny how Michael happened to stumble out to "the line that was not to be crossed" right when Jack and Kate were there."[4]

The idea that someone is "meant to be" in a particular place at a particular time could be a description of one of three related but different philosophical theories: divine providence, fate, and determinism. The theological theory of divine providence is the idea that God has a plan for all of us. To say that the plane crash in *Lost* was providential is to say that it happened under the "watchful eye" of God, that what occurs does so because God wills it. Desmond would surely disagree. As he says, "Not even God can see this island!" ("Live Together, Die Alone").

We've all heard people make comments concerning someone's fate, like "He was fated to die in a plane crash" (as we could perhaps say of the unfortunate Boone). There are also generally fatalistic comments like "It was inevitable that she would go insane" (as maybe some people say of Rousseau and her time on the island). Fatalism is the idea that no matter what choices a person makes, a certain thing will happen to them. The most famous story concerning fate is *Oedipus Rex*. Oedipus is told that his fate is to kill his father and sleep with his mother. He desperately wants to avoid this, and so leaves what he thinks is his family, not knowing that he was adopted. Even though he does everything he can to prevent these events from coming to pass, his rash nature makes him kill a stranger who has insulted him at a crossroad, and marry a woman who turns out to be his widow.[5] Unwittingly, he has fulfilled the prophecy, because the man at the crossroad was his father, the widow his mother.

Determinism is the idea that every event is necessitated by previous events and natural laws, and this, unlike the idea of fate, includes

3  Hanner80, The Tailsection, www.buddytv.com/forum/showthread.php?t=4501, posted on 06/05/06 at 07:47p.m., accessed on 10/04/06.

4  biggest lost fan, Lost Plot Message Board (www.abc.com), posted on 06.05.06 at 06:46p.m., accessed on 10/04/06.

5  Sophocles, *Oedipus the King*, trans. H. D. F. Kitto (Oxford: Oxford University Press, 1962).

233

human thoughts and actions. So whereas if one's doing X is fated, one will do X no matter what one decides or chooses, if one's doing X is determined, that's because one can only choose to do X given previous events and the laws of nature (the natural laws that govern how things work in the world, for example the law of gravity). With fate it seems that human choice is ineffective, whereas with determinism, human choice is effective, within certain limits, as it forms links in causal chains. So we might say that Jack's being on Oceanic Flight 815 was determined, not because he would've been on the flight no matter what decision he made, but because given certain facts about the kind of man he is, his choice to fly to Australia to find his father was itself inevitable.

All three theories seem to create problems for free will. If you believe in divine providence, and everything happens according to God's plan which was formulated before your birth, how do you freely choose anything? If events in your life are fated, no matter what you do, how are you in control of anything in your life? If every event in the universe is determined, then that includes all the choices you will ever make, in which case how are they really choices?

All three theories – divine providence, fatalism, and determinism – are linked to the idea of coincidence. Sometimes a belief in one of these theories will be sparked by an experience of an amazing and seemingly meaningful coincidence. If a man's plane crashed on an island where his brother's plane crashed years before, and he was a religious man, he might come to believe that it was part of God's plan. If a man who had believed it was his destiny to go on a spiritual quest in a harsh, physically challenging environment crashed on an uninhabited island he might believe it was fate. Sometimes the strange coincident events that happen to us seem so incredible that we suppose that there must be some explanation other than chance or randomness. The explanation sometimes given is a transcendental force (providence), or of a more mysterious destiny or inevitability (fate), or of a kind of necessity (determinism).

In the third season, the viewer discovers Desmond's experience of going "back in time," of revisiting past experiences with "memories" of the events on the island, which seems to have been a result of being blown up with the hatch. We discover that Desmond has flashes, apparent visions of the future, which resemble the memories of the future he had in that revisitation. He meets a woman (Mrs. Hawking, in "Flashes Before Your Eyes") who tells Desmond that everyone has a path, and that the universe "has a way of course-correcting." So when Desmond precognizes Charlie's death, he knows that no matter how many times he saves Charlie, the universe will "course-correct" and that Charlie will die. This idea seems to fit with fatalism, as Mrs. Hawking assures Desmond that choice isn't a factor: "it's your path to go to the island. You don't do it because you choose to, Desmond. You do it because you're supposed to." It appears that Locke's talk of what's "supposed to happen" (in "Through the Looking Glass") isn't far off the mark.

## Does Locke Believe in Jungian Synchronicity?

Carl Jung (1875–1961), the famous Swiss psychiatrist, was intrigued by the stories of meaningful and improbable coincidences that he came across in his investigations of what he termed the "collective unconscious." Through the theory of "synchronicity" Jung attempts to explain such coincidences. Some coincidences are simply meaningless, those which don't involve any kind of psychic or mental state (for example, a dream or an idea) in an individual that would cause him to perceive the coincidence as meaningful. By contrast, meaningful coincidences consist in the concurrence of:

A person having a dream, idea, image, premonition or some other kind of unconscious mental state
and
Some objective, external event which shares some significant feature with the mental state.

Jung offers as an example of a meaningful coincidence a patient who recounts to him a dream that she had the night before about a golden scarab. At that moment a gentle tapping on the window draws Jung's attention to a scarab beetle (or its closest European equivalent) at the window.[6]

---

[6] C. G. Jung and W. Pauli, *The Interpretation of Nature and the Psyche* (London: Routledge and Kegan Paul, 1955), p. 31.

Jung sees synchronicity as a way of explaining certain kinds of acausal (uncaused) events that involve the psychic (or mental) and physical worlds. Such uncaused events require explanation (beyond saying that they are purely random or chance events) because they seem to be ordered. Acausal events which involve the mental and the physical worlds are governed by synchronicity in the same way that most events are governed by the principle of causation.

Locke seems to believe that at least some events, both on the island and leading up to the plane crash, are too improbable to be mere coincidence, but it is unclear whether he believes in fate or synchronicity. In the episode "What Kate Did" he has a conversation with Mr. Eko about the pieces of the orientation film, and says: "I mean, think about it. Somebody made this film. Someone else cut this piece out. We crash – two halves of the same plane fall in different parts of the island – you're over there, I'm over here. And now, here's the missing piece right back where it belongs. What are the odds?" Eko replies: "Don't mistake coincidence for fate." In the episode "Man of Science, Man of Faith," Jack mocks Locke's belief by saying, "Is this what you were talking about, Locke? Is this your destiny? All roads lead here." So it seems that the other characters think that Locke believes in fate. However, in the flashbacks of the episode "Walkabout," Locke has a strong feeling that he is meant to experience a situation with none of the comforts of western lifestyles that would change him spiritually, and we see that his trip to Australia was an attempt to have that experience by being part of a "walkabout" (an ancient aboriginal spiritual journey forming a special relationship with the land). When this ambition is thwarted, Locke gets on Oceanic Flight 815 to travel back home, which of course crashes on the island and starts a chain of events leading to him having the exact experience that he believed he was meant to have. The belief plus the coincidence of his experience on the island could thus be seen as an example of synchronicity. Whatever the case, it seems clear that Locke has faith that the events and coincidences are not just accidental or random.

## Attributions of Coincidence

One of the central elements of a coincidence is that it is improbable. If I walked out of my front door and bumped into my neighbor, we would not call this a coincidence because it is pretty likely that this will happen on a somewhat regular basis. If, on the other hand, I walked out of my front door and bumped into my long lost cousin who had returned from the other side of the world with his new wife who just so happened to live on my street, this highly improbable occurrence would be a coincidence. Still, as Locke observes, if something is *too* unlikely or improbable this may suggest that it cannot be a coincidence. So we have a sliding scale of probabilities: too probable to be called a coincidence, just improbable enough to be called a coincidence, and too improbable to be called a coincidence.

But how good are our natural abilities at judging how probable an event is? Let's look at some examples. If there are 23 people in a room, how likely is it that two of them have the same birthday (excluding year)? Many people are surprised to learn that there is a 50 percent chance that two of those people will share a birthday. We're inclined to reason that if there are 367 people, two of them will definitely share a birthday, and so for a 50 percent chance we just have to divide this figure in half. They therefore expect that for a 50 percent chance of two people sharing a birthday there would have to be a group of roughly 183. This is known as the Birthday Paradox, and it is a famous example of how people go wrong in guessing probabilities. This example seems to suggest that we often judge situations to be more improbable than they actually are. This could affect whether we deem something to be an amazing coincidence or not, as well as whether we view it as too improbable to be coincidental.

Another way that our intuitions about probability lead us astray is thinking about the probability of a particular hand in cards. Taken in itself, a bridge hand containing 13 hearts is no more unlikely than any other bridge hand. There are a possible 635,013,559,600 different 13-card bridge hands, and any particular hand is equally improbable: 1 in 635,013,559,600. Of course, the odds of getting a hand specified in advance are much longer. Consider also the Law of Truly Large Numbers. This law states that with an extremely large number of events, you would expect all kinds of events to occur, even occasionally very improbable events. For example, if you played enough poker, eventually you would expect to see a perfect hand of cards dealt to you. It would be highly improbable if no highly improbable events occurred! Statisticians Diaconis and Mosteller explain: "Events rare per person occur with high frequency in the presence of large numbers of people."[7] The nature of true randomness, combined with a large number of events, ensures that some very unlikely events will occur. For example, with a fortune the size of Hurley's, imagine the number of business transactions, clients, and employees that his companies deal with. That large number makes it less unlikely that he should bump into someone with whom he has had business dealings (Locke works for a box company that Hurley owns) than if he only owned a small business.

When we are assessing reasoning about apparent coincidences, we need to consider the possibility of *confirmation bias*: the tendency to ignore evidence that contradicts our theory or preconceptions, or to search for information that supports them. In part to combat confirmation bias, the philosopher of science Karl Popper (1902–1994) emphasized the importance of falsifiability. Scientists must construct hypotheses that are in principle falsifiable and then seek to falsify them.

Confirmation bias connects with what is happening when people register "amazing" coincidences. We hear about and experience a great many events each day, but when one event coincides somehow with one of the great many dreams, thoughts, and images we have recently experienced, we notice. We tend to ignore two considerations, because they would falsify, or at least undermine to some extent, the remarkableness of the coincidence. Firstly, all the other different events that might've happened and would've been considered just as much of an amazing coincidence, and secondly, the number of chances there are for us to experience something coincidental when we don't. We also tend to ignore the problem of multiple endpoints. Whereas the odds of a particular coincidence, specified in advance, in other words a single outcome or endpoint in a specified window of time, may be very low, the odds of any coincidence or a set of coincidences which could include any number of outcomes or endpoints in a vague or not at all defined window of time, none of which are specified in advance, could be pretty high. So, for example, it seems really unlikely for Jack to meet Desmond on the island when he's already met him in LA. But when we consider the amount of people that someone like Jack (a social, professional man in his

[7]  P. Diaconis and F. Mosteller, "Methods of Studying Coincidences," *Journal of the American Statistical Association*, Vol. 84, 1989, pp. 853–861.

thirties, who lives in a huge city) comes into contact with, along with the fact that if it were any of those people that Jack met in the hatch it would seem to be an equally amazing coincidence, the coincidence doesn't seem quite as unlikely.

Noticing patterns and coincidences is a very important human skill. Much learning in children, such as the ability to learn a language, depends on it, and many discoveries in the sciences also depend on it. When a scientist observes a coincidence or regularity the scientist postulates that there is some kind of explanation for it, that it is not just random, and proceeds on that basis, thinking about and inferring from the data what the best explanation for the phenomenon might be. This is called *Inference to the Best Explanation* (IBE). The scientist then has a hypothesis or a theory that he can test by attempting to falsify it. So maybe, if we were to approach *Lost* theorizing scientifically, we too should make the assumption that the regularity (the coincidence of the connections between the characters) isn't just random, make an inference to the best explanation, and then test the hypothesis that we formulate.

## Human Connections, Social Networks, and a Small World

Are the connections between the Losties really that unlikely or improbable? In the 1960s, the famous psychologist Stanley Milgram did a series of experiments called the Small World Study. The experiment was set up so that randomly selected "starters" in one part of the USA were given a folder. The object was to get the folder to a specified person, the target, in another part of the country by sending the folder on to an acquaintance who may know the target. The results of these experiments was the famous phrase "six degrees of separation." Milgram thought it proved that each person in the USA was connected to any other through an average of six others.[8] A popular game based on this idea among movie fans is "Six degrees of Kevin Bacon," where players have to connect any actor to Kevin

---

[8]  In fact, Milgram's experiment was subsequently criticized for apparently targeting and looking for connections between the professional upper classes, making the "six degree" results perhaps less surprising.

Bacon in as few connections as possible. For example, Matthew Fox, the actor who plays Jack, was in the TV show *Party of Five* with actress Neve Campbell, who was in the movie *Wild Things* with Kevin Bacon. Connections between people is a theme which fascinates *Lost*'s co-creator, J. J. Abrams. In fact one of his other shows, which chronicles the lives of six New Yorkers and the ways their lives intersect in seemingly random ways, is titled *Six Degrees*.

So whether or not the connections between the characters are really something that need to be explained is questionable. Maybe if you took any event, even if it is a random (?) disaster like a plane crash, you could trace connections between the lives of everyone involved.

## Coincidence, Conspiracy, and Dharma

Most recent historical events have some conspiracy theories attached to them. There are conspiracy nuts who, for example, think that the moon landings were faked by the Americans in order to win the space race and get one up on the Russians in the Cold War. Conspiracy theorists often cite strange, highly improbable coincidences surrounding events such as the moon landing as proof that there is more going on than meets the eye, because they find the coincidences too improbable to be truly coincidental. They call anyone who disagrees, and believes they are simply weird coincidences, "coincidence theorists." Theories about *Lost* can be divided into these two categories – those who feel the need to incorporate an explanation of the connections between the characters (the conspiracy theorists) and those who don't (the coincidence theorists). The conspiracy theorists usually give some kind of theory which includes the Dharma Initiative handpicking the Losties and engineering their lives so that they are on the plane when it crashes.

In true *Lost* style I will leave you with questions! What's your *Lost* theory? Do you think that the connections between the Losties are significant? Do you think they require explanation because they are "too coincidental" to be true coincidences? Or are they just examples of a Small World? Are you and your theory about *Lost* and coincidences suffering from confirmation bias? Are the apparent coincidences really unlikely, and do they fit the other criteria of what it is to be a coincidence? Are all the characters on fatalistic paths?

Good luck with answering them!

# 20

# Aquinas and Rose on Faith and Reason

## *Daniel B. Gallagher*

If there is one thing Rose Henderson's fellow castaways know about her, it is this: Rose "knows." Hurley knows that Rose does not merely hope her husband Bernard is still alive, she knows he is. Charlie knows that Rose does not merely think he will receive help from on high if he asks for it, she knows he will. Locke knows that Rose not only surmises that their plight will come to an end, she knows it will – and knows that Locke knows the same. Her husband Bernard knows that Rose not only feels that the island has healed her from terminal cancer, she knows it has. Everybody knows that Rose knows. But nobody can refrain from asking, "How does Rose know?" She baffles everyone, including her husband Bernard, with a rather ordinary response: "I just know."

The island Rose and her castaway companions find themselves stranded on becomes a place where everyone is challenged to give reasons for hope – not only in words, but in action. Some, placing their hope in an unseen satellite, decide to pitch in and help Bernard construct a large SOS sign on the beach. Others, placing their hope in what lies beyond the sea, get to work building an ersatz raft. Some gradually begin to place their hope in the island itself and relocate themselves inland. Some place their hope in the transceiver, others in firearms. Every time the castaways act upon certain hopes, they find themselves wrestling with how to best articulate them – to others and to themselves. All are confronted with the issue of whether hope is reasonable or unreasonable, rational or irrational. Rose, however, sets herself apart. While never wavering, she offers no explanation for her faith.

Thomas Aquinas (1225–1274), one of the most brilliant philosophical minds of the medieval era, taught that such a response holds no water (the one thing never lacking on the island!). Faith and knowledge are interdependent upon each other and interpenetrate one another. Aquinas would have admired the unshakeable certainty of Rose's faith, but he would have cautioned her against letting faith trump the role of her natural ability to reason. Aquinas turned to Christian scripture in support of his conviction that faith cannot do without solid reason to buttress it: "Always be ready to give an explanation to anyone who asks you for a reason for your hope" (1 Peter 3:15).

The character of Rose Henderson spurns us diehard Lostaways to confront the same issue week after week as we throw ourselves onto the living room couch and join our friends on the island: just what is the relationship between faith and reason? Are they absolutely separate and distinct? Do they overlap? Or are they one and same thing? Is faith a type of knowledge? If so, can we give a more convincing rationale for why we believe the things we believe than simply, "I just know?"

## What Can We Know?

Humans, of course, did not have to wait until the crash of Oceanic Flight 815 to begin asking such questions. They have been around as long as philosophy itself. Socrates, in fact, could not help but wonder whether *all* of our "knowledge" might not be anything more than mere "opinion." Socrates' star pupil, Plato, in his *Republic*, continues to refine these two types of cognition. Knowledge (*epistēmē* in Greek) is the type of certitude we have only after all the sensible, changeable characteristics of things are somehow left aside. Consequently, knowledge of a thing is only had when we fully possess the "idea" or pure "form" (*eidos*) of a thing. Opinion (*doxa*) refers to the imperfect, but by no means false, knowledge that we have of things through our senses.

So is faith one of these? Is it something like "knowledge" (*epistēmē*) or "opinion" (*doxa*)? When Rose says that she knows her husband is still alive, does she mean that her certitude even surpasses the concrete, sensible experience she had of him when they shook hands for the first time on that blistery winter night in Brooklyn ("SOS")? If so, then perhaps faith is something like *epistēmē*. Or does she mean that she is quite satisfied with accepting even the fuzziest of premonitions as if they were cold hard facts? If so, then maybe faith is something like *doxa*.

Aquinas, following the lines of a highly influential definition of faith proposed by Hugh of St. Victor in the twelfth century, asserts that faith is actually "mid-way between knowledge and opinion."[1] He believes that faith shares both in the certainty we associate with knowledge, as well as in the imperfection characterizing opinion. In fact, "to be imperfect as knowledge is the very essence of faith."[2]

The ongoing saga of *Lost* teaches us that we can begin to penetrate this paradox only after we have clarified the object of faith. We must ask ourselves what, or whom, we ultimately place our faith in. Aquinas, who is a master at making distinctions, begins by distinguishing between the "formal" object of faith from the "material" object of faith. Though the material object of faith is God, the formal object – that is, the aspect under which the believer views God as the object of his or her belief – is "first truth."[3]

Just what is Aquinas up to here? He is making what philosophers like to call a "conceptual distinction." A conceptual distinction is a distinction based on the variety of ways we can conceive a single identical object. A single piece of wood, for example, can be "conceived" either as a branch (when it is attached to a tree), a stick (when it is lying on the ground), or a walking-staff (when I pick it up and use it during my hike). Similarly, "God" and "first truth" refer to the same object (i.e., the divine being), but through different conceptual lenses. "God" refers to the omnipotent, omniscient being that is the source of everything. "First truth" refers to that same being, but with reference to the fact that such a being is the ground of all other truths. We could say that "God" refers to the divine being in a descending way (i.e., all things proceed "downward" from God),

[1] Thomas Aquinas, *Summa Theologica: Complete English Edition in Five Volumes* (Westminster: Christian Classics, 1981), Vol. 2, pp. 873–874 (I-II, q. 67, a. 3).

[2] *Summa Theologica*, Vol. 2, pp. 873–874 (I-II, q. 67, a. 3).

[3] *Summa Theologica*, Vol. 3, pp. 1185, 1191, 1193 (II-II, q. 4, a. 1; q. 5, a. 1; q. 5, a. 3). See also *The Disputed Questions on Truth*, trans. Robert W. Mulligan (Chicago: Henry Regnery, 1952), Vol. 2, pp. 204–206 (*Quaestiones disputatae de veritate*, q. 14, a. 1).

whereas "first truth" refers to God in an ascending way (i.e., all truths lead "upward" to God). Someday, when we behold God face to face, we will know the divinity perfectly and directly simply as "truth." In the meantime, since our knowledge of the divinity is only imperfect and indirect, we are only able to conceive God as the "first truth" among many truths. We reason to the existence of a "first truth" because other truths appear to us as contingent and dependent. As we shall see, Rose falls into the trap of equating the power of "first truth" with all contingent truths. Her faith in a higher power tends to trump the uncertain and imperfect contingencies in the finite world. She claims to "know" things that she really only "believes."

Let's take the filming of the show we love so much as an example. I believe that the episodes of *Lost* are truly being filmed on the Hawaiian island of Oahu. I have not been there to watch the filming take place, nor can I deduce from watching the television program itself that it is indeed filmed there. I accept the statement that "*Lost* is filmed on the island of Oahu" as true because I believe the producers are credible. Based on their testimony, I *believe* that *Lost* is filmed on Oahu; I don't really *know* it as scientific knowledge. I have reasonable grounds for believing that when the producers tell me that *Lost* is filmed on Oahu, they are telling the truth. Although knowledge and belief seem at first to be the same, they are in fact quite different. The actors who have been filmed on Oahu have direct knowledge that the show has been filmed on Oahu. My belief that the show has been filmed on Oahu is indirect: it depends on the truth of the producers' testimony, which in turn depends on where the filming has taken place. This is to say that my belief depends on a prior truth.

## Chain of Truth

The truths to which the *Lost* survivors most often give their assent depend on prior truths. The truth of what Shannon claims to hear though the transceiver depends on the accuracy of her translation of the French. Assuming her translation is accurate, the truth of what is being said by the mysterious French voice (which ends up belonging to Rousseau) depends on whether the call for distress is still valid 16 years later. The list of dependencies goes on and on. All of the castaways' deliberations are, in fact, based on an "if." If there are other people on the island, then perhaps they can work together to find a way off. But this depends on whether or not the "others" are truly friendly. The dependence of every truth on a prior truth is what in fact keeps us coming back for the next episode.

The writers of *Lost* capitalize on the fact that human beings tend to place their ultimate hope in something, someone, or somewhere that ultimately fails to satisfy. In his life prior to the air crash, Jack placed his hope in his ability to cure people ("Man of Science, Man of Faith" and "The Hunting Party"). Kate placed her hope in her ability to deceive people ("Born to Run" and "Tabula Rasa"). Jin placed his hope in the employment offered to him by his father-in-law (". . . In Translation" and "Exodus"). Charlie placed his hope in his big brother Liam ("The Moth" and "Fire + Water"), Claire in the psychic Mr. Malkin ("Raised by Another"), and Locke in his biological father Anthony Cooper ("Deus Ex Machina"). The Virgin Mary statues containing contraband become a potent and multi-layered symbol of the human tendency to place ultimate hope in something non-divine, even when that something – or someone – should ultimately lead us to the divine ("House of the Rising Sun," "Exodus," and "The 23rd Psalm"). Because the hopes of so many of *Lost*'s characters had been shattered even before they found themselves on the island, they wander around carrying a heavy load of betrayal and regret during their plight.

## Rose Colored Glasses

Except perhaps Rose. While everybody around her anxiously tries to make sense of what has happened, Rose is merely grateful to be alive. While others see only doom and gloom on the horizon, Rose accepts the small blessings that come her way.

Rose keeps her distance from what Aquinas calls *acedia* in Latin, the greatest sin against faith. Though it is often translated as "sloth," *acedia* is a much more technical term. It designates a type of torpor preventing a person from enjoying things that are genuinely good. It is a spiritual paralysis that stymies the ability to look beyond the bad. It is "to look upon some worthwhile good as impossible to achieve, whether alone or with the help of others," and it can "sometimes dominate one's affections to the point that he begins to think he can never again be given aspirations towards the good."[4]

No one on the island shows clearer signs of *acedia* than Charlie Pace, to whom Rose offers comfort early in the first season of the series. At that time, Charlie and Rose were standing on opposite ends of the spectrum spanning from hope to despair, from faith to *acedia*. Charlie was once religious, faithful, and repentant. He sought reconciliation for the sins he committed during the wild, early days of DriveShaft, only to be lured back into heroin addiction by none other than his big brother Liam – the handsome lead singer ("The Moth"). Charlie has been so deeply hurt through relationships with his father ("Fire + Water"), his brother, and Lucy – the one person whose trust he won only to abuse ("Homecoming") – that he is all but completely incapable of entrusting himself to anybody or anything. Though he remembers how he was once a religious man, he now thinks he can "never again be given aspirations towards the good."

Just at the moment when it seems Charlie would never dig himself out of his deep *acedia*, Rose reminds him that faith is never impossible ("Whatever the Case May Be"). "It's a fine line between denial and faith," she says to him as they sit together in the dark on the beach. "It's much better on my side." She then reminds Charlie of what he once knew, but finds impossible anymore to do: "You need to ask for help." At this, Charlie breaks down and sobs, preparing him for the grueling road to recovery from addiction with Locke's help.

## Does Rose *Really* Know?

Rose herself, however, misdirects her faith. While she seems to rise above the fickle fortunes that distress everyone else, she is not immune from the temptation to mistake what Aquinas calls "first truth" for the truth itself. In other words, she claims to *know* what in reality she only *believes*. To understand the temptation, we have to take a closer look at what Aquinas teaches about the relationship between faith and reason.

---

[4] *Summa Theologica*, Vol. 3, p. 1256 (II-II, q. 20, a. 4).

Reason, Aquinas teaches, is the faculty by which human beings attain knowledge of what is real. Any such knowledge, Aquinas holds, must be acquired through the senses. "Nothing comes to exist in the intellect which does not first exist in the senses."[5] In this way, Aquinas distinguishes himself from the Platonic tradition we considered earlier. Though it is true that sensible realities are always in a state of flux and instability, our intellect is able to abstract a stable nature from reality that allows us to call it "x."

The fact that we can be mistaken about the natures of things, or the fact that we can have sensible experience of things without being able to articulate fully their respective natures, need not bother us too much. For the first several episodes, the "smoke monster" remained just as enigmatic to *Lost*'s characters as it did to its viewers. Later, Locke encounters it in the jungle ("Walkabout"), though we the viewers are not given a chance to look at it. Finally, when Mr. Eko stares it down "face to face" during his hike with Charlie ("The 23rd Psalm"), we are offered a good, long look at it. We see that it is composed of dark, black smoke, and that it seems to contain vague, flashing images within. There is more we would like to know about it, but we know enough about it to call it the "smoke monster" to distinguish it from other things. Our understanding of what (or who) the smoke monster is waits to be expanded, but it would be hard for us to doubt whether we have knowledge of it.

## Do *We* Really Know?

If, as Aquinas teaches, all our knowledge comes through the senses, how can we ever attain knowledge of supersensible things? God, having no sensible qualities that can be seen or heard or touched, would be included among such things. Aquinas argues that although we can have no direct, sensible experience of God, we can come to know God's existence by exercising our natural power to reason. Using Aquinas's own terminology, the existence of God is not something obvious or knowable in itself (*per se notum*), but only by way

---

[5] *Summa Theologica*, Vol. 4, pp. 1896–1897 (II-II, q. 173, a. 2) and Vol. 3, pp. 278–279 (I, q. 55, a. 2).

of demonstration.[6] Among the most famous of Aquinas's demonstrations are his "five ways" in which he "proves" that God exists: by motion, efficient cause, possibility and necessity, the hierarchy of beings, and the government of things.[7]

The first two of these five proofs most manifestly begin with sensible realities and proceed to demonstrate that all finite things are dependent on a first efficient cause. In philosophical lingo, an "efficient cause" is not one that happens to be unusually successful in producing its effect. Rather, in the words of Aristotle, it is the cause which is "the primary source of the change or coming to rest" in a thing.[8] The first of these efficient causes, Aquinas concludes, "is what all call God." Philosophers continue to argue over whether the five ways can maintain their persuasive power if detached from the monotheistic Christian context in which they were formed, but Aquinas clearly believes that there is a reasonable, logical basis for the assertion "God exists." *That* God exists is wholly within the grasp of natural reason; *what* or *who* God is can be partially penetrated by natural reason, but only comes to fuller light through revelation and faith.

According to Aquinas, faith, insofar as its divine object infinitely surpasses the finite capabilities of the human intellect, can ultimately only be given by grace. Though unaided human reason can come to know that the divine being exists, it is unable to know the full nature of that divine being without the divine being's aid. But we can prepare to receive faith through what Aquinas calls the *praeambula ad articulos*, or the "preambles to the articles of faith."[9] Philosophy can assert that God exists, God is one, and God is "first truth." Philosophy can make other similar assertions because the human mind is able to deduce truths regarding supersensible realities based on its direct experience of sensible realities. Human reason, however, could never have come to know that God exists as a Trinity of persons, or that the second person of the Trinity took on human flesh, if it were not for the self revelation of God and the gift of faith.

---

[6] *Summa Theologica*, Vol. 1, pp. 11–12 (I, q. 2, a. 1).

[7] *Summa Theologica*, Vol. 1, pp. 13–14 (I, q. 2, a. 3).

[8] *Introduction to Aristotle*, ed. Richard McKeon (New York: Random House, 1947), p. 122 (*Physica*, Book II, Ch. 3).

[9] *Summa Theologica*, Vol. 1, p. 12 (I, q. 2, a. 2).

## "I have made my peace" – Rose

Accepting God's revelation is not such an easy thing to do. It is, so to speak, an all-or-nothing proposition. Rose shows clear signs that she has given everything to this divine proposition. This becomes more evident through her relationship with Bernard and the contrast between their attitudes of acceptance and non-acceptance. It begins the moment when Bernard makes his all-or-nothing marriage proposal to Rose at Niagara Falls ("SOS"). Only then does Rose return his proposition by informing him of what he must accept if she says "yes": a wife who is terminally ill. This, so to speak, is the return proposition to him. He also accepts.

It is one of the more moving moments in *Lost*, but we soon learn that there are two different worldviews at work in Rose and Bernard's relationship. Rose is at peace with the fact that she is dying. Bernard, though he initially accepted her, cancer-and-all, believes it's worth taking every conceivable measure to stop her from dying.

Hence the trip to Australia to visit the faith healer Isaac of Uluru ("SOS"). Though it seems at first that Bernard's efforts to find a cure for Rose are magnanimous, we discover a hint of selfishness in his motivations. In answer to her protestations against going through with the faith-healing ritual, Bernard begs her: "Will you try Rose? For *me*?" Bernard cannot help but put his faith into each and every worldly means that might lead to Rose's recovery. Rose, on the other hand, has put all her faith in divine providence. "I have made my peace with what is happening to me." She has accepted the all-or-nothing proposition of trust.

Aquinas teaches that the only thing that can elicit such a complete act of trust from us is a wholly perfect being – the first truth. Because this is a being which can neither deceive nor be deceived, it is the only being worthy of our complete trust. Aquinas quickly adds that this perfect being in no way undermines our freedom. Yet whatever trust we place in God is based wholly on the basis of God's own credibility. The act of faith is an act that transcends reason, but is by no means unreasonable.

Rose's complete trust in this perfect being makes it impossible for her to receive aid from any other source outside of this being. Despite Isaac's efforts to harness the geological energy that resulted in the miraculous healing of so many hopeless cases before Rose, he tells her, "There is nothing I can do for you" ("SOS").

Though Rose calmly accepts, she makes a stunning decision: she will tell Bernard that she has been healed. She will lie to him.

## Does Rose *Presume* to Know?

This is a critical turning point in Rose's journey of faith. Her faith begins to trump everything else – even the moral rectitude of telling the truth. There is a strong allusion during the scene with Isaac that the "place" where Rose might find a home may not be the divine "heaven" she has hoped for.

The contrast between the respective theological and secular world-views of Rose and Bernard comes to a climactic point only after they are reunited on the island after the crash. While Bernard drums up support for his plan to construct a large SOS sign, Rose seems to have found a "home" on the island ("SOS"). Just as Bernard once searched frantically for a way to save Rose from imminent death, he now works furiously to save everyone from being perpetually lost. And this drives Rose crazy. "Why can't you just let things be?" she asks him in exasperation.

Whereas at Isaac of Uluru's house it was Bernard whose reasons were partly selfish, now it is Rose. What Isaac was unable to do for her, the island now has done for her. She "knows" that she has been cured of her cancer. Bernard feels as if he must do everything he can to help their desperate situation and get them off the island. Rose has found that the island has already saved her from a desperate situation. Whereas Charlie was guilty of *acedia*, Rose is now guilty of an opposite sin which Aquinas calls *praesumptio* (presumption). Aquinas defines "presumption" as "a certain type of immoderate hope."[10] The presumptuous person, though a person of faith, directs her hope (often unconsciously) toward one of God's powers rather than toward God alone. Rose believes that this mysterious island has become an instrument through which God has worked a miracle in

---

[10]   *Summa Theologica*, Vol. 3, p. 1256 (II-II, q. 21, a. 1).

her life. Indeed, she even suggests that the island itself is the source of the cure. It has become the "place" of which Isaac spoke.

## To Know . . . *and* Believe

The tension between two different ultimate horizons – secular and supernatural – is symbolized by the simultaneous construction projects of Mr. Eko's church and Bernard's large SOS signal ("SOS"). The church is a sign that the immediate, visible world is not the ultimate horizon. The letters in the sand are a sign that human beings must do everything within their power to save themselves. When Bernard insists that he is only trying to save everyone, Mr. Eko confidently remarks, "People are saved in different ways."

Aquinas teaches that it is entirely possible to come to certain knowledge of certain basic realities – including God – that we tend to relegate exclusively to the realm of faith. The certain knowledge of those things, however, can only attain its true goal if one further assents to that which is revealed by God. Faith and reason are in harmony with one another, not in opposition. Faith does not abrogate the role of reason, but neither can reason wholly take the place of faith.

Rose is an inspiration to her companions because she is a woman of faith. But her faith has left little room for the role of natural knowledge. What she claims to "know," she actually "believes"; not in the sense of *doxa* or opinion, but in the sense that those things she holds by faith pertain to a transcendent essence so as to be uniquely distinguished from those things she knows by the light of natural reason. The knowledge involved in faith is radically different from the knowledge involved in natural cognition. The latter begins in the senses, whereas the former is beyond the senses. According to Aquinas, the respective objects of natural knowledge and supernatural faith grant them each a legitimate autonomy. Rose is guilty of a confusion of idioms. She mistakenly believes that the type of knowledge distinctive of faith is interchangeable with the type of knowledge distinctive of natural reason.

Aquinas thought differently. "One should not presume that the object of faith is scientifically demonstrable, lest presuming to demonstrate what is of faith, one should produce inconclusive

251

reasons and offer occasion for unbelievers to scoff at a faith based on such ground."[11] Rose doesn't necessarily presume that she can "scientifically" demonstrate her faith, but her experience of being cured elevates all the things she once held by faith to the level of certain knowledge – *epistēmē*, to be precise. Rose knows, but Rose also believes. Aquinas admonishes her, and us, to know the difference between the two. At the same time, he urges us to probe what we believe with our minds, and to allow our minds to lead us to belief.

---

[11]   *Summa Theologica*, Vol. 3, p. 1166 (II-II, q. 1, a. 5).

# 21

# *Lost* and the
# Problem of Life after Birth

## *Jeremy Barris*

> Perhaps the self-same song that found a path
> Through the sad heart of Ruth, when, sick for home,
> She stood in tears amid the alien corn;
> The same that oft-times hath
> Charmed magic casements, opening on the foam
> Of perilous seas, in fairy lands forlorn.
> John Keats, Ode to a Nightingale

Unlike science, philosophy does not discover unknown things, or give us new information about familiar things. Instead, strangely at first sight, it deals with things that we actually all already know very well. It helps us understand the nature of these familiar things more deeply than we did before. This interest in a deeper understanding of familiar things is expressed in a sense of wonder about the things in the world around us, a feeling that we all sometimes experience. Plato (428–347 BCE) wrote that "wonder . . . is characteristic of a philosopher . . . this is where philosophy begins, and nowhere else."[1]

What each of us is *most* familiar with is our own life. In fact, our lives are so basic that we find other things meaningful only to the extent that they connect with something in our lives. As the great Spanish philosopher José Ortega y Gasset (1883–1955) argued,

---

[1] Plato, *Theaetetus*, trans. M. J. Levitt, revd. Myles Burnyeat (Indianapolis: Hackett, 1992), p. 155C–D.

"every other reality, different as it is from my life, is made known by some modality of my life. . . . God Himself, should He exist, will begin to be for me by existing somehow in my life." And so life is "the foundation of all other realities. . . . In the final analysis, every other reality will be a reality *in it*." My world "is only made up of whatever is lived by me."[2]

An understanding of life itself is necessary for us to understand the meaning of everything else that affects us. This is why the meaning of life is the most overwhelming question: it affects everything, including all other questions. And as I shall soon discuss, it also affects the meaning of, and the questions we ask about, *Lost*.

We often puzzle over whether there is a life after death, and what that life might be. But even that question has meaning for us only in the context of our lives, of the interests and concerns that cause us to ask that question in the first place. So an even more important question is the question of life after birth. As the German philosopher Martin Heidegger (1889–1976) pointed out, the clue to *all* questions about the nature of reality or being is the nature of the *asker* of the questions about reality or being, namely *us*, here and now as we ask these questions in our lives. Heidegger wrote, "Looking at something, understanding and conceiving it" are all part of the being of "those particular entities which we, the inquirers, are ourselves. Thus to work out the question of Being adequately, we must make an entity – the inquirer – transparent in his own Being."[3]

Our lives are what our understanding of the world most depends on, and so what we most need to understand. And because our lives are also what we most take for granted as obvious, they are also what we least understand, and so most need help to understand.

TV shows, like anything else, have meaning for us only because they connect with our lives. And when they are not only meaningful, but gripping and fascinating, it is because they connect with something important or basic to our lives. *Lost* in particular connects with our lives in an especially full way. In fact, *Lost* expresses, not just

2   José Ortega y Gasset, *What Is Knowledge?* ed. and trans. Jorge García-Gómez (New York: State University of New York Press, 2002), pp. 66, 111.
3   Martin Heidegger, *Being and Time*, trans. John Macquarrie and Edward Robinson (New York: Harper and Row, 1962), pp. 26–27.

some common experiences in our lives, but aspects of the basic nature of each of our lives, as a whole, themselves. In other words, *Lost* expresses what life itself basically *is*.

## Why Are We Here?

*Lost* pays a lot of attention to why and how each person happened to arrive on the island. In many respects, the way the show presents and explores this issue echoes the way in which we, in our more reflective moments, are troubled by the question "Why are we here?" There are other senses of this life-question that we'll discuss a little later, but one of its meanings is certainly this: "How did we happen to be put here, where did we come from?"

Like each of our births, the castaways' (assuming that this is what they really are) actual arrival, in the plane crash, is the result of a series of extraordinary chances. Their back-stories show what unpredictable, coincidental, and intricately interwoven circumstances led to their being present on that particular plane at that particular time. The crash itself was caused entirely accidentally by a series of events having to do with Desmond's own life and his own purely personal concerns. As we discover in the second season, he had, just once, neglected to reset the counter that had become his responsibility by sheer circumstance, and whose purpose he didn't even know. As a result, a powerful electromagnetic field took effect at just the moment the castaways' plane happened to be flying overhead – something that itself happened only because instrument failures led the pilots to go wildly off-course – and brought it down.

It's true that, unlike our births as we understand them in the most common perspectives, these events can be and are explored in terms of lives the castaways led before arriving on the island. But through these explorations, *Lost* highlights the mysterious circumstances that led to each of these people arriving in precisely this situation. For example, the simple explanation that Desmond let the counter lapse is kept hidden for most of two seasons. And the background information about the hatch that houses the counter, the counter itself, and the electromagnetic field is, in each case, given very gradually in enigmatic hints. As a result, the show is about the mystery. The back-stories of each of the characters similarly emphasize the strange turns their lives take, and the remarkable coincidences between their lives, which we'll consider shortly.

This mystery of the castaways' arrival on the island is at the heart of all our lives, making us ask the life-question, "Why are we here?" In Heidegger's language, we, like the characters of *Lost*, find ourselves "thrown" into our life situation, as parts of an ultimately bewildering environment and history, neither of which we made, and both of which are in many ways indifferent to our concerns and to our existence itself.

Another sense of the question "Why are we here?" is whether there is a purpose to our being here, and if so what is that purpose? *Lost* pays close attention to this sense of the question, too. Are the castaways there to carry out an important task, to serve some important although unknown goal, as Locke believes? Or are they perhaps there to be spiritually or morally redeemed? Mr. Eko believes so, and it's a possibility that former heroin addict Charlie certainly has to consider. It's also a possibility that has potential significance for Kate, with her tortured criminal past, and for Sawyer, who has spent his life on a bitter quest for revenge.

Is the island a place for second chances of other kinds? Locke, Rose, and perhaps Jin are healed from incurable physical conditions (paralysis, cancer, and infertility, respectively). Shannon, Boone, Sayid, Sawyer, and Jin each get the chance to change, or rework, their destructive dealings with others.

Or – a possibility that Hurley finds himself troubled by – is the entire experience only a delusion, a kind of dream, in which "all is vanity," and from which it would be better to wake to reality?

Again, the fascination of these themes doesn't lie in the answers – *Lost* hasn't given any of these answers yet. Clearly, what keeps our interest is the mystery itself.

All of these experiences and concerns are, in one way or another, basic possibilities in all of our lives. At some point, we all want to feel that there is a point to our lives, to our being here. We want to feel that at least something we do is worth doing, or that we are making a difference, or contributing something. And we are always faced with the possibility of finding that we have been living lives that don't work for us, lives that we feel have not been satisfactory or worthwhile or good, so that we might feel the need to find a way of starting over. And as the existence of our many religions and philosophies shows, we are all liable to wonder, at times, whether this abundantly imperfect and painful reality can be the real deal, whether there isn't a very different reality that we simply can't see.

*Lost*, then, expresses themes that are basic, not to this or that area of life, but to life itself as a whole. These themes belong to the very nature of our lives, as an experience that begins, endures, and ends in circumstances mostly indifferent to us and our concerns, and that offers little idea of what we should do with ourselves now that we are here.

## How Does It All Make Sense?

As the castaways' back-stories and experiences unfold, all sorts of connections emerge between their stories and between their present challenges or opportunities and their histories, hinting at a meaning to the castaways' situation and to their being in it together. But the suggestions of meaningful patterns really organize and heighten the enigma of their situation. They raise the question of how it all makes sense, rather than answer it. And this character of incomplete sense, or of the mysterious nature even of what we already know, is another of the basic structures of life.

Living a life naturally raises the question, "How does it all make sense?" This question belongs to the nature of life because our lives are thoroughly shaped by being limited, by being an experience with boundaries, in space and time and reach. As a result, while things do make some sense to us (otherwise we wouldn't even know enough to be puzzled by them), they only make sense to an extent. The events of our lives always fit into a larger context that extends beyond our awareness, and so they are shot through with elements of what does not make sense to us, and which may or may not have a sense we haven't been able to grasp. Because of this wider context, the things and events of our lives, on the one hand, never make full and final sense, but, on the other hand, don't even give us the security of knowing that we can dismiss them as making no sense at all, and so move on.

Existentialism, a school of twentieth-century philosophy, explores themes of the nature of human existence (as we are doing now). Martin Heidegger, Jean-Paul Sartre (1905–1980), and Albert Camus

257

(1913–1960) were perhaps the most famous existentialists. Some of them argued that life is simply absurd, without rhyme or reason, that we really are "lost" in the universe. We must therefore create our own meanings and purposes. But I think these existentialists didn't come to terms with just how lost we are. We really don't even have *that* much definite information about our situation – that we *are* definitely or completely lost.

It seems to me that life, instead, is only in part a fabric of arbitrariness, accidents, and apparently inexplicable events. There is the "other hand": life is also shot through with strands and connections of sense. And this presence of both understanding and lack of understanding makes life neither reliably understandable nor reliably senseless, but more like a riddle or a mystery: deeply puzzling, but with enough things we do understand to give us "clues" to wonder in particular directions for answers.

We definitely do understand some things to some extent. Otherwise, we couldn't even understand the possibility that we can't understand: this possibility is *itself* something we understand. And we couldn't have *that* understanding, in turn, without understanding all sorts of other things. The Austrian philosopher Ludwig Wittgenstein (1889–1951) made this clear. To understand that we might not understand, we need to understand the meanings of the words we use in expressing that thought. And to understand those, we need to understand a great deal about the things those words refer to, and about the society in which we learned the words. Otherwise we couldn't have learned to apply the words successfully in our environment (which is the same as learning them at all), or to work successfully with and so learn from the people who taught them to us. "If you are not certain of any fact, you cannot be certain of the meaning of your words, either."[4] And, beyond the meanings of words, "If you tried to doubt everything you would not get as far as doubting anything. The game of doubting itself presupposes certainty." For, Wittgenstein asks, "Doesn't one need grounds for

---

[4]  Ludwig Wittgenstein, *On Certainty*, ed. G. E. M. Anscombe and G. H. von Wright, trans. Denis Paul and G. E. M. Anscombe (New York: Harper and Row, 1969), p. 17e. Subsequent citations of this work will be given in parentheses in the text, as *On Certainty* with the page number.

doubt?" (*On Certainty*, p. 18e). As a result, because even not understanding things, or experiencing them as senseless, depends on understanding or grasping the sense of some other things, we simply can't get to the point of finding everything senseless. We can only fool ourselves that we're doing that!

Because we do understand some things to some extent, we can never rule out the possibility that we might come to understand more. But because our lives are finite, the things we understand always have a wider context, and so we always only partly understand them. There are always things that we do understand, but there are always also things that we don't understand.

Our understanding and lack of understanding interact with each other. The sense which things do make tells us that we don't yet have the whole story. But the fact that we can never get the whole story makes the sense we already have unsatisfactory. And so we're always aware that there is more to know even about the familiar things and events of our lives, and we're impelled to keep asking questions, and find out more of the story.

As in life, the story on *Lost* unfolds in patterns and connections that hint at sense or meaningfulness. Connections exist between different characters, who often turn out to have been involved in some significant part of another character's life, and even involved in the circumstances that directly led to that character's being on Oceanic Flight 815 and so on the island. For example, before Jack and Sawyer met for the first time on the island, Sawyer happened to encounter Jack's father in a bar, and had a conversation with him about his troubled relationship with Jack. (He had just failed to get up the nerve to call Jack and reconcile with him, something he had apparently tried to do many times.) Shortly after that, Jack's father died without yet having managed to tell Jack what he meant to him. His father's death was what brought Jack to Australia, the flight's place of departure, and also made it necessary for Jack to take that particular flight to bring him home. This brought him to the island, where he met Sawyer – who could then tell him what his father wasn't able to tell him about his father's feelings.

Another example is the connection between Hurley and Libby. They establish a love relationship on the island, but, apparently without either of them being aware of it, they turn out to have been patients together in the same psychiatric ward. And it was in this

259

ward that Hurley came across the numbers that later won him the lottery but also brought him terribly bad luck, which led him to Australia to try to undo their curse, which in turn brought him to Flight 815, and so to the island.

Then there is the pre-island meeting between Jack and Desmond, in which Desmond offers the despairing Jack a perspective on possible miracles which leads to Jack's healing the patient that he later marries. And within minutes of that conversation Desmond is provoked to leave on the dangerous sailing trip that brought *him* to the island – where his unknowing negligence later caused the crash of Flight 815.

As we know, Mr. Eko finds his own brother's dead body in a drug-courier plane that just happened to have crashed on the very same island on which Mr. Eko is marooned: a plane his brother had boarded in the first place because of Mr. Eko's unexpectedly misfiring actions.

As a final example, Locke's abusive, con-artist father turns out also to be the man Sawyer has spent his life hunting for bringing about the deaths of his own parents. What is more, he uncannily appears on the island, resulting in their cooperation to get rid of him.[5]

A central feature of *Lost*, then, and one that rivets our interest, is that everything seems to hint, but only to hint, at making sense. Tantalizingly, this is not enough sense to be quite understandable; it is a sense just beyond our grasp. In exploring this theme, *Lost* mirrors an important aspect of our lives: their character of being a perpetual mystery, which we also can never rightly give up on.

Because this is an aspect of the *nature* of our lives, and not just a particular experience *within* our lives, it is an aspect of what our lives, and so our selves, *are*. As a result, when *Lost* expresses this dimension of the nature of our lives, it is, like philosophy, expressing not just something *about* us, but what we *are*.

And expressing what we actually *are* (and not just something *about* what we are) is exactly the same as *being* what we are. It *is* what we

---

[5] It's also interesting that several of this small group have the names of great eighteenth-century philosophers: John Locke, (Desmond) Hume, and (Danielle) Rousseau. And, what's more, the character Henry Gale is played by actor Michael *Emerson*. Coincidence? Or has the island's electromagnetic field burst free of the writers' control, and now started drawing our own world into its reality?

are, emerging, actively being itself, carrying itself out. Both philosophy and *Lost*, then, are not just "spectator sports." In expressing basic aspects of our nature, they are both an activation of what most makes us "us."

## Is There A Life After This One?

*Lost* also pays attention to a third very basic feature of human life, namely that being where the castaways are is not enough for most of them. They feel the urgent need to find a home beyond where they are. And while some of them do need to huddle where they are and forget about the troublesome world beyond, this is also a way of shaping their lives by awareness of and reference to somewhere other than where they are.

In the light of this need to be or focus on somewhere else, along with not knowing why we're here, and not knowing how it all makes sense, the theme of being "lost" wonderfully captures a basic part of our human situation.

Part of being alive and conscious is to be driven by desire for what we do not have, or have not achieved, to be partly dissatisfied with our situation in our lives. And, as we discussed, part of what it means to be alive and conscious is also to be unsure of the sense of the world that is our context. In other words, we're unsure, among other things, of whether and how we fit in or belong. One way of saying and experiencing both of these is that we are not fully at home in life – and that our true home therefore lies somewhere beyond our always partly alien life circumstances.

The needs for sex and romance, for bonding or "fusing" with someone else, are two kinds of especially compelling expression of this structure of our lives: of the general need to connect with what is beyond our finite selves and our finite situation, to be more complete and to belong. *Lost* actually demonstrates that this more general need really *is* deeper and more basic for us. *Lost* has comparatively little of either lust or love in the island present (and not all that much in the back-stories either), and when they do feature, they usually play little role in the ongoing developments of the story. But we don't feel the lack of them. So it seems that the more general need to "find a real home," which *is* constantly featured in the show, is deep enough

261

to have an even more compelling appeal, and so to override our usual interest in its particular expressions in sex and romance.

## Art and Entertainment

Enjoying *Lost* means having a deep, existential experience, one that connects with the themes basic to our human existence. *Lost* produces this kind of experience in an especially clear and direct way, and so can also help us understand why other programs appeal to us so much, including the many detective and other puzzle-solving programs that continue to keep our interest.

Cultural critics sometimes compare contemporary western culture unfavorably with ancient Greek culture, whose storytelling art did not mainly provide a means of escape from life, but instead was a standard way of experiencing deep questions about it. I suggest, however, that the lesson of *Lost* is that our culture's standard entertainment is sometimes also that kind of deep art.

We may not be conscious of our depth. But that doesn't mean it goes away. Whether we know it or not, we never stop being entirely who we are, and in one way or another experiencing and living out all of who we are. This is also true in our entertainments, whether we are their creators or their audience. And it is true, as well, whether these entertainments are famous public efforts, or just our chatting with each other in our everyday lives.

# About the Authors

**Briony Addey** is a graduate student in the Philosophy Department at the University of Bristol. Her research interests are freedom, philosophy of biology and neuroscience, ethics, moral psychology, and philosophy of action. She is convinced that she would have gotten the fish biscuits quicker than the bears (and much quicker than Sawyer!).

**Robert Arp** is currently a visiting assistant professor of philosophy at Florida State University. He is editor of *South Park and Philosophy: You Know, I Learned Something Today*, and co-editor of *Batman and Philosophy*. He has also contributed to numerous other Philosophy and Pop Culture books. Among other publications in philosophy of mind, philosophy of biology, and the history of western philosophy, he has authored *Scenario Visualization: An Evolutionary Account of Creative Problem Solving*. He likes John Locke's character best because his name sounds just like the famous empiricist philosopher, John Locke.

**Michael W. Austin** is associate professor of philosophy at Eastern Kentucky University. He is the author of *Conceptions of Parenthood* (2007) and editor of *Running & Philosophy* (Blackwell, 2007). He has never hated Hugo.

**Deborah R. Barnbaum** is associate professor of philosophy at Kent State University. She has published extensively on research ethics, has served on hospital ethics committees, and served on several Institutional Review Boards for the protection of human research subjects. She doesn't recall being a research subject in any of the medical or psychological studies she reviewed, but since some of the more recent ones were deception studies, she cannot be certain.

**Jeremy Barris** is professor of philosophy at Marshall University in Huntington, West Virginia. His publications include *Paradox and the Possibility of Knowledge: The Example of Psychoanalysis* and *The Crane's Walk; Plato, Pluralism, and the Inconstancy of Truth*. He lost his bearings years ago and has been wondering ever since.

**Shai Biderman** is a doctoral candidate in philosophy at Boston University, a visiting fellow in the IWM in Vienna, Austria, and an instructor in the College of Management, Israel. His research interests include philosophy of culture, philosophy of film and literature, aesthetics, ethics, existentialism, and Nietzsche. His essays appear in the following volumes: *Movies and the Meaning of Life*, *Hitchcock and Philosophy*, *South Park and Philosophy*, *The Philosophy of TV Noir*, *Star Trek and Philosophy*, and *Family Guy and Philosophy*. He considers himself one of the Others, but refrains, on principle, from snatching babies from stranded castaways.

**Sandra Bonetto** has worked as a philosophy lecturer and tutor in Ireland for the past nine years. She teaches a variety of courses, currently at University College Dublin (Adult Education) and Dublin City University (Oscail), including ethics and political philosophy, contemporary philosophy, and conspiracy theories. She has published several articles, most recently on Shakespeare, Nietzsche, and Hegel. When asked how she felt about writing her chapter, she replied: "Lost!"

**Patricia Brace** teaches humanities and art history at Southwest Minnesota State University. A lifelong science fiction fan, she has annoyed friends and family for years with her encyclopedic knowledge of TV cult favorites like the *X-Files*, *Buffy the Vampire Slayer*, and *Lost*, and they are pleased to see her at last put it to some good use.

**Richard Davies** read philosophy at Trinity College, Cambridge, where he also did his PhD. He now lives in Italy, where he teaches theoretical philosophy at the University of Bergamo. He has written books on Descartes and published articles on logic, ontology, ethics, and the status of literary criticism; he is currently working on an exposition of the logical tools of analytic philosophy for an Italian readership. He thinks we are all in this together.

**William J. Devlin** is assistant professor at Bridgewater State College and visiting lecturer at the University of Wyoming. His research interests include eastern philosophy, philosophy of science, and Nietzsche, and he has written articles on Nietzsche, time travel, personal identity, and art. He currently walks through his hometown of Boston, waiting for a sign from the city to tell him what to do.

**Jessica Engelking** is a PhD candidate at the University of Iowa. This is her first publication. She is 23 at the time of writing this, but that's just a coincidence . . . right?

**Peter S. Fosl** is professor of philosophy at Transylvania University and a Kentucky Colonel (yes, really). Specializing in skepticism and early modern philosophy, Fosl is a contributing editor to *The Philosophers' Magazine* and co-author with Julian Baggini of *The Philosophers Toolkit* and *The Ethics Toolkit*. In his spare time he serves as the executive director of the Dharma Project of Kentucky.

**Karen Gaffney** is an assistant professor of English at Raritan Valley Community College in central New Jersey. She teaches classes on composition, gender, race, and popular culture. She is currently working on a book project about the "divide-and-conquer" mentality that tends to pit racial minorities against each other. In her spare time, she thinks about whether or not to push the button.

**Daniel B. Gallagher** is assistant professor of philosophy at Sacred Heart Major Seminary in Detroit. He is the author of numerous articles in metaphysics, aesthetics, and Thomistic philosophy, and is the translator of several books. He currently serves as editor of the *Values in Italian Philosophy* series. Although Father Gallagher was quite saddened to see fellow priest Mr. Eko get squashed by the smoke monster, he is quite pleased at the longer lines outside his confessional ever since.

**Charles Girard** is a PhD student at La Sorbonne – Paris 1 University in France. He teaches classes on moral and political philosophy. His researches focus on the theories of public debate and the news media. Being a self-proclaimed man of science, he would be very grateful if you could all please stop mistaking coincidences for fate.

265

## About the Authors

**Tom Grimwood** teaches philosophy at Lancaster University, UK. He has published articles in hermeneutics, feminist philosophy, and the history of philosophy, and his current research is concerned with the theorizing of irony within the philosophy of interpretation. In his free time, he travels from village to village, solving local mysteries.

**Dan Kastrul** is the founder and executive director of Chez Nous, Inc., a company which has provided residential and training services since 1983 to people considered developmentally disabled. He earned a BA in Psychology from the University of Wisconsin, Milwaukee, and a MPH in Health Education from the University of Minnesota. Dan discovered through past life regression that in a previous incarnation he was a noted but Oscarless Hollywood movie director. Having found his way through a long hatch into his current lifetime, Dan aspires to bring home that Academy Award.

**Sharon M. Kaye** is associate professor of philosophy at John Carroll University in Cleveland. She has published numerous articles, mostly in medieval philosophy, as well as a number of books, including *Philosophy for Teens* (2006), *More Philosophy for Teens* (2007), and *Medieval Philosophy: A Beginner's Guide* (2008). If you see her, please report her whereabouts to local authorities immediately.

**Sander Lee** is a professor of philosophy at Keene State College, New Hampshire. He is the author of *Eighteen Woody Allen Films Analyzed: Anguish, God, and Existentialism* (2002), as well as other books and scholarly essays on issues in aesthetics, ethics, social philosophy, and metaphysics. He remains convinced that the guy without an eye is Patchy from Spongebob.

**David Meulemans** is a graduate student at the University of Provence, in the south of France. He has been giving lectures on aesthetics and TV for a few years. He has not turned off his TV for a few years as well. If you happen to find the missing remote, please go to www.whereismyremote.com and let him know.

**Scott Parker** is a PhD student in philosophy. He was once denied health insurance for three years because of asthma that he didn't have, and at times felt like torturing someone for answers. It's a long story. He'll gladly tell it to you on a long flight or a tropical island.

**Brett Chandler Patterson** is assistant professor of theology and ethics at Anderson University in South Carolina. His writings explore the importance of narrative for theological reflection and the expression of theological themes in literature and culture (including pop culture). He has recently taught a course (and is designing a book) on theology and the imagination, which examines the works of MacDonald, Lewis, Tolkien, Card, and Wolfe, as well as *Lost* episodes. He is hoping that the Others do not turn out to be aliens, so that he won't have to admit that his mother was right all along.

**Charles Taliaferro** is professor of philosophy at St. Olaf College and the author or editor of seven books, including *Evidence and Faith* (2005). He is the son of an airline pilot who crash landed his plane in a lake. Everyone survived, but they would have been happier if Kate and Jack had been on hand to assist with the medical attention.

**Rebecca Vartabedian** is an adjunct professor in the philosophy departments at the Metropolitan State College of Denver and Regis University. She's also continuing her study in the Graduate Interdisciplinary Program at the University of Colorado-Denver. Her work is mainly focused on the links between epistemology, ethics, and film theory. Her feet went missing for a few hours overnight during a 2001 climbing excursion in the Nevada desert. She's glad they returned safely.

**David Werther** is a faculty associate in philosophy in the Department of Liberal Studies and the Arts, University of Wisconsin-Madison. In addition, he teaches theology in the extension program of Trinity Evangelical Divinity School. He is primarily interested in philosophical theology and has published papers in *Ars Disputandi*, *Philosophia Christi*, *Religious Studies*, and *Sophia*. Like Boone (Daniel, that is, the hunter and trailblazer, not Shannon's stepbrother), David allows that "I have never been lost but I will admit to being confused for several weeks."

**George Wrisley** is finishing his dissertation at the University of Iowa. His primary research interests are in metaphysics and the philosophy of language, particularly issues concerning realism and antirealism, and the relations between language and world. He recently set sail to save the survivors only to find that the boat he was on belonged to Neurath. Alas, due to the need for constant repairs he hasn't gotten very far.

# Index

# Index